SCOTTISH ODYSSEYS

THE ARCHAEOLOGY OF ISLANDS

SCOTTISH ODYSSEYS

THE ARCHAEOLOGY OF ISLANDS

EDITED BY GORDON NOBLE, TESSA POLLER,
JOHN RAVEN AND LUCY VERRILL

First published in 2008
Reprinted 2013

The History Press
The Mill, Brismcombe Port,
Stroud, Gloucestershire, GL5 2QG
www.thehistorypress.co.uk

© the individual authors, 2008

The right of the individual authors to be identified as the Authors of this work has been asserted in accordance with the Copyrights, Designs and Patents Act 1988.

All rights reserved. No part of this book may be reprinted or reproduced or utilised in any form or by any electronic, mechanical or other means, now known or hereafter invented, including photocopying and recording, or in any information storage or retrieval system, without the permission in writing from the Publishers.

British Library Cataloguing in Publication Data.
A catalogue record for this book is available from the British Library.

ISBN 978 0 7524 4168 9

Printed in Great Britain

CONTENTS

Preface   7

List of contributors   9

1. Island Stories
   Andrew Fleming   11

2. West Voe: A Mesolithic-Neolithic transition site in Shetland
   Nigel D. Melton   23

3. An island of fluctuating perceptions: the landscape and archaeology of Bute
   Gordon Noble & Fay Stevens   37

4. Islandscapes and Standing Stones: changing perceptions
   Joanna Wright   61

5. Peeling Back the Layers: reconstructing a vanished Iron Age landscape
   Deborah Lamb   73

6. Splendid Isolation? Changing perceptions of Dùn Èistean, an island on the north coast of the Isle of Lewis
   Rachel C. Barrowman   95

7. All quiet on the Western Front? Landscape survey on Foula, Shetland
   Helen Bradley   112

8. At the crossroads: the historical archaeology of Rathlin Island
   Wes Forsythe & Rosemary McConkey 132

9. A Fifer in the North: William Bruce and the Laird's Houses of Early Modern Shetland
   Sabina Strachan 150

10. The western islands: Ireland's Atlantic islands and the forging of Gaelic Irish national identities
    Aidan O'Sullivan 172

PREFACE

The Scottish Archaeological Forum (SAF) was set up in 1969 in order to provide 'an opportunity to hear, discuss and assess some of the important new discoveries and reinterpretations of material, either published or unpublished as yet, by all those working in the archaeological discipline in Scotland'.

The Forum is run by a committee of archaeologists and since its foundation it has included some of the most prestigious names in Scottish Archaeology. One of its main aims is to organise conferences and workshops which further the study of archaeology in Scotland. A large number of conferences have been organised over the years and the proceedings of many were made available as published volumes, either as one of the SAF's own publications or separately. Recent conferences in the last five years have included subjects as diverse as Nationalism and Archaeology, Medieval or Later Rural Settlement, Industrial Archaeology, Roundhouses and Modern Views of Ancient Lands.

On the 28th and 29th of October 2005, the Scottish Archaeological Forum held a conference: *Scottish Odysseys: The Archaeology of Islands*. The resulting conference was one of the SAF's most successful; papers were presented by academics, island communities, historical societies and field archaeologists, amongst others. The conference aimed to promote the study of island archaeology in Western Europe, building on recent developments made in the theoretical approaches to the study of island archaeologies in the Mediterranean and the Pacific. Islands were studied in their many forms, whether they were small sea-bound islands, inland islands, island archipelagos, symbolic islands, or larger 'Mainland' landmasses. An eclectic mix of subjects were covered from a number of different perspectives. There were summaries of recent projects and research programmes taking place on Scottish islands, studies of how islands have been perceived by scholars from the Middle Ages onwards, how Scottish island communities interact with and perceive both archaeology and archaeologists, and several of them reanalysed island architecture, material culture and landscapes. Stimulating Irish comparisons were also presented.

The papers contained in this volume were all presented at the Scottish Odysseys conference. Andrew Fleming's paper serves as a thought-provoking introductory chapter; he analyses the way islands have etched themselves onto academics' subconscious, taking on an iconic and mythic status throughout scholarly thinking in the western world. Nigel Melton presents exciting new evidence of the Mesolithic-Neolithic transition at West Voe, Shetland. Gordon Noble and Fay Stevens look at the multiple ways of understanding 'islandness' in the study of the prehistory of the Isle of Bute. Joanna Wright identifies the way in which antiquarians' and archaeologists' preconceptions of islands has informed and biased their approach to studies of standing stones located on islands. Then, using the Isle of Mull as a case study, she illustrates how an awareness of these preconceptions can be used to create new discourses. Deborah Lamb peels back the layers of evidence for administration across the landscapes of islands in order to reconstruct Iron Age infrastructures. Rachel Barrowman explores how communities in the Isle of Lewis have reacted to, and fluctuated in, their perception of archaeology over the course of the Dùn Èistean project and Helen Bradley also explores this issue in a report on recent survey work in Foula, Shetland. Returning to Ireland, Wes Forsythe questions the place of Rathlin in the Irish Sea, examining the historical archaeology of the island, highlighting its ambiguities and asking to which cultural diaspora, Ireland or Scotland, its inhabitants belonged. Aidan O'Sullivan also provides an insight into the way the islands of the west coast of Ireland have been used to form and maintain identity. However, his contribution also serves as a glass through which Scottish archaeologists should analyse the development of their own fascination and discipline.

The stimulating papers presented in this volume should serve as a valuable contribution to future studies of island archaeologies.

Scottish Archaeological Forum
www.scottisharchaeologicalforum.org.uk

LIST OF CONTRIBUTORS

Rachel C. Barrowman
Glasgow University Department of
Archaeology
16 Eorodale
Isle of Lewis
HS2 0TR

Helen Bradley
Council for Scottish Archaeology
Causewayside House
160 Causewayside
Edinburgh
EH9 1PR

Andrew Fleming
Department of Archaeology and
Anthropology
University of Wales
Lampeter
Ceredigion
SA48 7ED

Wes Forsythe
Centre for Maritime Archaeology
School of Environmental Sciences
University of Ulster
Coleraine
BT52 1SA

Deborah Lamb
Department of Archaeological
Sciences
University of Bradford
Bradford, West Yorkshire
BD7 1DP

Rosemary McConkey
Centre for Maritime Archaeology
School of Environmental Sciences
University of Ulster
Coleraine
BT52 1SA

Nigel D. Melton
Department of Archaeological
Sciences
University of Bradford
Bradford, West Yorkshire
BD7 1DP

Gordon Noble
Department of Archaeology
University of Glasgow
The Gregory Building
Lilybank Gardens
Glasgow
G12 8QQ

Aidan O'Sullivan
College of Arts & Celtic Studies
School of Archaeology
Newman Building
University College Dublin
Belfield
Dublin 4

Fay Stevens
Institute of Archaeology
University College London
31-34 Gordon Square
London
WC1H 0PY

Sabina Strachan
Historic Scotland Images
Longmore House
Salisbury Place
Edinburgh
EH9 1SH

Joanna Wright
Archaeology
School of Arts, Histories and Cultures
The University of Manchester
Oxford Road
Manchester
M13 9PL

I

ISLAND STORIES

Andrew Fleming

I will start by posing the question which most of the contributors to this volume will already have asked themselves from time to time: just what is so fascinating about islands, from the perspective of those who work in historical disciplines? It is one thing to eschew geographical determinism, and to agree with my colleague Paul Rainbird (1999) and other commentators that we should not attempt to treat islands as laboratories for the study of culture process, as we were urged to do in the early 1970s (Evans 1973). However, anyone who has been involved with island archaeologies knows that to make light of their islandness and treat them simply as detached bits of the nearest 'mainland', is an equally problematic exercise. If we should try to refrain from exaggerating the Otherness of island communities – their remoteness and exoticism – it may be equally hard to get away with portraying them as Same, as variations on the familiar (Fleming forthcoming). Rainbird (1999; 2007) argues that 'island archaeology' as a topic has effectively become meaningless and is best subsumed within an archaeology of coastal and maritime communities, taking a more nuanced approach which recognises the particular characteristics of islanders' lifeways.

In this paper I wish to take a different tack and to discuss a feature of island history which must appeal to any writer – their potential for being treated not as laboratories, but rather as worlds in microcosm, locations which may bring particular themes and narratives into sharper focus. In the final analysis, the landscape historian is a story-teller. As Rainbird (1999) has reminded us, it is not by accident that some of the most compelling tales ever penned have been set on islands – and this seems to have the effect of making them more effective and potent as parables, analogues, metaphors, satires, etc. Doubtless those who work in historical disciplines will hesitate before wanting to write history, let alone prehistory, as a set of morality tales or 'just-so stories', imbued with a didactic 'author's message', and I sympathise entirely with this healthy instinct. However, I contend that a brief survey of island literature reminds us that, as writers of narratives of the past, we may avail ourselves of a wider and more attractive range of choices than contemporary and more narrowly-focused theoretical debates would suggest.

Recently, writing a new account of the history of St Kilda (Fleming 2005) I soon became aware that the archipelago has been the object of certain rather compelling narratives. Some writers have taken the long-term history of St Kilda, or the alleged character of the St Kildans, to be allegories of the human condition. It all started with Martin Martin, writing at the end of the seventeenth century (Martin 1986). He asserted that the islanders were essentially survivors of the Golden Age, and eulogised their 'innocence and simplicity, purity, mutual love and cordial friendship'; their 'freedom from solicitous cares and anxious covetousness; from envy, deceit and dissimulation; from ambition and pride and the consequences that attend them'. The St Kildans were, he claimed, 'altogether ignorant of the vices of foreigners, and governed by the dictates of reason and Christianity' (*ibid*). They had 'no designs upon one another, but such as are purely suggested by justice and benevolence'. For Martin, the only thing wanting to make the St Kildans the happiest people in the world was that they did not know how fortunate they were. Evidently our author was conforming to contemporary convention; the eulogy only takes up two paragraphs in his account, which seems otherwise quite shrewd and perceptive about what the St Kildans were really like. Nearly 70 years later, the author of Kenneth MacAulay's description of St Kilda (1974) – who wasn't always MacAulay himself (Powell 1940) – took a similar line, creating a text which was quite a candid, informative account, but also a morality tale. Apparently the St Kildans were not only innocent of the vices of the wider world, they also displayed many of the virtues of the old Germans, whose barbarian nobility Tacitus had long ago contrasted with the decadence of Imperial Rome (Schama 1995).

In 1965, Tom Steel took the evacuation of St Kilda in 1930 to be the event which defined its long-term history. He saw this history as a classical tragedy in two senses. In the first place, it was predestined. At the edge of the Atlantic, the inevitable winner of the 'struggle for existence' would be nature, not humanity. In the second place, the St Kildans had tragic flaws – their conservatism, their socialism, the intensity of their Christian faith, even their 'Celticity', made them unsuited to survive the onrush of modernity. At around the same time, the naturalists who had been involved in thinking about St Kilda's history and archaeology, as well as its wildlife, felt that St Kilda's story was essentially an allegory of the Fall of Man. With the coming of modernity, the St Kildans had lost their innocence. In an ideal world, they believed, St Kilda should now become a pure sanctuary for wildlife – essentially a Garden of Eden from which the descendants of Adam and Eve should be firmly excluded (apart from suitably qualified naturalists, of course). Not long afterwards, Charles Maclean (1972) took these ideas to their logical conclusion. He suggested that those who survived the impending ecological and social Armageddon might want to go back to St Kilda and think about it as a form of Utopia, learning lessons about the adaptive qualities of life in small, self-regulating communities (see Fleming 2005, Chapters 1, 9 and 10 for further commentary on outsiders' perceptions of St Kilda).

This late twentieth-century perception of St Kilda's history was essentially developed by two naturalists and a geographer, who carried out a survey for the National Trust for Scotland in the summer of 1957 (Williamson & Boyd 1960; MacGregor 1960). As the Trust assessed their newly acquired property, the bulldozers of the RAF got busy on the creation of a radar station to accompany the new rocket range on South Uist. The Hardrock Consensus, as I have called it, propagated more widely in Tom Steel's very readable book, was largely instrumental in developing the iconic status which the archipelago has enjoyed in the second half of the twentieth century. More recently, Paul Bahn and John Flenley, in their *Easter Island, Earth Island* (1992), have written a comparable account of the history of Rapa Nui. As the title of the book indicates, the history of the island is seen as a cautionary tale at the very least, or more ambitiously as an allegory of the catastrophic impact of humans on the ecology of planet Earth.

Most island narratives, however, involve invented islands. The imaginary island is a recurrent component of the writer's toolkit, offering instant escape from the rigours of direct engagement with the here and now, and total freedom to create the parameters of an imagined world. One might say, paraphrasing the psychologist in a famous episode of Fawlty Towers, that the topic of nesography (writing about islands) would provide enough material for an entire conference. In the francophone world there is indeed an annual conference, which takes place on the isle of Ouessant (Ushant) (http://jacbayle.club.fr/livres/salon.html). To list the authors who have written about imaginary islands virtually involves taking a roll-call of great writers and engaging with some great works of literature (not to mention the cinema) as well as lesser luminaries. Agatha Christie, of all people, quite liked the idea of owning an island (Christie Mallowan 1946, 25-6), but then she remembered that the only South Sea islanders she had ever seen were eating a meal swimming in grease, off a very dirty table-cloth. Balking at the difficulties of dusting, provisioning, doing the washing up, sorting out dustbins, and so on, she concluded: 'No; an island is, and should be, a dream island … [with] white sand and blue sea – and a fairy house, perhaps, built between sunrise and sunset; the apple tree, the singing and the gold …'. What must surely be one of D.H. Lawrence's worst short stories – *The man who loved islands* – is said to represent a dig at Compton Mackenzie and his nesophilia (not to mention his ownership of the Shiant Isles). Mackenzie himself was inspired to write *Rockets Galore* (1957) by the controversy over the construction of the South Uist rocket range; soon afterwards, Hammond Innes penned his *Atlantic Fury*, a military adventure set on a thinly-disguised St Kilda (1962).

The archaeologist who wishes to become acquainted with the literary freedom which comes with the invention of islands, without taking a degree in world literature, could do much worse than consult Manguel and Guadalupi's *Dictionary of Imaginary Places* (1981), the book which is the source of the examples chosen here (except where otherwise referenced). Evidently the invention of a fictitious island presents a writer with a licence to have a great deal of fun, with or without the development of a serious underlying message. Of course, some imagined otherworlds involve other, non-insular geographies – they lie beyond mountain ranges, on promontories, in woods or beneath the sea. But many of them, more than most of us would guess, are set on islands or archipelagos.

Reading about the inhabitants of islands which Charles Kingsley invented for *The Water Babies* I'm tempted to ask, in today's usage: 'What was he like?' (And to remind the reader that he actually became Regius Professor of Modern History at Cambridge). Why have so many people written about islands? The invention of islands just for fun has a long history. One might cite Floating Island, invented in 1673. This island only appeared in summer, in the middle of the Thames Estuary. Its people were noted for their sloth; they were too idle to make wine, in spite of the luxuriant vineyards, and too lazy to cultivate the land; they spoke a lingua franca and apparently smoked a great deal.

At another level, writing about an imaginary island can be a deeply serious project, a way of putting forward a political manifesto, expressing one's deepest political ideals, or engaging in potentially dangerous political critique without commenting directly on one's own society. Thomas More's Utopia, introduced in 1516, was, of course, an island, albeit a very large one which was difficult of access. Utopia was very different from the England of Henry VIII. It was a representative, consultative democracy (albeit with slavery) and it had a prosperous and efficient economy based on the application of science. There was no private property or money, chamber pots being made of gold in order to discourage the love of this metal. The people hated war and tried to mitigate its worst effects, and they practised religious tolerance. They treated the mentally handicapped kindly, they exercised euthanasia, and hated hunting, not being able to see 'why anyone should find pleasure in the barking and yapping of dogs, not to mention the mutilation of small animals for no reason at all'. I regret to say, however, that Utopia was entirely without beer.

Sexual politics also figures in the creation of imaginery islands. The feminist island of Babilary was conceived by the Abbé Desfontaines in 1730. The name Babilary meant 'To the Glory of Women'. Here the women were not only warriors and pirates, but also musicians and poets. The men received no education and need only worry about their appearance; wives could divorce their husbands, but not vice versa.

The island had been ruled by women ever since the queen defeated her weak husband in battle by the simple expedient of putting the youngest and most beautiful girls in the front line, literally disarming the opposing army. Then there was the island of Philos (the name is to do with love, but let us not confuse it with Love Island). This eighteenth-century French creation was governed by love, friendship and candour; the beautiful women of the island ruled over the other inhabitants through the love they inspired. The women apparently chose their lovers with great care, 'never bestowing their charms on the young, but rather on mature men who had proved reliable'. It is perhaps not too difficult to guess the author's approximate age…

We shouldn't forget the creation of the one-time archaeologist Jacquetta Hawkes. In her novel, *Providence Island*, published in 1959, a small team of archaeologists and anthropologists discover that descendants of the Upper Palaeolithic Magdalenians have survived on the small Melanesian island of Providence. Fortunately the Magdalenians speak a form of the Basque language – as, even more providentially, does one of the team. They discover that the islanders – who are magnificent human specimens in every way – have wonderful powers of thought transference, telepathy and hypnosis, powers which modern 'rational' people have long since lost. These powers enable the team to ward off the threat from a team of visiting American military personnel, who are prospecting for a site for testing nuclear weapons. Even more importantly, they allow Jacquetta Hawkes to speak up in favour of feeling, empathy and intuition, both in life and as the right way of thinking about the past. This was partly an expression of her feminist persona; such an approach would create a particularly significant role for female academics. Yet Hawkes was also, of course, in some sense a post-processualist, years ahead of the fashion. In her novel, the most rational young archaeologist can't hack the encounter with intuition and feeling among the Magdalenians, and retreats into science. 'If history could not be measured, then he would not be an historian, for exact measurement was what he liked' (Hawkes 1959). The wise old professor, on the other hand, decides to abandon his dusty life in Oxford immediately, realising that he will learn more in the touchy-feely world of the Magdalenians than by carrying on with a career of conventional scholarship. Later, Hawkes put her advocacy of this approach into a paper in *Antiquity*: 'The Proper Study of Mankind' (1968).

The island of Philos had many theatres, which showed 'mostly French plays of the classical period'. Here we encounter another recurring fantasy. What could be more satisfying for the struggling writer or frustrated intellectual than to conjure up an island where the arts and the life of the mind are properly appreciated, or at least saleable commodities? Then there was the archipelago created in eighteenth century France in a direct response to *Gulliver's Travels* – Poets' Island, where the people of course spoke in rhyme and within given metres, and an annual fair was held for the sale of tragedies, comedies, words for an opera, epic poems and epigrams; some were protected from export by customs officers. In quite a few imaginary islands an important role is played by academic institutions of one sort or another, though interestingly on Limanora – the Island of Progress, invented in 1903 – there were no schools or universities, 'as they were considered to be hotbeds of uniformity'. Nevertheless applied science was very prominent in the lifeways of the Limanorans.

Satire, whether bitingly political or gently fun-poking, is also well set on islands. Lilliput, after all, was an island. Irish readers may be disconcerted to read about Oceana, a fictitious island off the south coast of Ireland, created as recently as 1971. Its inhabitants are described as staid and extremely conservative; mail is delivered in horse-drawn vans and women in country areas still wear traditional dress. Witchcraft rituals still survive, including worship of the devil, naked orgies and a variety of sado-masochistic rites (shades of *The Wicker Man*). On Oceana there is only one national dish, the cold pudding made from bread and blayberries known as blayberrie breaddie.

Islands are also ideal environments on which to set one's darkest musings about humanity's capacity for evil, and the thin veneer of civilisation; think of *Lord of the Flies* (Golding 1954). Usually this means encounters with the Other – sometimes our own savage or barbarian past, sometimes an enemy race or ethnic group. Take the island known as Houyhnhnms Land which features in Jonathan Swift's *Gulliver's Travels*. This place was inhabited by a race of graceful and gentle horses, who had developed a calm, peaceful civilisation, governed by reason; they were wise and sophisticated and – surprise, surprise – very good poets. Yet unfortunately they weren't the only inhabitants of the island. They had had to face up the Yahoos, who looked like hairy versions of humans; they are described as extremely unpleasant with a natural affinity to nastiness and dirt. They also bred very rapidly. To counter the threat which the Yahoos posed to this equine Utopia, the horses had been compelled to hunt them systematically, and they ended up being kept in kennels and bred as beasts of burden. The Other, it seems, is inescapable. Thomas More's Utopia had its polar opposite, the island of Venalia, 500 miles to the east, inhabited by a primitive and savage people who lived by hunting and stealing. They were well paid by the Utopians to act as mercenary soldiers; they spent their wages on 'the most squalid and amusing forms of debauchery' and the Utopians did not care how many Venalians they sent to their deaths, since it was an act of philanthropy to rid the world of such scum.

Then there is Skull Island. On the western peninsula lay the ruins of an ancient city, and the remains of a gigantic wooden wall once built by its inhabitants to isolate them from the eastern half of the island. Alas, the descendants of this ancient civilisation had degenerated into savages, living in mud huts. They were negroes, ruled by a king, and they worshipped a giant gorilla. For this was the island of King Kong. To the east of the wall, in the realm of this assertive primate, tropical flora had achieved enormous proportions, and dinosaurs, huge lizards and flying reptiles roamed the land. Periodically, Kong came through the gate in the big wall, to be presented with a new bride by 12 of the tallest men of the village, dressed in rough black skins and furry skulls in order to resemble a pack of apes.

What of *The Land that Time Forgot*? Edgar Rice Burroughs' creation in 1917 – not long after the 'discovery' of 'Piltdown Man' – was an island called Caspak, which was only accessible by a submarine tunnel. In the interior were dinosaurs, pterodactyls and some very nasty carnivorous reptiles, crawling and leaping around in a flora which included giant maize plants some 50ft tall. Rather implausibly, perhaps, woolly rhinos, aurochs and horses were also to be found here. Caspak was inhabited by a whole evolutionary typology of hominids, from ape-men to Neanderthals, who kept themselves apart; the crudest of them were the ape-men who lived in the south of the island. As one travelled north, one encountered more progressive peoples – in terms of their evolutionary status and their cultural advancement. However all these peoples were equally aggressive, killing strangers on sight. Most of them started life in the form of eggs and tadpoles, incidentally. The most civilised people had migrated to the outlying island of Oo-Oh; I can't say I blame them.

Invented islands have to be seen in their historical contexts. It's not hard to comprehend the intellectual context of those island otherworlds which were conjured up in post-medieval and recent literature. In the background lurk the tales and iconographies of medieval Christendom. There is the voyage of Brendan the Navigator, taken these days more as a Christian allegory than as a challenge to experimental nautical archaeology or an expression of early geographical knowledge (McCone 2000; Wooding 2000). There are the strange beasts which prowl around at the edge of medieval world maps and in medieval bestiaries; some of them lived on distant islands. Yet it was of course post-medieval developments which stimulated the intellectual and imaginative freedom of the creative writers I've been talking about – the Renaissance, the impact of new (or revived) political philosophies and the discovery of new worlds and new peoples beyond Europe. Then came the growth of a spirit of scientific enquiry, rationalism and the Enlightenment. Still later, the islands of the Pacific, or even sometimes the west coast of Ireland, became targets for the anthropologist – and eventually for the writer of anthropological pastiche or satire.

Clearly, one does not have to be literate to find imagined islands stimulating, and their creation long pre-dates the Middle Ages. They crop up in classical literature, right back to Homer's *Odyssey*. There were some interesting islands beyond the pillars of Hercules and in north-west Europe. Island otherworlds also certainly figured in so-called 'Celtic' mythology – most famously, such islands were compounded and confused with various mariners' tales to create the island of Hy Brasil, to the west of Ireland. Hy Brasil wasn't removed from the charts until 1865 and was last 'sighted' by the archaeologist T. J. Westropp in 1872 (1912, 255 & 257).

At this point those of us who work in historical disciplines might well conclude that our role should be to tell plain tales of real islands, and leave fantasy to the fantasists. My purpose in presenting this brief review of 'island stories' is to point out that the all-too-evident character of an island as a microcosm makes it an attractive subject to write about. Conversely, from some points of view it is hard to avoid treating islands as microcosms, even when we are well aware that ultimately we must deal appropriately with the wider context. This review has highlighted the diversity of narratives available to those who write about particular places and regions. In this sense the essential sterility of the processual/post-processual debate becomes very clear. If we do not need to place our narratives in the service of culture-as-system, or of progressivist, teleological accounts of 'social evolution', neither should we feel pressurised by the fashionable spread of the 'people agenda' into 'going beyond the evidence' (Fleming 2006). We should be open to a much wider range of possibilities.

For the novelist, this is a matter of imaginative choice and artistic freedom. In historical disciplines, the subject of the enquiry may encourage particular forms of narrative. Islands are not uniform. Geography and topography may suggest particular lines of enquiry and recurrent themes; the nature of the evidence available may enable or constrain. If 'thick description' and Annales-type approaches afford the potential for nuanced treatments, rich in anecdote and textural diversity, it has to be conceded that the available material is quite patchy and variable. Let us consider briefly the three small island groups in Britain and Ireland which have arguably generated more literature than any others – St Kilda, Great Blasket and the Aran Islands. If, inevitably, the input is always the engagement of outsiders, the outcomes thus inspired display some interesting differences. Accounts of St Kilda's history and culture have been largely written as the avowedly 'objective' accounts of outside observers; discerning the perceptions of the islanders has been mostly a matter of trying to read between the lines. In contrast, the former inhabitants of Great Blasket, off the west coast of Ireland, have produced such a vibrant body of literature that the commentator's task must involve an attempt to understand their perceptions of what was expected of them as writers, what they chose to emphasise and what they preferred to omit, and so on; more conventional sources provide rather limited information about the history and archaeology of the archipelago. As for the Aran Isles, although their landscapes are archaeologically rich and visually spectacular, the voices of both islanders and external scholars/scientists are distinctly muted when set against the volume of novels, poetry, films and works of art which have taken Aran as their starting-point and inspiration (see Waddell *et al* 1994, especially Chapters 15-18; Robinson 1986, 1995 *passim*). As 'iconic' islands, both Great Blasket and the Aran islands must surely have the edge over St Kilda, in the sense that the perceived characteristics and values of their communities came to symbolise the self-image of the re-emergent Irish nation, most importantly in the first half of the twentieth century (see O'Sullivan's paper in this volume). Yet it must also be the case that the more imaginative and consciously impressionistic the texts stimulated by these iconic islands, the greater the potential and need for deconstructive critique, including that provided by the historical disciplines.

'Islandness' is a relative, contingent, situational matter. There are, of course, physical factors to take into account – size, distance from larger land masses, resources, productive potential, climate, ease or difficulty of access, and so on. There is also the trajectory of history to consider, in terms of both process and event – the traditional, customary relationships between the islanders and the outside world, variations in sea-faring competence, boat-building skills and so on over time. How far has the island under consideration been accustomed to a relative degree of autonomy, how far has it operated as a dependency of the nearest part of the 'mainland'? The island as concept has often tended to override the physical character of the island as geographical entity.

There is little space here to review the progress made in north-west Europe in developing intellectually challenging island archaeologies. As noted above, Scottish islands, even those which form compact and diverse archipelagos such as Orkney, Shetland and the Western Isles, have not generally been dealt with collectively as case studies in 'island archaeology' of the sort developed in the Pacific and the Aegean (Irwin 1992; Broodbank 2000). There is a good deal of scope for exploring this dimension within north-west Europe and within Scotland. It should be possible to do so without being silenced by fear of accusations of geographical determinism, or the feeling that post-modernism has somehow placed an indefinite fatwah on such ruminations. It might be argued that recent studies (Hau'ofa 1993; Gosden & Pavlides 1994; Rainbird 1999) have critiqued the subject of 'island archaeology' to extinction. In the longer term it is more likely that the subject has actually been amplified and improved by a greater critical awareness, as we move away from more simplistic early treatments. Within an Atlantic context, Cunliffe (2001) has insisted that we need to take maritime archaeology seriously, and islands will surely play a critical role in these narratives. Cooney's recent discussions of islands in the Irish Sea (2004) and Scarre's (2002) work in north-west France demonstrate that the subject is far from dead. As I have argued elsewhere (Fleming forthcoming) there is scope for thinking about the geography of St Kilda's history as neither Other (over-determining the archipelago's history in terms of its isolation and its perceived cultural exoticism) nor as Same (regarding it simply as a detached component of the nearby mainland, in a 'sea of islands' model). Rather, we should explore and delineate the unique set of interactions and relationships between the islanders and the outside world, in which 'islandness' is certainly a critical dimension.

As the earlier part of this paper has reminded us, there has been a dynamic and productive relationship between islands and imaginative literature. From a post-modern perspective, it is evidently possible to argue that there is no essential difference between the narratives of those who work in the historical disciplines and those who write well-researched historical novels, such as Margaret Elphinstone's excellent *Sea Road* (2000), a modern saga about the life of a particularly well-travelled Icelandic woman in the eleventh century. This question has become more critical and interesting recently, with the emergence of mixed treatments in which evocative, explicitly fictional narratives alternate with more factually-based essays written from the perspective of historical disciplines – such as Mark Edmonds' *Ancestral Geographies of the Neolithic* (1999) or Geoffrey Moorhouse's *Sun Dancing* (1997) which deals with the history of the monastic settlement at Skellig Michael, a small high island (or a large rock stack?) off the west coast of Ireland. As I have argued elsewhere (Fleming 2006), such experimental writing is to be welcomed, provided that it is not put forward as some kind of replacement for the more direct argument- and evidence-based form of landscape archaeology, on the spurious grounds that the latter has somehow been discredited. There is scope for various narratives; hyperinterpretive treatments face their own challenges. Those of us who want to engage with our readers as well as our source material may have to consider afresh our role as story-tellers. These recent writings have reminded us that we need to think about not just the nature of the story, but also how it is to be told. To insist on the truism that the past only exists as written in the present, to dismiss the quest for objectivity too sweepingly, may tempt us to forget that the historical disciplines are usually involved in investigation before they present their narratives. Many of us will recall the shock of meeting an excavation director – or for that matter a director of a television programme – at an early stage in the proceedings, and discovering that the story has already been more or less decided. We may have to ask ourselves which is the more honest and enduring course of action. Should we jettison the quest for objectivity, award ourselves the exhilarating freedom to 'go beyond the evidence', and create our own 'dreamworks' (Tilley 2004, 225)? Or would it be better to develop ways of re-asserting the primacy of our engagement with evidence and argument, taking readers into our mental workshops, presenting landscape history as an on-going investigation, always a work in progress, 'writing the past in the present' in a rather different sense? Whatever conclusion we come to on this matter, it seems to me that 'island stories' often sharpen our focus in special ways, reminding us of the narrative choices which may have to be made. For those who work in historical disciplines, islands, I contend, are 'good to think'.

REFERENCES

Bahn, P. & Flenley, J. 1992, *Easter Island, Earth Island*, London
Broodbank, C. 2000, *An Island Archaeology of the Early Cyclades*, Cambridge
Burroughs, E.R. 1924, *The Land that Time Forgot*, Chicago
Christie Mallowan, A. 1946, *Come, Tell Me How You Live*, London
Cooney, G. 2004, 'Neolithic worlds: islands in the Irish Sea', in Cummings, V. & Fowler, C. (eds), *The Neolithic of the Irish Sea: materiality and traditions of practice*, 145-59, Oxford

Cunliffe, B. 2001, *Facing the Ocean*, Oxford

Edmonds, M. 1999, *Ancestral geographies of the Neolithic: landscape, monuments and memory*, London

Elphinstone, M. 2000, *The Sea Road*, Edinburgh

Evans, J.D. 1973, 'Islands as laboratories for the study of culture process', in Renfrew, C. (ed.), *The Explanation of Culture Change*, 517-20, London

Fleming, A. 2005, *St Kilda and the wider world: tales of an iconic island*, Bollington

Fleming, A. 2006, 'Post-processual landscape archaeology: a critique', *Cambridge Archaeol J* 16(3), 267-80

Fleming, A. forthcoming, 'The islandness of St Kilda', in Sharples, N. (ed.) *Land and People: papers in honour of John G. Evans*, Oxford

Golding, W. 1954, *Lord of the Flies*, London.

Gosden, C. & Pavlides, C. 1994, 'Are islands insular? Landscape vs. seascape in the case of the Arawe Islands, Papua New Guinea', *Archaeology in Oceania* 29, 162-71

Hau'ofa, E. 1993, 'Our sea of islands', in Waddell, E., Naidu, V. & Hau'ofa, E. (eds), *A New Oceania: rediscovering our sea of islands*, 2-16, Fiji

Hawkes, J. 1959, *Providence Island: an archaeological tale*, London

Hawkes, J. 1968, 'The proper study of mankind', *Antiquity* 42, 255-62

Innes, H. 1962, *Atlantic Fury*, London

Irwin, G. 1992, *The Prehistoric Exploration and Colonisation of the Pacific*, Cambridge

Kingsley, C. 1880, *The Water Babies*, Oxford

MacAulay, K. 1974, *The History of St Kilda*, Edinburgh. First published in 1764

MacGregor, D.R. 1960, 'The island of St Kilda: a survey of its character and occupance', *Scottish Studies* 4, 1-48

Mackenzie, C. 1957, *Rockets Galore,* London

Maclean, C. 1972, *Island on the Edge of the World: Utopian St Kilda and its passing*, London

Manguel, A. & Guadalupi, G. 1981, *The Dictionary of Imaginary Places*, London

Martin, M. 1986, *A Voyage to St Kilda*, Edinburgh. Facsimile of 4th edition, 1753; first published 1698

McCone, K. 2000, *Pagan Past and Christian Present in Early Irish Literature*, Maynooth

Moorhouse, G. 1997, *Sun Dancing: a medieval vision*, London

More, T. 2003, *Utopia*, London. First published 1516

Powell, L.F. 1940, 'The history of St Kilda', *Rev Eng Stud* 16, 44-53

Rainbird, P. 1999, 'Islands out of time: towards a critique of island archaeology', *J Med Archaeol* 12, 216-34

Rainbird, P. 2007, *The Archaeology of Islands*, Cambridge

Robinson, T. 1986, *Stones of Aran: Pilgrimage*, London

Robinson, T. 1995, *Stones of Aran: Labyrinth*, London

Scarre, C. 2002, 'A pattern of islands: the Neolithic monuments of north-west Brittany', *Euro J Archaeol* 5, 24-41

Schama, S. 1995, *Landscape and Memory*, London

Steel, T. 1965, *The Life and Death of St Kilda*, Edinburgh

Tilley, C. 2004, *The Materiality of Stone*, Oxford
Waddell, J., O'Connell, J.W. & Korff, A. (eds) 1994, *The Book of Aran*, Newtownlynch
Westropp, T.J. 1912, 'Brasil and the legendary islands of the north Atlantic: their history and fable', *Proc Roy Irish Acad* 30C, 223-59
Williamson, K. & Boyd, J.M. 1960, *St Kilda Summer*, London
Wooding, J. (ed.) 2000, *The Otherworld Voyage in Early Irish Literature*, Dublin

2

WEST VOE: A MESOLITHIC-NEOLITHIC TRANSITION SITE IN SHETLAND

Nigel D. Melton

INTRODUCTION

Archaeological investigations undertaken in 2004 and 2005 on a midden exposed by coastal erosion at West Voe, Sumburgh, in the south of Mainland Shetland have provided the first direct evidence of Late Mesolithic hunter-gatherers in the Northern Isles. The midden deposits contained a sequence of dominant species of marine molluscs: oyster, limpet, mussel and cockle. Also present, particularly in the limpet-rich phase, were numerous seal and sea-bird bones. An activity surface within the midden deposits was associated with the mussel phase of deposition, whilst the final, cockle, phase was separated from the earlier deposits by *c.*0.4m of sands. This final phase of activity was associated with a substantial drystone wall. Radiocarbon dates indicate that the site spans the Mesolithic–Neolithic transition.

PRELIMINARY INVESTIGATIONS IN 2002

The eroding middens at West Voe described in this paper are located in the north-west corner of the Voe (*1*), directly opposite the multi-period site at Jarlshof where Bronze Age to post-medieval occupation phases have been recorded (Hamilton 1956), and lies in an area that is rich in prehistoric sites. These include an Early Neolithic cist that was found contain the remains of 18 individuals (Hedges & Parry

Scottish Odysseys: The Archaeology of Islands

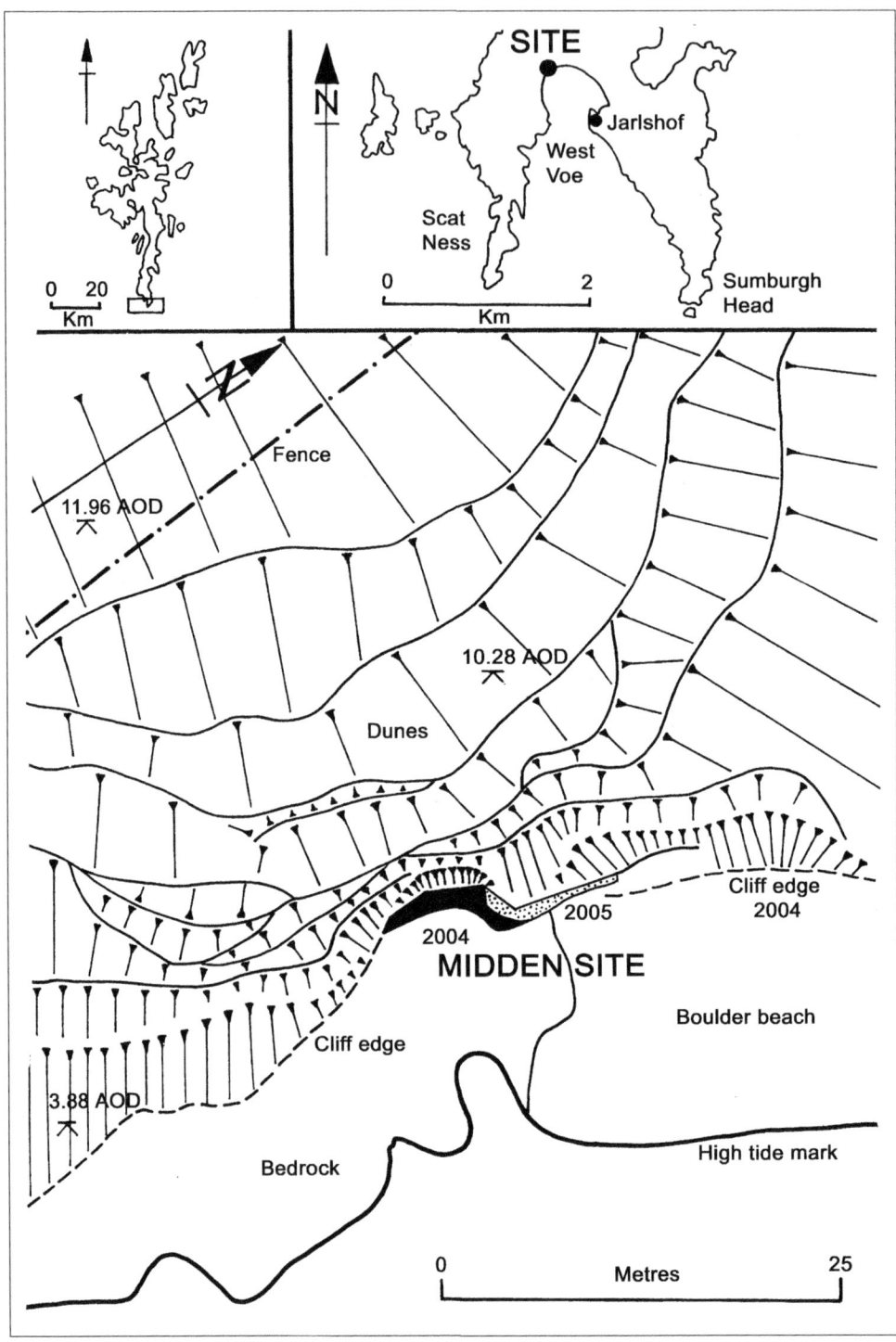

1 Plan showing location of the 2004 and 2005 investigations

1980). The fieldwork undertaken at West Voe in 2004-2005 followed on from a preliminary examination and sampling of the site in 2002 (Melton & Nicholson 2004) which had established that the site consisted of two midden deposits separated by a layer of sand *c*.0.4m thick. The lower of the middens overlay a dark greasy, sandy layer that sealed a natural of glacial deposits and the sandstone bedrock.

Only a short section of the lower midden was cleaned and recorded in 2002. It was found to contain large numbers of oysters (*Ostrea edulis*), together with limpets (*Patella vulgata*), mussels (*Mytilus edulis*), and seal and sea-bird bones. A sample from the upper midden, obtained from an unoccupied fulmar nest, was found to consist entirely of cockle (*Cerastoderma edule*). This latter midden appeared to butt onto a drystone wall and was sealed by in excess of 6m of dune sands. A shell from each of the middens was submitted for radiocarbon dating and these provided dates of 4320-4030 cal BC (95.4%, GU-11218) and 3750-3520 cal BC (95.4%, GU-11219) for the lower and upper middens respectively.

The dates confirmed that the site was early, with the two middens appearing to span the Mesolithic-Neolithic transition. This was significant, as no Mesolithic sites had previously been recognised in the Northern Isles, although there had been finds of Mesolithic-type artefacts on Orkney and Fair Isle (Mithen 2000, 15; Saville 2000, 94) and a Mesolithic human presence on Shetland had been proposed from pollen analyses (Bennett *et al* 1992; Bennett & Sharp 1993a, 1993b; Edwards 1996). Following the confirmation of the early date of the middens at West Voe, and the fact that the site was under threat from coastal erosion, further evaluation and excavation was undertaken in 2004 and 2005.

THE 2004 AND 2005 FIELDWORK

The aims of the 2004 season were to determine the extent and preservation of the eroding middens, to obtain additional samples and dating evidence from each of the middens, and to assess the threat to the site from coastal erosion. In 2005 the aims were to obtain information on the nature and the formation of the lower midden, and to examine the evidence for the Mesolithic-Neolithic transition within the midden sequence. The fieldwork concentrated on certain aspects of the lower midden that had been noted in the previous year's work. These included an activity surface of crushed mussel shells that was present within the sequence of midden deposits and a detailed investigation of the northern edge of the midden.

EXCAVATION AND SAMPLING METHODOLOGIES

The 2004-2005 excavations at West Voe were limited by the nature of the site. The thick deposits of unstable sands that sealed the middens restricted investigations

2 The site in 2004

to the cleaning of the lower part of the eroding section (*2*). The section, which extended from natural to the sands sealing the upper midden, was cut back to vertical, exposing a narrow, typically 0.5m wide, strip of the lower midden. In the centre of the section examined this exposed strip increased to in excess of 1m in width. Part of the increased exposure of the lower midden in this part of the section was the result of coastal erosion by the winter storms of January 2005 that also resulted in the loss of a small area of midden deposits. A 14m length of the coastline was examined in 2004-2005 (*3*). The strip of midden deposits and contemporary ground surface that was exposed by cutting back the section was divided into 0.5m sampling blocks. Each block was excavated stratigraphically and all contexts were totally sampled in order to maximise recovery of economic and artefactual evidence. The samples were processed using a siraf-style tank fitted with 1mm residue and 500 micron flot meshes.

In addition to the exposure of the strip of lower midden, in 2004 a second step, 2.5m long, was cut to the north of the wall feature in order to permit examination of a small area of a ground surface associated with the upper midden and to provide access to a column for taking OSL dating samples from the sands sealing the upper midden. In order to facilitate sampling of both the black Holocene layer and the

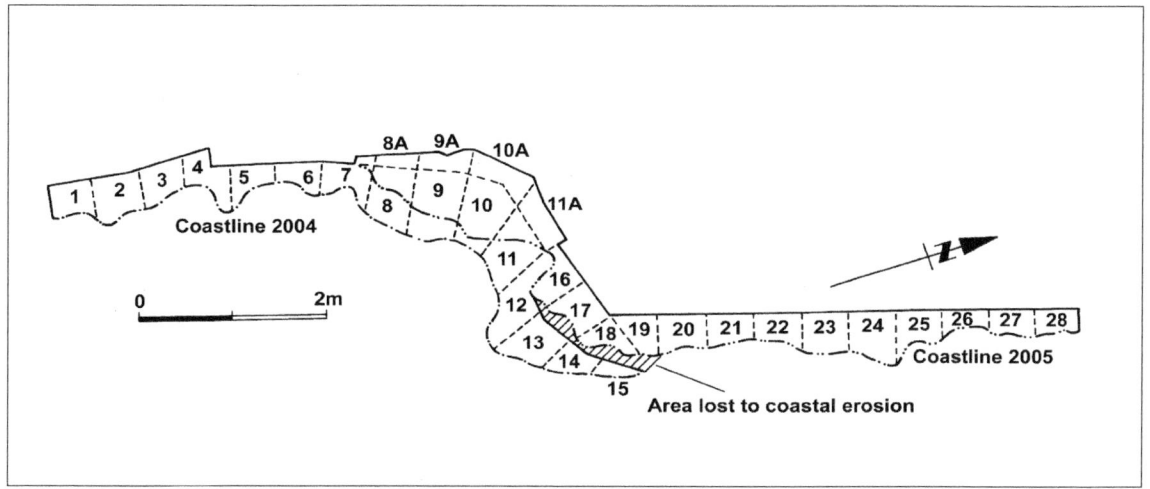

3 Plan showing midden blocks excavated in 2004 and 2005

sands that sealed the midden at a position clear of disturbance by human activity, an additional section of the eroding cliff face to the north of the main section was cleaned but not cut back to vertical. Column samples were taken in this extension to the main section for the detailed examination of the sands and for pollen and microtephra analyses of the Holocene layer. The lateral extent of the lower midden was determined in 2004-2005 by cutting a series of column samples to the south of the main section. These indicated that the midden extended for approximately 20m north to south. Auger samples taken to the rear of the section failed to locate the midden and it appears that it has now been almost completely lost to coastal erosion.

SITE STRATIGRAPHY

The basal Holocene deposit
Sealing the sandstone and glacial till natural was a thin layer of black silty sand. This layer was continuous throughout the section examined. It was of variable thickness, with pockets of local thickening where it had filled in hollows in the underlying natural. The lower midden deposits had been pressed into, and had become intercalated with, this deposit. To the north of the main midden, in sample blocks 20-28 where it was undisturbed, its upper surface was even, dipping gently to the north. This deposit was traced for a considerable distance to the south of the site. It contained fragments of charcoal and much microscopic charcoal, hinting at an earlier human presence in the area. Finds from this layer consisted of a number of tiny fragments of quartz debitage, the majority of

which were found on its upper surface in sample blocks 20-28. A charcoal sample, taken from this layer at a point where it was disturbed by the overlying midden deposits, provided a radiocarbon date of 7030-6640 cal BC (95.4%, OxA-14147).

The lower midden

The lower midden contained evidence for both stratified deposition and for lateral change. In sample blocks 1-6, in the southern end of the section examined in 2004, the midden consisted of a basal layer of large oysters, mixed with limpets and occasional razor shells, that had been pressed into the underlying Holocene deposit. This basal, predominantly oyster, layer was overlain by a layer of shells mixed with seal and sea-bird bones, and, finally, by a greasy layer that also contained shells and seal and sea-bird bones. This section of the midden lay to the south of a possible cut feature, located where the natural changed from sandstone in the south to glacial till in the north. This possible feature, which had vertical sides and a flat base, contained coarse angular gravel and is possibly geological, rather than archaeological, in origin. The midden deposits thinned at this point (in sample block 7) but thickened again to the north of it, the sequence of layers within it

4 The eroding midden section in 2005 (sample block 17)

becoming more developed, and the deposits attaining a maximum thickness of 0.3m (*4*). The sequence of deposits present in the northern part of the section, towards the northern edge of the midden, consisted of a basal deposit of horizontally orientated oyster shells, again co-mingled with the underlying Holocene layer, that was overlain by a layer containing a jumble of limpet shells and large numbers of seal and sea-bird bones, the latter two tending to occur in concentrated pockets. There was some evidence for articulation, particularly in the bird bones. These earlier oyster and limpet-rich phases of the midden had a common northern edge in sample block 19 (*5 & 6*). The mixed limpet/bone layer was sealed by an occupation surface formed from trampled mussel shells that was then sealed by the greasy black layer containing shells and seal and sea-bird bones which was also present in the south of the section. In sample blocks 17 and 18 a small deposit of uncrushed mussel shells represented the final phase of use of this midden (see *5*). Although the main midden sequence had its northern edge in sample block 19, there was evidence of continued activity to the north of this in the later, mussel, phase of use. A series of mixed sandy and organic deposits containing mussels continued as far as sample blocks 25 and 26, at which point

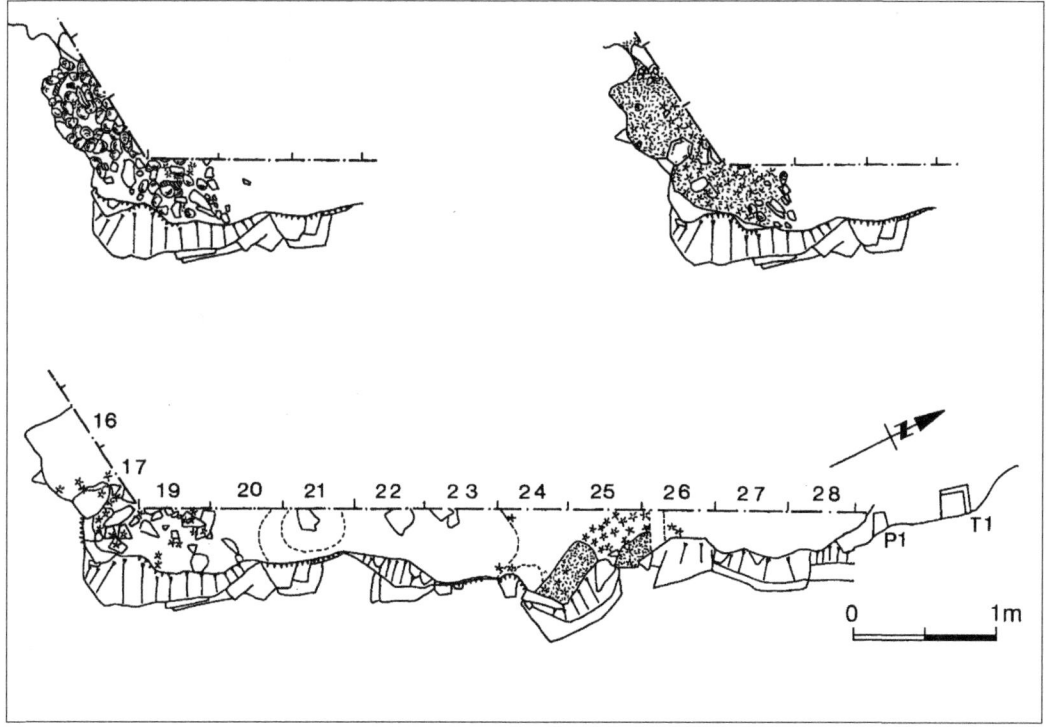

5 Plan of the lower midden in samples blocks 16-28, showing the northern edge of the midden in the oyster, activity surface, and mussel-rich phases of use and the northern extension to the midden in the final, mussel, phase of use

6 The northern edge of the midden in the limpet phase in sample block 19

there was a surface of crushed shell sealed by a small deposit of uncrushed mussels and clams (*Venerupis* sp(p.)) (see 5) that had been deposited directly on the black Holocene layer.

The sands between the middens
Sometime after the deposition of the small deposits of mussels and clams, the lower midden was sealed by approximately 0.4m of sand. A thin, gently undulating, black organic layer present in the 2005 section suggested that at least two deposition events are present in these sands and that there was time for a vegetation cover to develop between these.

A number of features had been cut into these sands. A series of intersecting pits and linear features was recorded above sample blocks 6 to 10. The two linear features present, both of which contained lenses of dark organic sand, ran at a shallow angle to the face of the section and were difficult to interpret. It may be that they represent a single feature that had been re-cut. The last in the sequence of cut features was a shallow pit containing cockles. Although the majority of these features were confined to the sands, one pit, containing a deposit of cockles in its base, had cut through the lower midden into the glacial till in sample blocks 11 and 12.

The upper midden and associated structure

Sealing the shallow pit that contained cockles was a double-faced wall, 0.6m wide and surviving to a height of 0.6m. A second structural element present was a 0.1m-diameter stake hole located 1m to the south of the wall. This stake hole was sealed by a 0.4m thick cockle midden that butted onto the southern face of the wall. The cockle midden extended for 4m to the south of the wall, at which point it thinned to less than 0.1m thick. Augering revealed that the midden extended in excess of 5m back from the cliff face. To the north of the wall, and associated with the cockle midden, was an extensive layer of cockles, *c.*0.05m thick. This layer was present as far as the cleaned section extended to the north and was also located in a series of auger samples taken to the rear of the section.

The sands sealing the middens

A series of sand deposits had accumulated against the northern face of the wall and within these, at a position level with the surviving top of the wall, was a thin layer of fragmented shells that also contained a cow tooth and a fragment of sheep or goat skull. This layer was sealed by *c.*0.8m of dune sands, above which was a more compacted sandy layer, 0.25m thick, that was then sealed by a thick sequence of dune sands in excess of 5m thick. This sequence of sands was OSL dated. Those immediately above the layer containing the cow tooth were Neolithic, the compacted layer dated to the Bronze Age, and the sands immediately above this were post-medieval, dating to the seventeenth century AD.

THE FINDS

The total sampling and wet sieving of all contexts resulted in the recovery of 289 lithic artefacts, the vast majority (286 items) being quartz and quartzite debitage, most of it recovered from the 1mm-5mm sieved fraction. The other six items present were three cores, two hammerstones and one quartz flake with edge-retouch (Ballin 2006). The assemblage consisted of 263 quartz, 23 quartzite, two sandstone and one rock crystal fragment. Some 83 per cent of the quartz and 100 per cent of the quartzite items were from contexts in the lower midden. All of the quartzite finds, a core and 22 flakes, were a light rose pink in colour and, although it was not possible to refit any of the debitage, it is possible that all derived from a single source nodule. The quartz items had been procured from both beach pebbles and from quartz veins, the nearest of which are only a few kilometres distant.

In addition to the lithic material, four small sherds of pottery were recovered from the lower midden. Two of the four sherds, both of which were sooted externally, were found in sample block 5 and are probably from the same vessel. The other sherds were found in sample blocks 4 and 13, the latter example being concreted to the activity surface of crushed mussel shell. All of the sherds are from the bodies of vessels, but are too small to provide any indication of the vessel forms. A radiocarbon date of 3710-3530 cal BC (95.4%, GU-13836) was obtained from a fragment of animal bone that directly overlay the pottery fragments found in sample block 5.

THE ECONOMIC EVIDENCE

Marine molluscs
As described above, a sequence of dominant marine mollusc species was present in the lower midden. The primary target for exploitation was oyster and the valves present were from large specimens, some more than 10 years old (N. Milner *pers. comm.*). Oysters were present in sample blocks 1-6 and 8-19, the latter marking the northern edge to the midden in its earliest phases. This bimodal distribution corresponded with the observed lateral changes in midden stratigraphy. The greatest concentrations of oysters were in sample blocks 1-3 and 5-6 in the southern part of the section, and in sample blocks 8 and 16-19.

The second phase present in the midden was associated with the exploitation of limpets. The distribution of limpets was similar to that of the oysters, with the limpets also having a bimodal distribution; in sample blocks 1-5 and then in blocks 8-19. The greatest concentration of limpets occurred at the northern edge of the midden, in sample blocks 12-19 (see 6). The distribution of mussels, the third of the species to be targeted, was somewhat different. There was still a bimodal distribution, with fairly small numbers of mussels being found in sample blocks 2-4, followed by an absence of shells in blocks 5-8 and their reappearance in block 9. The mussels, however, continued beyond sample block 19, the midden edge in the earlier phases. The northern limit of the mussel layer of the midden occurred in sample blocks 24-25, where they were associated with a small area of trampled shell (see 5).

Other species of marine molluscs were present in smaller numbers in the lower midden contexts. These included razorshells (*Ensis* sp(p.)), cockles (*Cerastoderma edule* (L)), dogwhelks (*Nucella lapillus* (L)), rough periwinkles (*Littorina littorea* (L)), topshells (*Gibbula/Monodota* sp(p.)) (Nicholson 2005a), and clams (*Venerupis* sp(p.)) (Newman & Russ 2006). In contrast, the upper midden was composed entirely of the shells of one species, cockles. There was a pocket of predominantly complete shells against the southern face of the wall, but, in general, this midden was composed of fragmented shells.

Marine mammals
Work on the faunal material is ongoing, but preliminary assessments have revealed that in excess of 1200 fragments of seal bone were recovered in 2004-2005 (Worley

2005, 2006). Both grey seal (*Halichoeus grypus*) and harbour/common seal (*Phoca vitulina*) were present and many of the bones were from juveniles. The majority of the seal bones were recovered from the second, limpet, phase of the lower midden and, although the bones were present across much of the site, they often occurred in discrete pockets in sample blocks 11-19.

Terrestrial mammals

A small number of bone fragments were identified as being from terrestrial mammals (Worley 2005, 2006). Two rib fragments from large (cow-sized) ungulates were recovered from the upper part of the lower midden, whilst a humerus fragment from a medium (sheep- or dog-sized) animal was found on the top of the glacial till in sample block 9 – the point where the midden deposits thinned down. A cattle molar and a fragment of petrous bone, possibly sheep or goat, were found in a layer of shell fragments within the sands that had accumulated against the northern face of the wall and represent the latest evidence for a human presence on the site.

Sea-birds

Only half of the 370 fragments of bird bone recovered were identifiable, and of these many were those of shag (*Phalacrocorax aristotalis*) or shag-sized birds, with both mature and immature individuals being represented (Nicholson 2005b, 2006). Other species present included eider duck (*Somateria mollissima*), puffin (*Fratercula arctica*), swan (*Cygnus* sp.) and greater black-backed gull (*Larus marinus*). The bird bones, like those of the seal, were from the second, limpet, phase of the lower midden. They were mainly mixed within the pockets of seal bone and included a number of examples that had evidence for articulation.

Fish

A small number of fish bones were recovered from the sieved residues (Nicholson 2006). All were from small or tiny fish and the majority were found in contexts associated with the final, mussel, phase of the lower midden. Identified taxa include herring/sprat (Clupeidae), mackerel (*Scomber scombus*), cottid(s) (Cottidae), butterfish (*Pholis gunnellus*), ray (Rajidae) and gadids (Gadidae).

THE DATING EVIDENCE AND THE MESOLITHIC–NEOLITHIC TRANSITION

The radiocarbon dates obtained in 2002 from shells from each of the middens, namely 4320-4030 cal BC from the lower midden and 3750-3520 cal BC from the upper midden, suggested that the former dated from the Late Mesolithic and the latter from the Early Neolithic. Furthermore, the layer of sands between the two middens hinted that the fundamental social and economic changes had coincided with a dramatic change in the local coastal environment. The more detailed programme of dating that was undertaken in the 2004-2005 seasons of fieldwork revealed that this preliminary interpretation needed modification. The later samples dated the initial, oyster, phase of the lower midden to $c.$4000-3700 cal BC, and the second, limpet, phase to $c.$3700-3600 cal BC. One of the large ungulate ribs was dated at 3710-3530 cal. BC (95.4%, GU-13836), which is in close agreement with the activity surface of crushed mussel shells dated to $c.$3700-3600 cal BC. The final phase of use of the lower midden, the deposits of complete mussels in sample blocks 17-18 and 25-26, was dated to $c.$3650-3500 cal BC. These dates suggest that the Mesolithic-Neolithic transition took place within the accumulation of the lower midden. The appearance of ceramics in the upper part of the midden, the date provided by the ungulate bone and the shift in the boundary of the midden in its final phase of use, all suggest that this transition occurred somewhere around the time of the formation of the activity surface in 3700-3600 cal BC.

Subsequent to the deposition of the lower midden the picture is one of rapid environmental change, with the 2004-2005 dates from the cockle midden indicating that it was deposited within the period $c.$3500-3250 cal BC. This means that the whole sequence of events that occurred after the final, mussel, phase of deposition of the lower midden, that is the deposition of the sands, the cutting of a sequence of features into them, the construction of the wall and the deposition of the cockle midden, is likely to have occurred within the span of two centuries or less. The site, the first of this period to be found in this region on the north-western fringe of Europe, therefore has the potential to provide vital new information on the Mesolithic-Neolithic transition and its relationship to environmental change in the North Atlantic/North Sea region in the fourth millennium cal BC.

ACKNOWLEDGEMENTS

This project has been funded by research grants from Historic Scotland, NERC (NER/B/S/2003/00779) and The Prehistoric Society. The midden site lies within the boundary of Sumburgh Airport and I am grateful to Scotair Properties and to Mr N. Flaws, Airport Manager, for permission to carry out the investigations and for providing indoor space for finds processing and storage.

Dr Becky Nicholson (Oxford Archaeology) coordinated and supervised the programme of environmental sampling and analyses. Thanks are also due to Dr C. Christiansen, Shetland Amenity Trust, for provision of GPS coordinates of the site survey stations.

REFERENCES

Ballin, T.B. 2006, 'West Voe, Sumburgh, Shetland: the lithic assemblage' in Melton, N.D., *Late Mesolithic-Early Neolithic middens at West Voe, Sumburgh, Shetland: 2005 Field Season*, 38-44, University of Bradford

Bennett, K.D., Boreham, S., Sharp, M.J. & Switsur, V.R. 1992, 'Holocene history of environment, vegetation and human settlement on Catta Ness, Lunasting, Shetland', *Journal of Ecology* 80, 241-273

Bennett, K.D. & Sharp, M.J. 1993a, 'Holocene vegetation and environment', in Birnie, J., Gordon, J., Bennett, K. & Hall, A. (eds) *The Quaternary of Shetland: a field guide*, 18-22, London

Bennett, K.D. & Sharp, M.J. 1993b, 'Holocene environmental history at Dallican Water, Northeast Mainland, Shetland', in Birnie, J., Gordon, J., Bennett, K. & Hall, A. (eds), *The Quaternary of Shetland: a field guide*, 77-82, London

Edwards, K. 1996, 'A Mesolithic of the northern and western isles of Scotland? Evidence from pollen and charcoal', in Pollard, T. & Morrison, A. (eds), *The Early Prehistory of Scotland*, 23-38, Edinburgh

Hamilton, J.R.C. 1956, *Excavations at Jarlshof, Shetland*, Edinburgh

Hedges, J.W. & Parry, G.A. 1980, 'A Neolithic multiple burial from Sumburgh, Shetland', *Glasgow Archaeol J* 7, 15-26

Melton, N.D. 2005, *A late Mesolithic midden at West Voe, Sumburgh, Shetland: archaeological evaluation 2004*, University of Bradford

Melton, N.D. 2006, *Late Mesolithic-Early Neolithic middens at West Voe, Sumburgh, Shetland: 2005 Field Season*, University of Bradford

Melton, N.D. & Nicholson, R.A. 2004, 'The Mesolithic in the Northern Isles: the preliminary evaluation of an oyster midden at West Voe, Sumburgh, Shetland, U. K.', *Antiquity* 78, no. 299. Accessed by http://antiquity.ac.uk/ProjGall/nicholson/index.html

Mithen, S. 2000, 'The Scottish Mesolithic: problems, prospects and the rationale of the Southern Hebrides Mesolithic Project', in Mithen, S. (ed.), *Hunter-gatherer landscape archaeology: the Southern Hebrides Mesolithic Project 1988-98*, 9-37, Cambridge (McDonald Institute for Archaeological Research Monogr)

Newman, E.K.J. & Russ, H. 2006, 'Shells', in Melton, N.D., *Late Mesolithic-Early Neolithic middens at West Voe, Sumburgh, Shetland: 2005 Field Season*, 23-24, University of Bradford

Nicholson, R.A. 2005a, 'The Shells', in Melton, N.D., *A late Mesolithic midden at West Voe, Sumburgh, Shetland: archaeological evaluation 2004*, 23, University of Bradford

Nicholson, R.A. 2005b, 'Bird bone', in Melton, N.D., *A late Mesolithic midden at West Voe, Sumburgh, Shetland: archaeological evaluation 2004*, 24, University of Bradford

Nicholson, R.A. 2006, 'Bird bone', in Melton, N.D., *Late Mesolithic-Early Neolithic middens at West Voe, Sumburgh, Shetland: 2005 Field Season*, 27-28, University of Bradford

Saville, A. 2000, 'Orkney and Scotland before the Neolithic period' in Ritchie, A. (ed.), *Neolithic Orkney in its European Context*, 91-100, Cambridge (McDonald Institute for Archaeological Research Monogr)

Worley, F. 2005, 'Mammal bone', in Melton, N.D., *A late Mesolithic midden at West Voe, Sumburgh, Shetland: archaeological evaluation 2004*, 25-27, University of Bradford

Worley, F. 2006, 'Mammal bone', in Melton, N.D., *Late Mesolithic-Early Neolithic middens at West Voe, Sumburgh, Shetland: 2005 Field Season*, 28-30, University of Bradford

3

AN ISLAND OF FLUCTUATING PERCEPTIONS: THE LANDSCAPE AND ARCHAEOLOGY OF BUTE

Gordon Noble & Fay Stevens

INTRODUCTION

The research from which this chapter derives considers the landscape and archaeology of the island of Bute, in south-west Scotland, within a framework that reconsiders current definitions of islands. The project involves an exploration of the landscape and associated archaeology of the island. Utilising recent developments in 'island archaeology' in the Mediterranean and Pacific (e.g. Broodbank 2000, Fitzpatrick 2004) and incorporating these with theoretical approaches more common in Western European archaeology, we hope to suggest new methodologies for the study of islands and to promote 'island archaeologies' in an under-studied geographical area (i.e. western Britain). Our fieldwork should offer insight into how island 'scapes' and island identities are constructed, maintained and altered through time. We aim to challenge present definitions of what constitutes an island through an examination of the archaeology and physical geography of the island of Bute, using a study of the sites and artefacts dating from the Mesolithic to Early Bronze Age and through an analysis of the topography of the island. Our research has explicitly aimed to address the concept of 'insularity' both in a methodological and theoretical manner through the study of the archaeology of a small Scottish island. Utilising a landscape approach to the archaeology of the island we hope to contribute to the wider theoretical debate on how island landscapes (and their associated seascapes) can be studied in relation to concepts of insularity, island-mainland relationships, connectedness (or lack of) and changes through the course of time. Our fieldwork methodology involves site visits to all archaeological sites dating from the Mesolithic to Early Bronze Age on the island to identify patterns (or lack of) in the landscape location (topography, soils, environment, land capability, access to sea, relationship to the mainland, etc.) view-sheds, orientations, architecture and the contexts of archaeological material.

AN INTRODUCTION TO THE ISLAND

Geology and topography and location
The island of Bute is situated in the Firth of Clyde in western Scotland. The island is one of a number of islands in this area, located close to the mainland. Bute is just over 24km (15 miles) in length and between 1.5-8km wide (1-5 miles). To the north, the island is separated from Cowal in mainland Argyll by a short stretch of seawater. To the east is Ayrshire in lowland Scotland, to the west the peninsula of Kintyre and to the south the larger island of Arran. There are a number of smaller islands grouped around Bute itself. The island has a rich archaeological resource, with sites and monuments from the Mesolithic to more recent times.

The island of Bute is divided into two main geological zones by the Highland Boundary Fault (*1*), a geological split which separates highland from lowland Scotland (Whittow 1977; Munro 1973). The divide runs south-west across the island from the main town of Rothesay towards Scalpsie Bay on the west coast. The northern half of the island is made of metamorphic rocks, schists, grits and phyllites, which tend to support poor, thin, acidic soils, giving the north a barren moorland-like appearance only occasionally broken by more productive land. In the south, the land is composed of Old Red sandstones, which support a more arable landscape. The southern tip of Bute provides another contrast. Here, the sandstones have been engulfed by basaltic lavas of Carboniferous age, which create another area of rough, undulating and comparatively barren moorland (Whittow 1977, 80).

Bute is not as mountainous as the larger island of Arran to the south, whose distinctive profile can be identified from great distances. The northern and southern tips of Bute are generally higher than the more low-lying areas between. However, this does not mean that these areas are more distinctive. The northern end of the island, for example, is nested amongst the jutting peninsulas of the Cowal area of mainland Scotland. As Munro notes, it often becomes difficult to distinguish between island and mainland in this area of the island (Munro 1973, 11). Indeed, the topography in the northern Clyde is such a maze of peninsulas, bays, sea lochs, mountains, land and sea that it becomes difficult to identify where islands end and mainland begins. The chief exception to this, as mentioned already, is the island of Arran, whose great mountains and distinctive profiles mark the island as an important landmark in this area of western Scotland.

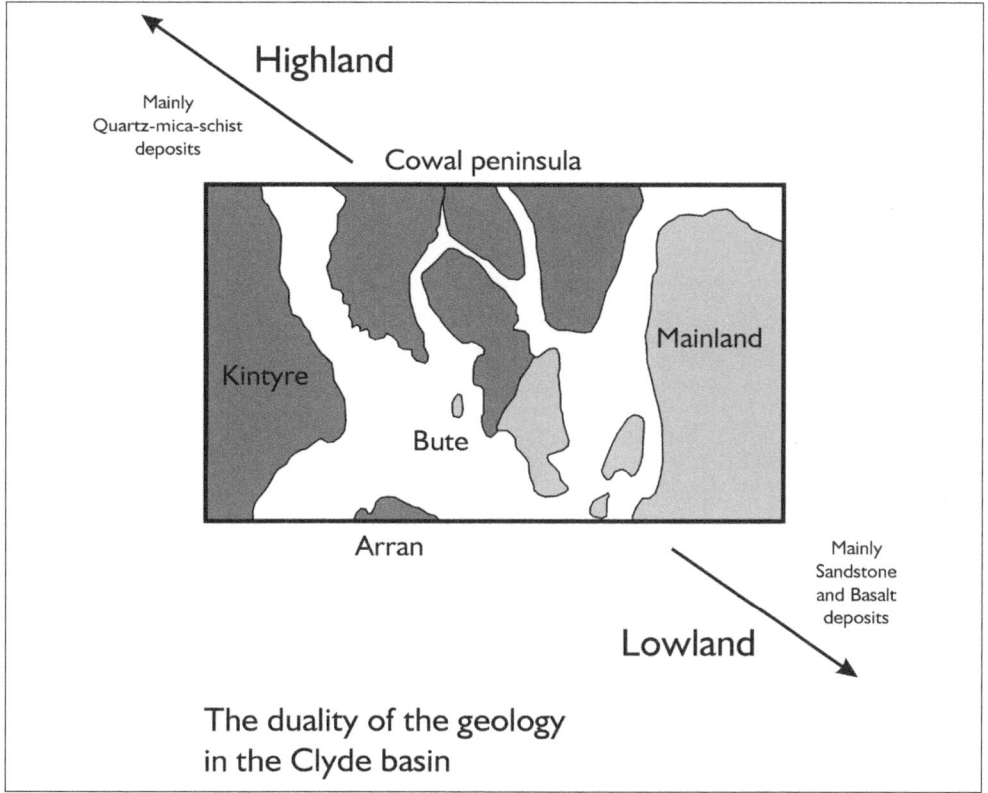

1 Schematic diagram of the geology in the Firth of Clyde demonstrating the way in which the island of Bute is bisected by the Highland Boundary Fault

What is an island?

As noted above, our research aims to consider the landscape and archaeology of the Island of Bute, in south-west Scotland, within a framework that explicitly reconsiders the definition of an island. In the past, islands have often been seen as bounded areas of land open to limited outside influence and often displaying evidence of insularity. This has often led to the consideration of an island as a relatively isolated geographical and social laboratory, framed within an evolutionary paradigm (e.g. Kirch & Green 2001) and as both physically and socially insular (*contra* Gosden & Pavlides 1994). For example, Evans (1973) argued that islands are made for 'closed communities', as being surrounded by the sea imposes restrictions on communications with groups elsewhere (Evans 1973, 516). Consequently individual islands in this view could be studied is isolation in order to elucidate interpretations that could then be applied to other areas. In contrast, more recent ideas on islands have seen the potential for these places to be dynamic, innovative locations that may have had wider significance beyond the so-called boundaries of the sea and have highlighted the dangers of studying individual islands in isolation

(Broodbank 2000; Noble 2003). In the Clyde area, the physical layout of the islands and mainland means that island and mainland are never far away and the layout encourages inter-island and island-mainland communication. The islands form an excellent example of an island nursery – where a favourable configuration of islandscapes in close proximity actively encourages sea travel and communication (Broodbank 2000, 131). However, many current studies still accept the boundaries of island landmasses at face value and rarely question whether an island forms a single entity rather than seeing the island itself as composed of a variety of fragmented, but inter-connected landforms, some of which may have closer relations to adjacent mainland areas than other parts of the island. In fact, Fitzpatrick comments on how the archaeological study of islands and island regions has itself developed in partial isolation compared to other areas of the world or landforms (Fitzpatrick 2004, xiii).

We would like to begin this study of the landscape location of the Neolithic and Bronze Age archaeology of Bute by questioning the very unity of Bute as an island. Rather than a single monolithic landmass, it is possible to suggest that Bute is in fact made up of a myriad/mosaic of areas, defined by distinct topographic locales, which at times seem to almost act like islands themselves. Some of these areas undoubtedly had significance to areas beyond the coastline of Bute and this should become evident in the case studies presented below. In our study we suggest that through the Neolithic and Bronze Age different parts of the island were marked by monuments and material culture in strikingly different ways, which suggests any notion of centrality on the island may have shifted through time. The changing pattern of monumentality and material culture distribution on the island suggests that at times the island acted as an insular island, while at others it functioned as part of a complex interplay of communication networks between the mainland, islands and the sea. In this respect the concept of what defined the island, or for that matter whether it was thought of as an island at all, may have fluctuated over time.

The North-South Divide
The definition of the island must consider the 'bones' of the land itself and how the very fabric of the island might have affected human practice. As noted earlier, the Highland Boundary Fault runs across the island. The fault cuts the island in two, creating at least two different 'islands', each with distinctive characters. The southern part of the island is more like the adjacent mainland to the east. This part of the island tends to be low-lying with gentle rolling hills where arable and pastoral farming dominates and where the main concentrations of population are found today. In the north the landscape is more akin to what many people envision Scotland to be like – mountainous, bleak and barren in places, and sparsely populated, yet spectacularly beautiful. The north is similar to the northern and western highland landscapes of Scotland and at times seems to meld with the mainland on the north. The northern

part of the island is nested between the jutting peninsulas of the Cowal mainland and at times the northern part of Bute is visually indistinguishable from this mainland area and hardly seems like an island at all. The Highland Boundary Fault creates highland and lowland regions within the island, in this respect Bute, like the isle of Arran to the south, is like 'Scotland in miniature' (Munro 1973), a microcosm of the Scottish landscape. These geological divides are not merely of interest to the geologist. These basic divides in the island have had an effect on the islanders themselves. For example, until the end of the nineteenth century, Gaelic, the language of the western highlands, was spoken by people living in the north, whereas Old Scots, more closely related to the southern, English, language was the dominant means of communication in the rest of the island (Munro 1973, 208). These divisions have implications for the construction of island identities and the orchestration of relations between social groups on the island and beyond.

Dividing Topography

The notion of Bute as a single island entity can be further questioned if we also consider topography. The landscape of Bute is even more variable if topographical distinctions are also taken into account. In 1973, Munro identified three 'natural' divisions to the island:

> The north – mainly wild moorland, bog and hilly ground
> Mid island – valleys and lochs
> The south – a basalt raised plateau with cliffs (Munro 1973)

During our fieldwork on Bute we identified at least five basic divisions of the landscape (2). These can be characterised as such:

The northern zone – Similar to Munro's description, this zone is characterised as upland moorland with very limited agricultural use, isolated, with little evidence for settlement. Thin strips of agricultural land on the west and east coasts with some limited settlement.

Northern bisecting valley (Ettrick to Kames Bay) – this wide, open valley separates the mid part and the northern parts of the island. This valley forms an important communication route between the eastern and western parts of the island.

Mid island zone – this part of the island is the main agricultural area on the island with rich resources and extensive settlement. Low lying, rolling hills with a number of lochs running down the centre of this area. These run north-east to south-west, further subdividing the mid-island area.

Southern bisecting valley (Stravanan to Kilchattan Bay) – This smaller valley separates the middle of the island from the southern rocky headland area. This valley also forms an important linking point between the eastern and western sides of the island.

Scottish Odysseys: The Archaeology of Islands

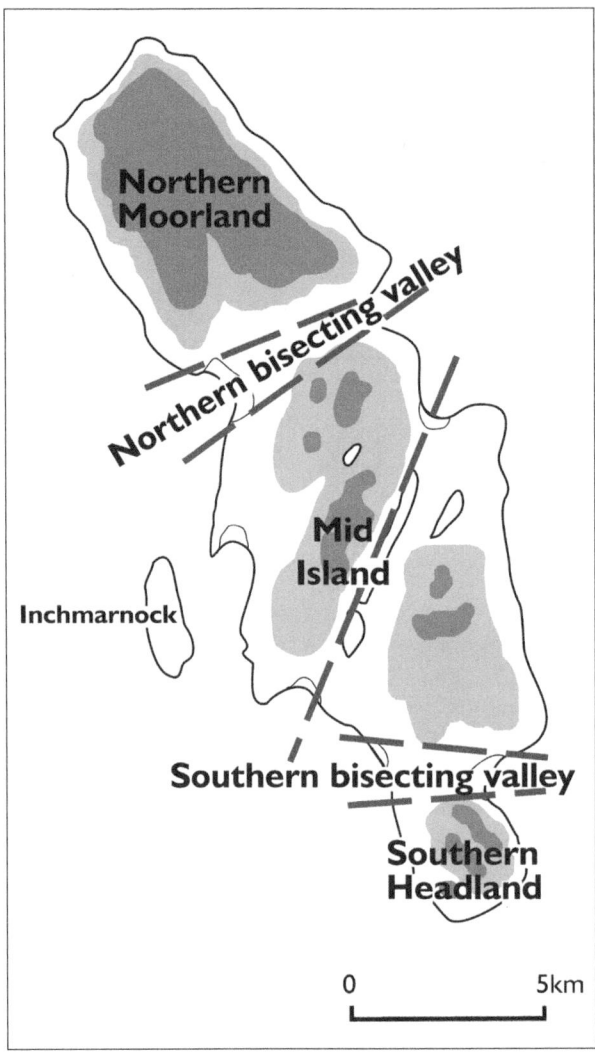

2 The topographic zones of Bute

The southern zone – a large basalt dome creates a projecting headland at the southern end of Bute. Rocky and rugged, this part of the island is dramatic and distinct.

Topographically, we would also like to highlight the importance of the main bays on the island (*3 & 4*), which would have been important places for arriving at and departing from the island by boat and the places where visitors would have first encountered the many islands of Bute. The consideration of these topographic zones is crucial for a more critical understanding of island inhabitation. The largest of the bays on the island are found at the ends of both of the bisecting valleys, further strengthening their role as important routeways and communication corridors. Further bays are also found at either end of the highland boundary fault

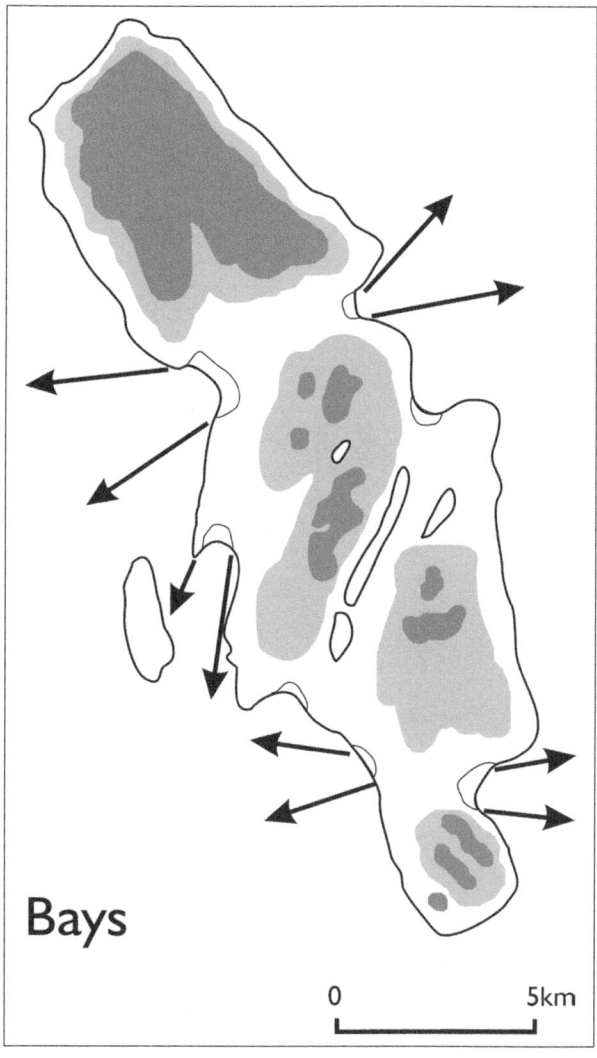

3 The bays of Bute

and at St Ninian's Bay on the west coast. We would argue that these topographical divisions had real impacts on people's perceptions and experiences of the island, and were at times physically demarcated or monumentalised. There is a later example from the Early Medieval period, when the southern zone of Bute was divided from the rest of the island by the inhabitants of the early Christian church settlement at St Blane's (Hewison 1895, 166-93; Munro 1973, 51-5). A wall was constructed from sea to sea, effectively creating an island within an island. This barrier may have been as much symbolic as physical, the placement of early Christian religious establishments on isolated islands is a well-known phenomenon, the wall effectively achieved such a location, separating the barren rocky headland from the larger islandscape of Bute and beyond.

Scottish Odysseys: The Archaeology of Islands

4 Ettrick Bay looking towards the island of Arran

Islands of time

Topographical distinctions complicate the definition of Bute as a single entity and the concept of a single island fragments upon closer consideration. Instead we are left with a series of different landscapes, each of which could have formed different taskscapes in prehistory (Ingold 1993; Sturt 2005). Each of these island zones would have been suitable for different forms of activity in the Neolithic and Bronze Age, but at the same time these may have been intimately connected through seasonally shifting settlement lifestyles (Cooney 2000, ch.3; Edmonds 1999; Thomas 1999). However, it is likely that these zones would still have been seen as distinct locales, associated with different experiences, seasons and activities. For example, the bays would have been locations where people came in contact with people who did not reside on the island and/or locations where people left the island world behind. The northern area of the island may have been associated with the seasonal grazing of animals, whereas the central area of the island may have been where cereals were grown and harvested. Indeed the topographical areas identified above may have been of fluctuating importance throughout the Neolithic and Bronze Age. The very definition of what constituted the island we now identify as Bute may have altered radically over time, but how can we get any sense of how the islandscapes were viewed in the past? This is where the archaeological remains of past island inhabitations may be crucial, giving us clues as to how the islandscapes of Bute were constructed and restructured over time. The archaeological evidence from the Earlier Neolithic, Later Neolithic and Early Bronze Age periods seems to indicate that different areas were emphasised through time on the island, both through the construction of monuments and through the structured depositions of what we refer to here as 'non-visual cultural markers' in the landscape; the places where material culture was deposited or inscribed on the island. If the island of Bute can be seen as a series of interconnecting island zones, it is important to assess how these might have been conceptualised and utilised in the past and how this might have impacted on the perceptions of the islandscape. We would now like to explore some of these themes through a case study that considers the distribution of archaeological remains from the Neolithic and Early Bronze Age on the island.

THE EARLIER NEOLITHIC AND THE CHAMBERED CAIRNS OF BUTE

The remains of the Earlier Neolithic period on the island of Bute consists of six chambered cairns and a small number of settlement locations. The number of cairns on Bute forms a distinct concentration of chambered cairns which is only matched by the number of cairns found on the island of Arran to the south (5). The cairns are sited in a group of five on the northern topographic zone of the island, on the margins, or above the agricultural strips of land near the coast. In the past these cairns have been interpreted as the territorial markers of small agricultural communities (Renfrew 1973; 1976). However, a close examination of the location of the cairns on Bute suggests more complex reasons were behind the construction and location of these Earlier Neolithic chambered cairns. If a regional view is adopted, it can be seen that the concentration of cairns on Arran and Bute are not matched by similar numbers elsewhere. In a 1988 study, Isobel Hughes argued persuasively that this was not due to preservational factors alone (Hughes 1988).[1] It seems more likely that these islands had a more central role in the treatment of the dead in the Firth of Clyde during the Earlier Neolithic and this forces us to consider the more complex ways these islands may have fitted into a wider geographic context, governed by more extensive social connections than have previously been suggested. The clustered location of cairns on Bute are difficult to explain within a territorial model. Five of the six cairns are in the northern zone of the island in some of the least productive areas of land. While these cairns form a distinct grouping, it is important to note that not all of these may be contemporary.

Of the five cairns in the main concentration in the northern zone of the island, two appear to be of an earlier form. Glecknabae (6) and Michael's Grave (7) are small round cairns of the type that tend to be earlier examples of Clyde cairns (Bryce 1903-4, 33-52; Henshall 1972, 408-14). In contrast, the others are more complex:

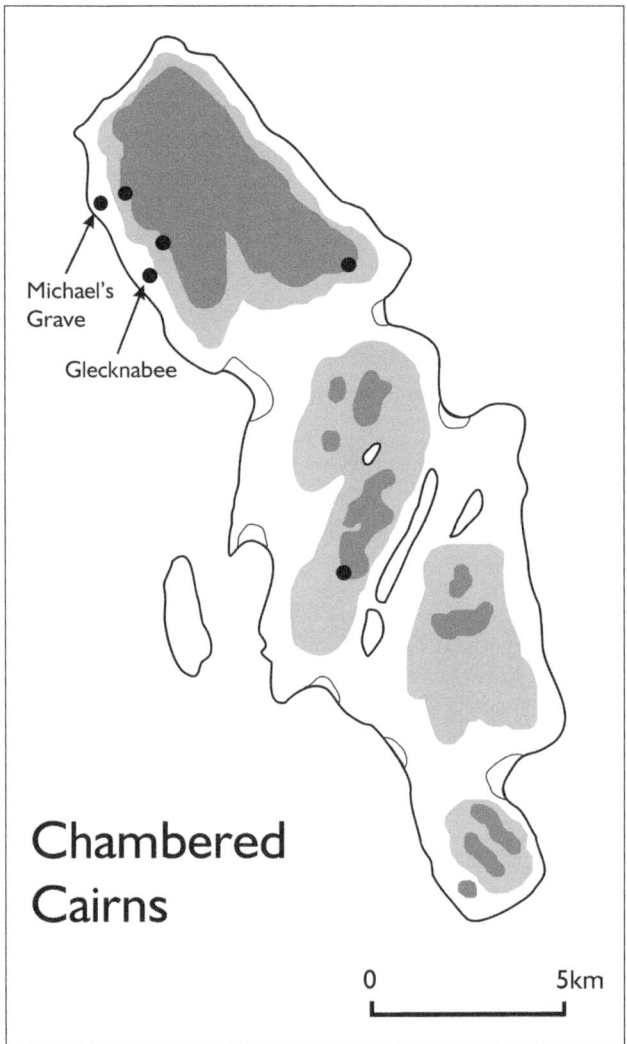

5 Distribution of chambered cairns on Bute

Glenvoidean has three chambers which are encased in a trapezoidal cairn, while Carnbaan is a massive long cairn with multiple chambers (Marshall & Taylor 1976-7; Henshall 1972, 410-11). Hilton was found in a dilapidated state, but probably resembled Glenvoidean in its finished condition (Marshall 1976). The structural sequence at Clyde cairns monuments suggests that simple round cairns were the early phases of Neolithic monuments in this area (Noble 2005; Corcoran 1969; Scott 1969). For example, at Mid Gleniron in Wigtownshire, two round cairns with small chambers were later subsumed within a massive trapezoidal cairn (Corcoran 1969). The later trapezoidal phase is strongly similar to the cairn at Glenvoidean. The relative dating of these cairns on Bute is also confirmed by the artefact types discovered in the tombs. While Glecknabae and Michael's Grave only contained

An island of fluctuating perceptions: the landscape and archaeology of Bute

6 Glecknabae chambered cairn from the north

7 Michael's Grave from the north, Arran is in clouds on the right hand horizon of the picture

relatively plain Earlier Neolithic pottery, the chamber at Glenvoidean contained decorated vessels. The plain pots at Glecknabae are close in style to the Traditional Carinated bowl pottery found in the earliest phases of the British and Irish Neolithic, while the Glenvoidean vessels are representative of slightly later styles (Herne 1988).

The reason for the locations of these early chambers in the northern zone of the island is suggested by the presence of what appears to be a Mesolithic shell midden below the cairn of Glecknabae (Cormack 1986). The earlier midden may have been deliberately monumentalised as a symbol of the continuing bonds to a location important to the earlier, perhaps seasonal, Mesolithic inhabitants of this zone of Bute. The location of the other cairns in this zone of the island may have been a means of referencing the past importance of this place due to the presence of the now monumentalised midden at Glecknabae. Over time, the cairns in this zone of Bute became more complex and the capacity of the chambers increased, perhaps indicating the increasing importance of mortuary ritual in Neolithic society and the importance of this zone of Bute in the patterns of social interaction in the Firth of Clyde region. In this way, the cluster of chambered cairns on Bute can perhaps be best interpreted as an island cemetery of wider significance in the Firth of Clyde. This would best explain the large numbers of monuments in this area. The presence of the shell midden, and its implied role in seasonal occupation in the Mesolithic, might suggest that mortuary ritual in the Earlier Neolithic was undertaken at particular times of the year and may have involved the gathering of dispersed communities from across the Firth of Clyde in the northern zone of Bute. Strengthening this suggestion is the location of the two early cairns in the northern zone of the island in close relation to the sea. Michael's Grave is located on a small peninsula that slopes sharply from the shore and when seen from certain directions seems almost to be falling into the sea itself (7). Similarly Glecknabae is located close to the shore and both the midden and the cairn are made up of elements found here; shells of course make up a large proportion of the midden and the quartz stones in the cairn are to be found in abundance on the shore. This relationship with apparently early forms of Neolithic monument and the sea is a common one across the British Isles (Sturt 2005; Cummings & Whittle 2004; Davies 1946).

Both of the early monuments at Glecknabae and Michael's Grave were found to contain material that strengthens the links between the users of these monuments, the sea and the wider island geography of the Firth of Clyde. In the chamber at Michael's Grave, and in both chambers at Glecknabae, pitchstone was found. Pitchstone is a type of volcanic glass found on the island of Arran, located around 10km from the southern part of Bute[2] (Thorpe & Thorpe 1984). The pitchstone and the coastal location perhaps indicate the importance of links to Arran and suggest sea-routes between the two islands. Arran contains the largest concentration of Clyde-type cairns in the whole of Scotland. In this respect, the two early cairns on Bute can be seen as part of the wide connections apparent at the beginnings of the Earlier Neolithic, when new forms of material culture and new lifestyles were adopted over a relatively short period of time across large areas of Britain and Ireland.[3] The early cairns referenced places where other cairns of a similar type were found and were part of a distribution that had significance beyond the immediate island location in the northern zone of Bute.

While these two early cairns share a strong relationship with the sea and other islands, the two later cairns appear to be more closely related to the island of Bute itself. Both Glenvoidean and Carnbaan are located away from the shore and appear to be placed at transitional points between the uplands and the lower ground of the island. Carnbaan is located on a sloping hillside in an elevated position, some distance from the shore. Glenvoidean is also located in an elevated position on a steep hillside in rough grazing at a point between the upland moorland area of northern Bute and the lower coastal areas. Both cairns seem to be more closely related to the islandscape of Bute itself than the two early cairns. Indeed, Glenvoidean and one further cairn in the north (Hilton) may have been located over former settlement locales and in this way the cairns perhaps memorialised former zones of domestic activity on the island (Marshall & Taylor 1976-7; Marshall 1976).

The location of the cairns was due to a range of complex and changing priorities, none of which can be reduced to the territorial concerns of a static, isolated island society. The early cairns seem to have been located in relation to the sea and contained material that referenced other islands amongst the sea-routes of the Firth of Clyde. The sequence and form of Glecknabae also seem to signify continuity with the Mesolithic period, it being situated directly over a Mesolithic shell midden. The later cairns seem to be more insular in character, related to former settlement sites and located further away from the sea. These cairns were more elaborate than the early cairns. However, they continued to be located in the northern zone of the island, seemingly in relation to the position of the earlier cairns. In this period, the northern zone of Bute appears to have been one of the central areas in the transformation of the dead in the Earlier Neolithic of the Clyde region. That this was not simply due to terrestrial, territorial concerns is reinforced by the location of Neolithic settlement finds on the island which are spread more evenly, concentrated in areas away from the location of the chambered cairns.

'LANDSCAPES' OF SETTLEMENT

Most of the settlement evidence on Bute has been found in the mid-zone of the island, in the region that is still today the main arable area of the island. For example, in contrast to the chambered cairns, stone axe finds are more widely distributed, with particular concentrations in the mid zone of the island and in the southern bisecting valley (*8*). In these two areas, axes are found in close proximity to inland, freshwater lochs. With the exception of a find from the southern rocky zone of the island (a group IX, porcellanite-type axe from Tievebulliagh or Rathlin in Northern

Scottish Odysseys: The Archaeology of Islands

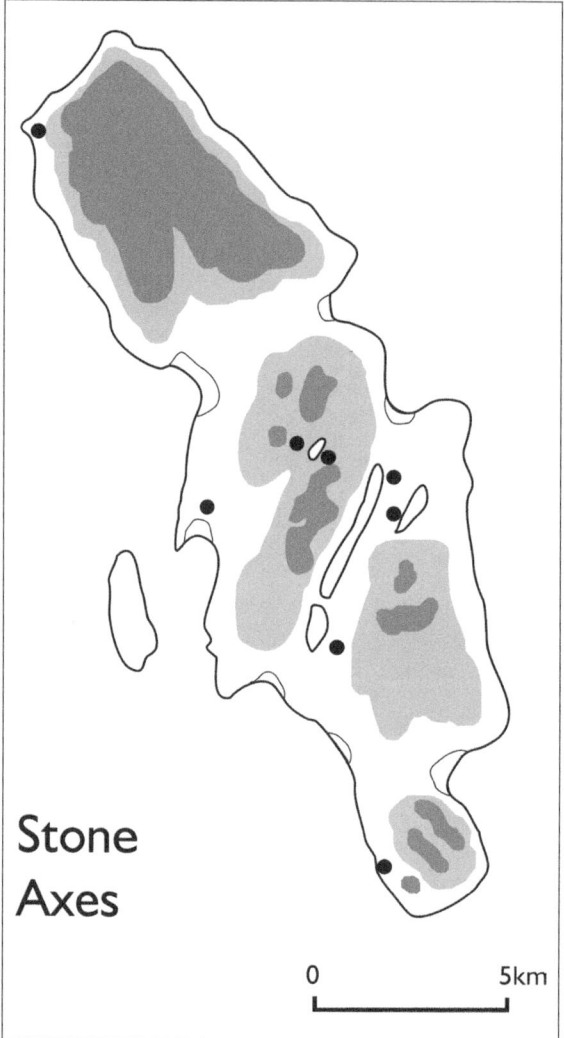

8 Distribution of stone axes on Bute

Ireland) the other axe locations have associations with the central inner areas of the island, the very zones which are the main agricultural and settlement locales of Bute today. These axes include examples, such as the polished stone axe from Townhead (group VI Langdale tuff) which was found in an area identified as a Neolithic settlement site, from which finds and features such as a saddle quern and rubbers, pottery fragments, postholes, hearth features and charred remains including nuts and cereals, indicate the processing of wild and agricultural foodstuffs. The finds of lithic scatters and known settlement locales extends the stone axe distribution further, with traces of what can be identified as settlement in a number of additional locations (9). These include the site at Townhead, which is located near to a natural spring, and Loch Fad, in an enclosed area, with a range of resources close at hand.

An island of fluctuating perceptions: the landscape and archaeology of Bute

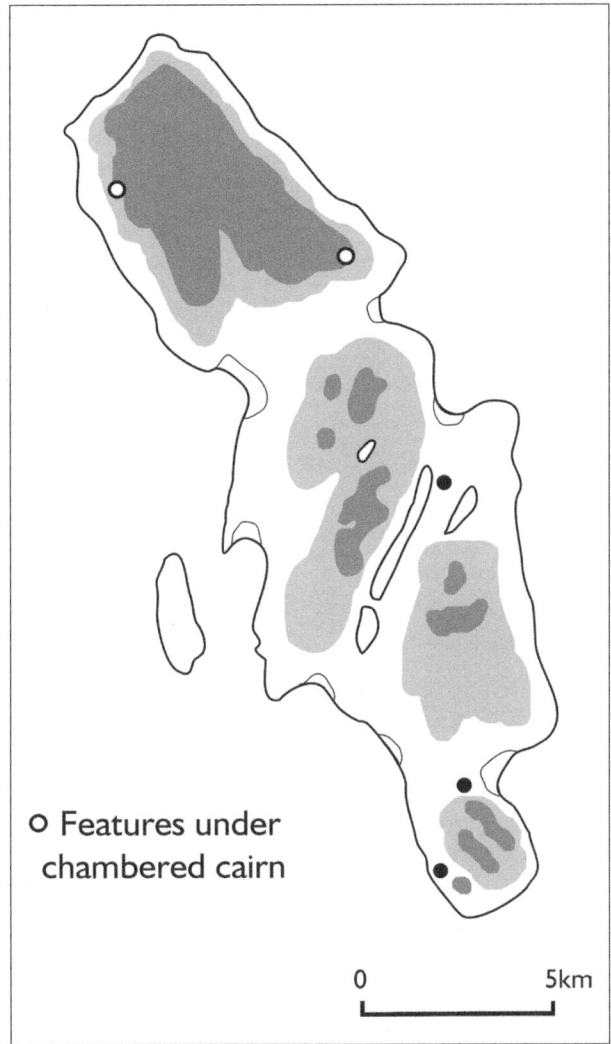

9 Known Neolithic/Early Bronze Age settlement locales on Bute from lithic scatters and excavation

The lithic scatter at Blackpark is located in one of the major bisecting valleys, in an area intensively cultivated area today. There are also possible settlement traces from under the cairns at Glenvoidean and Hilton.

These settlement finds demonstrate that Bute was by no means an island of the dead. While the northern zone of the island formed a regional focus for burial ritual in the Clyde region in the Earlier Neolithic, the fragmentary settlement remains show that nearly all the other zones of island were also used for the more everyday tasks of woodland management and subsistence. Overall, the settlements and stone axe finds suggest that settlement may have shifted across the island depending upon season, but that the main occupation zones were concentrated in the mid part of the island, in the main arable area of the island today. This contrasts with the overwhelming distribution of cairns in the more marginal upslope and northern zone locations. This may suggest that some degree of separation between ceremonial and subsistence activity was maintained, but the presence of possible settlement traces under the cairns at Glenvoidean and Hilton demonstrates that this was not absolute. The real separation may not have been between domestic and ritual, but a distinction between the public and private, or in terms of identity, between a wider Firth of Clyde regional identity and the more intimate bonds that maintained smaller scale family and kin bonds in the Neolithic.

THE LATER NEOLITHIC STONE CIRCLES AND STANDING STONES

While the location of the Earlier Neolithic cairns seems to have been dictated by a number of changing priorities, the location of monuments in the Later Neolithic seems to have been more deliberate and constant. The location of a number of stone circles and other standing stone monuments seems to be concerned with the deliberate orchestration of movement across, onto and off the island. This is evidenced by the location of the major Later Neolithic monuments in the main bisecting valley zones of Bute (*10*). For example, Ettrick Bay stone circle is placed in the northern bisecting valley that crosses and divides the northern and mid zones of the island. The valley is one of the major routeways across the island, allowing easy access between the east and west coasts of Bute. In addition to the circle at Ettrick, two standing stones are situated to the east of the circle, emphasising the linear east–west nature of the valley. The circle is located towards Ettrick Bay, but set back on ground that overlooks the bay. The circle is visible from the sea, and the two bays at either end of the valley would have been important landing places for the islanders and for people from more distant places. At Ettrick Bay, the architecture of the circle seems to emphasise an orientation towards Arran, where a distinct concentration of similar architectural traditions are found. The circle today consists of only four standing stones which are aligned towards Arran in the south. With the other stones in place it is likely that this impression would still be valid, as judging from the stumps of the broken stones, these were much smaller, thinner and have a different, rougher surface texture. The west coast route to Arran would have been the main routeway between the two islands (Davies 1946) and the circle is well placed on this route. The stone circles and standing stones of Arran are similarly concentrated in linking valleys and bays as they are in Bute (Noble 2006a, 186). The main concentrations of sites on Arran are situated at either end of the string road valley that divides the island in two. There is a group of stone circles at Machrie Bay in the west and a series of standing stones in Brodick Bay in the east.

The circles on both of these islands are placed in areas that are likely to have been transitional points between the insular islandscape and the outside world and also

An island of fluctuating perceptions: the landscape and archaeology of Bute

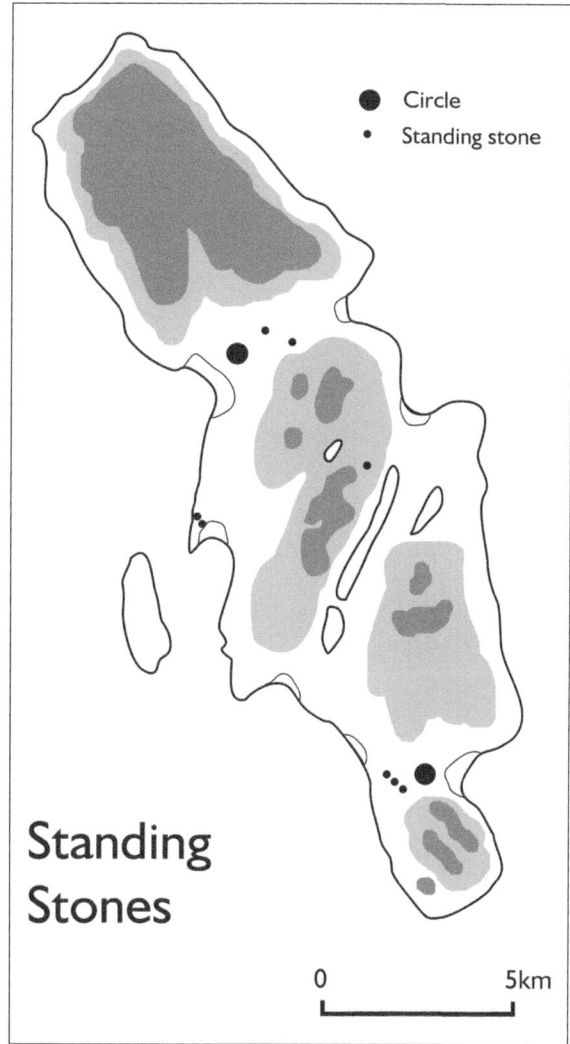

10 Standing stones and stone circles on Bute

important points in terms of movement and communication between groups of people on the island itself. In a similar manner, the stone row at Largizean is also located in one of the major bisecting valleys of Bute (in this case the southern). The stone row is orientated to the sea and Stravanan and Scalpsie bays to the north-east, linking the bays of the valley and emphasising connections with movement on and off the island as occurs at Ettrick (*11*). Further to the east of the same valley is Blackpark stone circle, located on a ridge, allowing excellent views of both eastern and western parts of the bisecting valley. Again, this valley, like the one to the north, is an important route between the east and west coasts of the island. The paired standing stones at St Ninian's Bay represent a further stone setting situated close to a bay with it associations of landing and disembarking. The nearby early Christian

11 The bay setting of Largizean stone row

chapel at St Ninian's Point is a reminder of the importance of pilgrimage and movement by sea in the past.

THE EARLY BRONZE AGE: CIST CEMETERIES

Early Bronze Age cist monuments have the widest distribution of any monument type discussed so far, being found in most of the topographic zones highlighted above, with the exception of the two bisecting valleys (*12*). Cists and barrows are found across the island in many different types of location: coastal areas, upland areas, and in the north, south and mid zones of Bute. The adjacent small island of Inchmarnock also contains more evidence for use in the Early Bronze Age than previous periods, perhaps indicating an expansion in settlement onto the smaller islands during this period. While cists are found in a variety of locations, many of the sites seem to be situated in relation to defined areas of land suitable for agriculture. Many are within nested/enclosed areas of agricultural land. The cairns or barrows, however, do tend to be located at higher elevations than the flat cists and often have wider views. For example, the Watch Hill tumulus is located on a ridge overlooking the western sea-routes and has views over the northern bisecting valley and areas of agricultural land (Bryce 1903-4, 72-3).

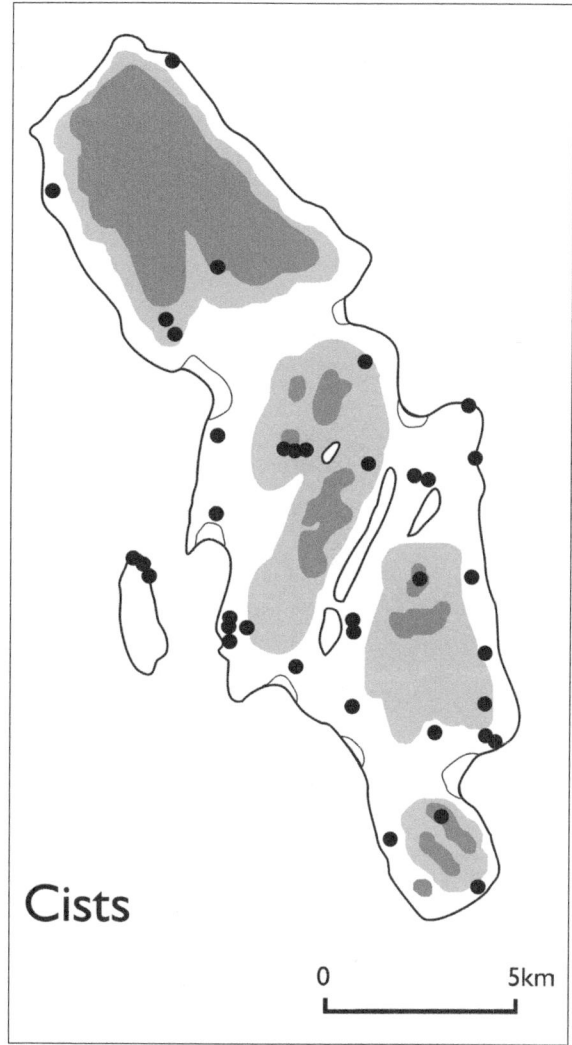

12 Early Bronze Age stone cists on Bute

There may have been a burial hierarchy in operation across the island, with the largest mounds positioned at the highest elevations overlooking larger areas of land. However, some of the richest burials, such as the Mount Stuart cist with a jet necklace, were found in the low-lying areas, making this distinction of dubious value (Bryce 1903-4, 63-9).

While the chambered cairns do not seem to be located in relation to territorial divisions of the island, such as the distinct areas of good agricultural land, which Renfrew (1976) argued for in the case of Arran, the cists can be seen to more fully match Renfrew's criteria for establishing a territorial role for monuments. Renfrew's idea of a segmentary society, with relatively autonomous groups who maintain their own area of land, seems to fit the Early Bronze Age evidence much better. The cists,

13 The rolling agricultural setting of Ambrisbeg stone cist in the mid zone of the island

as mentioned previously, have a stronger relationship with agricultural land and are the only monument type which are found in modern settlement locales. While the ratio of chambered cairns on arable land to those on grazing or limited agricultural value land is low (2:4), a much higher proportion of the cist sites are located on good quality arable land in comparison to those that are not – a ratio of 16:8. These figures suggest a close relationship between cists and agricultural land (*13*). In the Early Bronze Age the main focus of monumentality and activity seems to have been in the mid zone of Bute, where the main agricultural resources and settlements are found. This part of the island contains the burials with the richest burial goods and the goods that travelled the furthest distance before being deposited in the cists. However, the Early Bronze Age monuments on the island do not seem to be overtly placed with long distance connections in mind. The valleys that were monumentalised in the Later Neolithic do not appear to have been important in this period. Instead the Early Bronze Age can be argued to be a period when land and resources became the focus of more localised group identities. While some exotic objects were imported onto the island (such as the Yorkshire jet in the Mount Stuart cist) and the idea of single burial was adopted (ultimately originating on the Continent as part of the Beaker 'package') many of the grave goods were simple and of a local character. The only Beaker pottery found on the island was in the reused Glecknabae chambered cairn. Most of the ceramics found in the cists are of the Food Vessel type

– a ceramic form which derived from traditional Neolithic pottery forms. Thus, while new forms of burial and some exotic goods were introduced to the island, the cists seem to be more closely related to insular, island relationships between the social groups living on the island.

CONCLUSIONS

An interesting aspect of Bute (and one of our reasons for selecting it as a study area) is that it is an island encased within a complex regional landscape and seascape. As such, it does not represent an isolated, insular island in terms of its location. From this case study we hope to have shown the ways in which the islandscape of Bute was constantly reworked over time, including the ways in which the topographic zones of Bute increased and decreased in importance as social and economic priorities changed and the island fluctuated between a regionally important locale and one of more insular concerns. The case study presented here suggests ways in which human relations were embedded in the topographic and environmental setting of the Clyde region. In the Earlier Neolithic, for example, the location of chambered cairn monuments appears to have been due to a range of complex and changing priorities. At this time, the northern zone of Bute appears to have been one of the central places in the treatment of the dead in the Earlier Neolithic in the Firth of Clyde. In the Later Neolithic, the bisecting valleys and bay areas were monumentalised. Standing stone monuments were placed in areas that would have been transitional points where people would have moved onto and off the island and also where people would have moved across the island itself. The standing stone monuments were all located close to landing places, where boats could have been brought onto shore and where people would have begun and ended journeys. These landscapes represent the places at which the widest audiences would have regularly experienced these monuments. These monuments too, were not concerned merely with insular relations, but were perhaps designed to impact on Bute's role in the wider communication networks that developed between regions in Britain and Ireland during the Later Neolithic.

The perhaps idiosyncratic placement of stone monuments on Bute can be seen in other island cultures too. John Robb (2001, 196), for example, has noted that the design and location of megalithic architecture of Neolithic Malta presents a deliberate expression of identity and difference. From our research on the spatial organisation of stone monuments on Bute this has proved to be an interesting perspective, not only to the study of island cultures, but also to how the Neolithic is perceived. The Earlier Neolithic cairns are similar to, but not exactly the same as, their mainland counterparts, expressing forms of localised identities and differences. In contrast, the Later Neolithic stone circles and stone rows present Bute as having an identity that functioned as part of a dynamic wider network of cultural contact within and beyond the island confines of Bute and the Clyde region.

While this paper has drawn predominately upon evidence of Neolithic monumentality, and touched upon settlement evidence and stone axes, we can see in the Early Bronze Age that the focus of monumentality and activity seems to have shifted to the central part of the island, the main agricultural zone. The valleys that were monumentalised in the Later Neolithic do not appear to have been important in this period. Instead, the Early Bronze Age seems to have been a period when land and resources became the focus of more localised group identities. In this respect the island became divided and monumentality was no longer focused on the public spaces of the island. However, there is still some evidence for the continuation and development of the culture contacts established in the Later Neolithic into the Bronze Age, with grave evidence from the early Bronze Age cists demonstrating culture associations with broader networks (e.g. the jet necklace found at the Mount Stuart cist; Balfour 1910, 103) as well as more local connections.

This paper has focused on the methodological approaches to the study of island archaeology, the outcomes of which indicate the fluctuating significance of Bute in the Firth of Clyde region. The changing significance of the topographic zones on the island highlights the fact that the boundaries of an island should not be taken as given. This is not, however, the only approach that can be made, or indeed should be made, in the study of island archaeology. Other areas that could be considered are interregional island interactions, in the case of Bute, with the nearby island of Arran, or with other outlying islands and the mainland. These are all potential routes into considering a more detailed study of human societies and their island environments. We hope in this chapter to have highlighted the complexities of island archaeology and presented a range of material evidence that supports the idea that islands are not necessarily socially insular. Moreover, we have presented an argument that suggests that the study of islands should not distinguish between physical landscapes and island societies, but that both rather shape each other. As such we hope to have shown how an 'island archaeology' approach to the study of islands can produce much more detailed accounts of the ways in which people understood and reconfigured an island-centred geography over time.

NOTES

1 See also Noble 2006b for a similar critique of Renfrew's modelling of territorial divisions on the island of Rousay, Orkney.
2 This is within a day's there-and-back boat journey in a small boat.
3 For a full consideration of this in the west of Scotland see Schulting and Richards 2002.

REFERENCES

Balfour, J.A. (ed.) 1910, *The Book of Arran*, Glasgow

Broodbank, C. 2000, *An Island Archaeology of the Early Cyclades*, Cambridge

Bryce, T.H. 1903-4, 'On the cairns and tumuli of the island of Bute. A record of explorations during the season of 1903', *Proc Soc Antiq Scot* 38, 17-81

Cooney, G. 2000, *Landscapes of Neolithic Ireland*, London

Corcoran, J.X.W.P. 1969, 'Excavation of two chambered cairns at Mid Gleniron Farm, Glenluce, Wigtownshire', *Trans Dumfries Galloway Natur Hist Antiq Soc* 41, 29-90

Cormack, W.F. 1986, 'Glecknabae (N. Bute): Mesolithic core', *Discovery Excav Scot* 26

Cummings, V. & Whittle A. 2004, *Places of Special Virtue: Megaliths in the Neolithic Landscapes of Wales*, Oxford

Davies, M. 1946, 'The diffusion and distribution pattern of the megalithic monuments of the Irish Sea and North Channel coastlands', *Antiq J* 26, 38-60

Edmonds, M. 1999, *Ancestral Geographies of the Neolithic*, London

Evans, J.D. 1973, 'Islands as laboratories for the study of culture process', in Renfrew, C. (ed.), *The Explanation of Culture Change: Models in Prehistory*, 517-520, London

Fitzpatrick, S.M. (ed.) 2004, *Voyages of Discovery: The Archaeology of Islands*, Westport

Gosden, C. & Pavlides, C. 1994, 'Are islands insular? landscape vs. seascape in the case of the Arawe Islands, Papua New Guinea', *Archaeology in Oceania* 29, 62-171

Henshall, A.S. 1972, *The Chambered Tombs of Scotland*, Edinburgh

Herne, A. 1988, 'A time and a place for the Grimston Bowl', in Barrett, J.C. & Kinnes, I.A. (eds), *The Archaeology of Context in the Neolithic and Bronze Age: Recent Trends*, 9-29, Sheffield

Hewison, J.K. 1895, *The Isle of Bute in the Olden Time*, Edinburgh

Hughes, I. 1988, 'Megaliths: space, time and the landscape – A view from the Clyde', *Scott Archaeol Rev* 5, 41-58

Ingold, T. 1993, 'The temporality of the landscape', *World Archaeology* 25, 152-75

Kirch, P.V. & Green, R.C. 2001, *Hawaiki, Ancestral Polynesia: An Essay in Historical Anthropology*, Cambridge

Marshall, D.N. 1976, 'The excavation of Hilton Cairn', *Trans Buteshire Natur Hist Soc* 20, 8-26

Marshall, D.N. & Taylor, I.D. 1976-7, 'The excavation of the chambered cairn at Glenvoidean, Isle of Bute', *Proc Soc Antiq Scot* 108, 1-39

Munro, I.S. 1973, *The Island of Bute*, Devon

Noble, G. 2003, 'Islands in the Neolithic', *Brit Archaeol* 71, 20-22

Noble, G. 2005, 'Ancestry, farming and the changing architecture of the Clyde cairns of Southwest Scotland', in Cummings, V. & Pannett, A. (eds), *Set in Stone: New Approaches to Neolithic Monuments in Scotland*, 25-36, Oxford

Noble, G. 2006a, *Neolithic Scotland: Timber, Stone, Earth and Fire*, Edinburgh

Noble, G. 2006b, 'Harnessing the waves: monuments and ceremonial complexes in Orkney and beyond', *J Maritime Archaeol* 1, 1-18

Renfrew, C. 1973, 'Monuments, mobilisation and social organisation in Neolithic Wessex', in Renfrew, C. (ed.), *The Explanation of Culture Change: Models in Prehistory*, 539-58, London

Renfrew, C. 1976, 'Megaliths, territories and populations', in Laet, S. De (ed.), *Acculturation and Continuity in Atlantic Europe*, 198-229, Bruges

Robb, J. 2001, 'Island identities: ritual, travel and the creation of difference in Neolithic Malta', *Euro J Archaeol* 4(2), 175-202

Scott, J. G. 1969, 'The Neolithic period in Kintyre', in Powell, T.G.E. (ed.), *Megalithic Enquiries in the West of Britain*, 223-46, Liverpool

Sturt, F. 2005, 'Fishing for meaning: lived space and Earlier Neolithic of Orkney', in Cummings, V. & Pannett, A. (eds), *Set in Stone: New Approaches to Neolithic Monuments in Scotland*, 68-80, Oxford

Thomas, J. 1999, *Understanding the Neolithic*, London

Thorpe, O.W. & Thorpe, R.S. 1984, 'The distribution and sources of archaeological pitchstone in Britain', *J Archaeol Sci* 11, 1-34

Whittow, J.W. 1977, *Geology and Scenery in Scotland*, Hammondsworth

4

ISLANDSCAPES AND STANDING STONES: CHANGING PERCEPTIONS

Joanna Wright

INTRODUCTION

island. /'aIlənd/ n. 1. a piece of land surrounded by water. 2. anything compared to an island, esp. in being surrounded in some way. 3. = traffic island. 4. a detached or isolated thing.

The Oxford English Dictionary

The very word 'island' conjures up a vast myriad of instant images and impressions. The sense of islands as remote, cut off, bounded, insular, isolated and somehow slightly mystical is one that most people readily seem to identify with. These words are often used heavily in the opening pages of any island-specific book, be it academic in nature or appealing to the general public. That islands are perceived as peripheral, liminal or marginal in some way is implicit in the language used to describe them and, as Ritchie and Harman (1996, 11) stated, 'For most modern visitors to Argyll and the islands … the sea is a barrier …'. In other cases, the island, no matter its location, is often discussed in its wider context, the small part it plays in the larger network of trade routes and its role as a crossing point or point of cultural contact for the mainland. For instance, Ritchie (1997, 10) describes Fair Isle as lying '… 39 km to the south [of Shetland], like a stepping stone on the way to Orkney'. In other cases, islands have been considered in their economic terms, such as their usefulness in the acquisition of certain foodstuffs. A great deal of past research has focused upon the notion that in the past people visited islands simply to plunder them for produce or use them as convenient stepping stones to somewhere else, reducing their importance and role to one secondary to the mainland. The opposite extreme of this approach is to study the island in total isolation from that which surrounds it.

The most typical example of this latter method was championed by Evans (1973) in a paper entitled *Islands as Laboratories for the Study of Culture Process*, in which he discusses how the limitations of island life and the restrictive geography of the island itself make these places ideal for studying groups of people or cultures in isolation from outside influences. It is perhaps pertinent that the majority of people, the present author included, studying such islands are rarely native to them and may therefore be prone to seeing them as isolating or isolated. This may be especially true when we consider tropical islands, which also conjure up pictures of the mysterious and exotic. We also see islands as peaceful places to 'get away from it all' and this begs the question — are we drawn to islands in some way because of our perceived notions of their difference or isolation? I believe the answer to this question is certainly in the affirmative and I shall return to this point later.

When studying the Northern or Western Isles of Scotland in particular, the perception of islands as isolated entities is often exaggerated by the introduction of a further factor: the perception, and often the reality, of the climate. Descriptions of the weather itself are often utilised as a device to enhance feelings of the boundedness and 'otherness' around these places. Indeed, aspects of the weather, geography and accessibility are commonly embellished in the introductory pages of island specific books. A typical example states 'The islands of Orkney and Shetland … are wild, windswept and forbidding in the imagination of those who have never wandered in the far north' (Wainwright 1962, 1). In many cases the sense of remoteness that the word 'island' promotes, especially in the case of tropical islands, is turned into a hook for attracting tourists, a perception that is also deliberately exaggerated in the media.

Islands have always been a popular theme in literature, the more remote aspects of island life being played heavily upon in classics such as Daniel Defoe's *Robinson Crusoe* (1719) Robert Louis Stevenson's *Treasure Island* (1883) and *Kidnapped* (1886), right through to more recent works such as *Lord of the Flies* (1954) by William Golding, and the importance of this literature in shaping our perceptions has been noted in greater detail elsewhere by Rainbird (1999). In addition to this, the last couple of decades have seen a wealth of island-based television dramatisations and reality TV shows, and there have been a number of films where an island setting has been exploited to induce a sense of isolation from the outside. Films such as *The Wicker Man* (1973), *Castaway* (2000), *The Beach* (2000) and even *Jurassic Park* (1993) have played on the popular misconceptions and often exaggerated aspects of exclusion and boundedness. The island setting, a place surrounded by a watery barrier and somehow disconnected from the outside world, allows the reader or viewer to believe that anything is possible there.

EXPERIENCING ISLANDS

These stereotypical portrayals of island life have, in terms of academic study at least, come under close scrutiny during the last few years. The premise that an island is an isolated, bounded, inaccessible unit has been rightly challenged by people such as Rainbird (1999). I would agree strongly that islands cannot be studied in isolation. They are not separate bounded units, but form part of fluid flexible locales that encompass areas of both land and sea which are not obviously defined by their geography, a situation I would term an 'islandscape'. Until relatively recently, certain parts of an island may in fact have been more accessible via the sea and from the coast, than overland from another part of the same island. The small winding roads on many islands make land travel slow and laborious, and before modern upgrades to the road surfaces and modern forms of transport, visiting different parts of the same island may have preferably been via the sea. The remains of disused boat ramps and jetties can be found all around the coasts of the Isle of Mull indicating that once, sea travel was far more common than the few private boats and the two ferries that now dock at the two ports of Craignure and Tobermory. This means that connections between different islands and parts of islands and the mainland existed that may not be clearly visible to us today and we have to look beyond the island shoreline to get a clearer picture of life in the past. If, then, islands should ideally be studied as parts of a wider landscape such as this, should we abandon the idea of islands altogether? Is the study of an island still a worthwhile enterprise?

To answer this I need to address the questions — what is it that makes an island any different from a coastal mainland zone and what is the cause of this difference? To explain my reasoning I would like to turn for a moment to my own experiences on the islands. During the last few years there have been many incidences where I have felt lost or disorientated in the Western Isles. On visiting an island for the first time it has often taken me a while to get my bearings. Without stopping frequently to consult a map the changing views can be confusing, especially those in the distance. Often, it is difficult to tell what one is looking at; the peak of a mountain to the south of the island, on the mainland or on another island can be hard to distinguish until you have spent a while getting to know the look of the surrounding landscape from a variety of directions. Emotions can also become enhanced in the islands. On one occasion I was stranded for a while on a remote hillside in the fog, slightly alarmed and not daring to move far in case I strayed off the path. Another time I had a similar feeling when I became lost in an area of forest in the north of the Isle of Mull. Visiting the islands has not just involved a feeling of disorientation but also one of isolation. Often one is out of mobile phone range, public transport within and off the island is limited and sometimes you can walk for miles without meeting another person. I am certainly not alone in this feeling of boundedness. A colleague has described the feeling of undertaking fieldwork on the Isles of

Orkney as of being 'untouched' by external events, both of the wider world, such as news headlines, or of personal contacts (Colin Richards *pers. comm.*).

The above experiences, and others like them, have made me think a great deal about how I, as a stranger, an outsider, to the Western Isles, view these islands. My experiences, which I am sure I am not alone in, have undoubtedly shaped the ways in which I have interpreted and understood these places. In spite of the recent literature arguing the contrary I have used the words 'isolated', 'lost', 'remote', 'stranded' and 'disorientated', to reflect my own experiences of these places.

Would these experiences and feelings of isolation really have been any different if I had been in similar situations on the mainland? I would have to argue not. My feelings of seclusion on the islands have stemmed from my immediate physical experiences of particular locations and not the island landscape itself. It is surely the case that in familiar landscapes we feel safe; in unfamiliar ones we can feel isolated and disorientated. This is as true of island areas as anywhere else. So if being on an island can involve such similar basal perceptions and emotions as being on the mainland, then where does that leave the study of islands in terms of difference? Should we be thinking that being in a coastal location is qualitatively the same as being on an island? Island and mainland coastal landscapes can be remarkably similar; however, I still believe that a difference exists. It was perhaps the almost unconscious sense of 'otherness' in the island context that particularly unsettled me. The physical experience of being on an island can be exactly the same as that of being on the mainland coast; the critical factor is that of knowledge. Knowing that we are on an island, surrounded by the sea, does somehow enhance our physical and emotional state. Obviously, living on and visiting an island are of course very different experiences and my observations cannot and do not extend to those who actually live on the islands. To explore this is beyond the scope of this paper; I wish instead to discuss the problem of how we, as archaeologists, perceive islands and how this can affect our interpretations.

Although I would argue that islands cannot and should not be studied as isolated units, I believe there is something intrinsically different about being on an island as opposed to being on the mainland. It is problematical trying to define exactly what this difference is, and I have to return to the obvious answer – islands are physically surrounded by the sea. By knowing that you are on an island, you are aware that you are surrounded by a natural barrier and that knowledge arguably changes your perception of place. Yet where does this sense of difference stem from? I have already cited the media as a possible source but another, more obvious, one exists, that of maps.

MAPS AND ISLANDS

The connections and interconnections between different parts of islands and parts of the mainland are not visible when we look at a map. Maps do not show us the quality of roads, tracks that may be overgrown or impassable at certain times of year, the underwater currents or the directions of the winds and tides. The birds-eye view imposed by a map leads to a false reckoning of everything from ground conditions to distance and lines of sight. A map can never give you an understanding of an area in the same way that a photograph can, and even this does not really compare to being in a place. Even when using complicated (and often inaccurate) computer programs, it is very difficult to get a true sense of the surroundings from a map. This is especially true of those features that are more temporary; vegetation, impermanent farm buildings, vehicles or signs.

The modern overview imposed by a cartographic map has certainly contributed to a strong sense of islands as disconnected places. When islands are shown in this way they can inspire feelings of remoteness and isolation. On the ground, a direct feeling of disorientation or lack of knowledge of the landscape is no different from that experienced on the mainland, but I believe in the island context these feelings are intensified by the wider knowledge, provided by a map, of a separated geographical location. So, if the island setting feels somehow 'different' from the mainland, then should we be interpreting the archaeological monuments on these islands in the same ways that we interpret those on the mainland coast? Have people always felt that islands were special and can we see this in the archaeology? One way in which I have tried to approach this question has been to see if, in prehistory, there were differences between the standing stone constructions on the islands and those on the mainland coast. Was there a simple difference between the two or was the situation more complex? And what feelings of difference might we be able to see expressed through the archaeology?

DIFFERENT ISLANDS

This brings me on to another matter; so far I have been discussing 'islands' as if they are all analogous entities, due to their difference geographically from mainland areas. This tendency is prevalent in a great deal of literature, to treat all islands in the same manner, to use analogies from one, apply them to another and assume that the notion of an island is constant and cross-cultural (Rainbird 1999, 217). However, the evidence from people living on islands suggests that those on different islands have a very distinct sense of belonging to that particular island. This sometimes goes even further and islanders have an even stronger sense of belonging to a certain part of an island. An example of this comes from Clachan on the Isle of Lewis. The residents of this crofting community live in a small nucleated settlement. The outward appearance is one of a distinct, bounded territory, isolated from those which surround it. In reality, substantial kin and congregational links exist between the residents of this and neighbouring settlements and 'This means that Clachan is not discrete from these neighbours but rather that Clachanites *differentiate* their village from them' (Mewett 1986, 71, original emphasis). This situation can be used as an analogy for the study of islands. Although the outward appearance of boundedness and similarity may overpower, differences, connections and interconnections exist which may not be so obvious. One thing I have aimed to do is investigate if similar patterns can be detected in prehistory.

ISLANDS AND STANDING STONES

When the monuments of the Western Isles are closely examined it can be seen that arrangements of standing stones are markedly different between certain geographical areas. As a general rule, standing stones can be found in greater numbers on the islands than in adjacent coastal areas, although this may be due in part to greater land development on the latter. An example of this can be seen in figure 1; on the Isle of Mull more standing stones (of many different configurations) are found on the island than on the adjacent mainland. However, enough stones survive to make some general observations. As a general rule, single standing stones are the most common type of monument on both the mainland and across the islands. They are found almost everywhere with no discernable pattern and as such, little can usually be said about their geographical spread. However, distinct similarities exist between the locations in which they are set; a point I shall return to.

With regard to the other types of standing stone monument, there are a number of regional variations in design across Scotland, which can be seen clearly throughout the islands. For example, on the Isle of Mull there are the remains of no fewer than eight short stone rows in the north-west of the island, a unique type of monumental setting which does not occur on any of the other islands or the adjacent mainland. Discrete stone circle complexes appear on the Isles of Arran, Lewis and North Uist, but in each case there are differences in design. On the Isle of Arran at the site of Machrie Moor there are stone circles, a concentric circle, a (possible) five-stone ring, and a nearby four-poster and ring-cairn all of relatively small diameter, consisting of both tall red sandstone monoliths and small rounded granite boulders (Burl 2000, 90). On the Isle of Lewis, the tall Callanish stones are all of Lewissian Gneiss but the circles are generally quite small in diameter and, like those of Machrie Moor, vary considerably in form. In this complex can be found the unique site of Callanish I – a small oval ring with connecting rows and an avenue constructed around a small chambered cairn (Burl 1976, 148). On North Uist the four or five stone circles forming a complex to the south of the island are much larger and more open, and the stones smaller in size (Beveridge 2001 [1911], 259-61). In contrast again, in the Kilmartin Valley area of mainland Scotland a wide range of unusual, unique stone settings can be found, often with cup-and-ring markings, such as Temple Wood or Ballymeanoch. Of course the differences in stone are due to what is locally available

Islandscapes and Standing Stones: changing perceptions

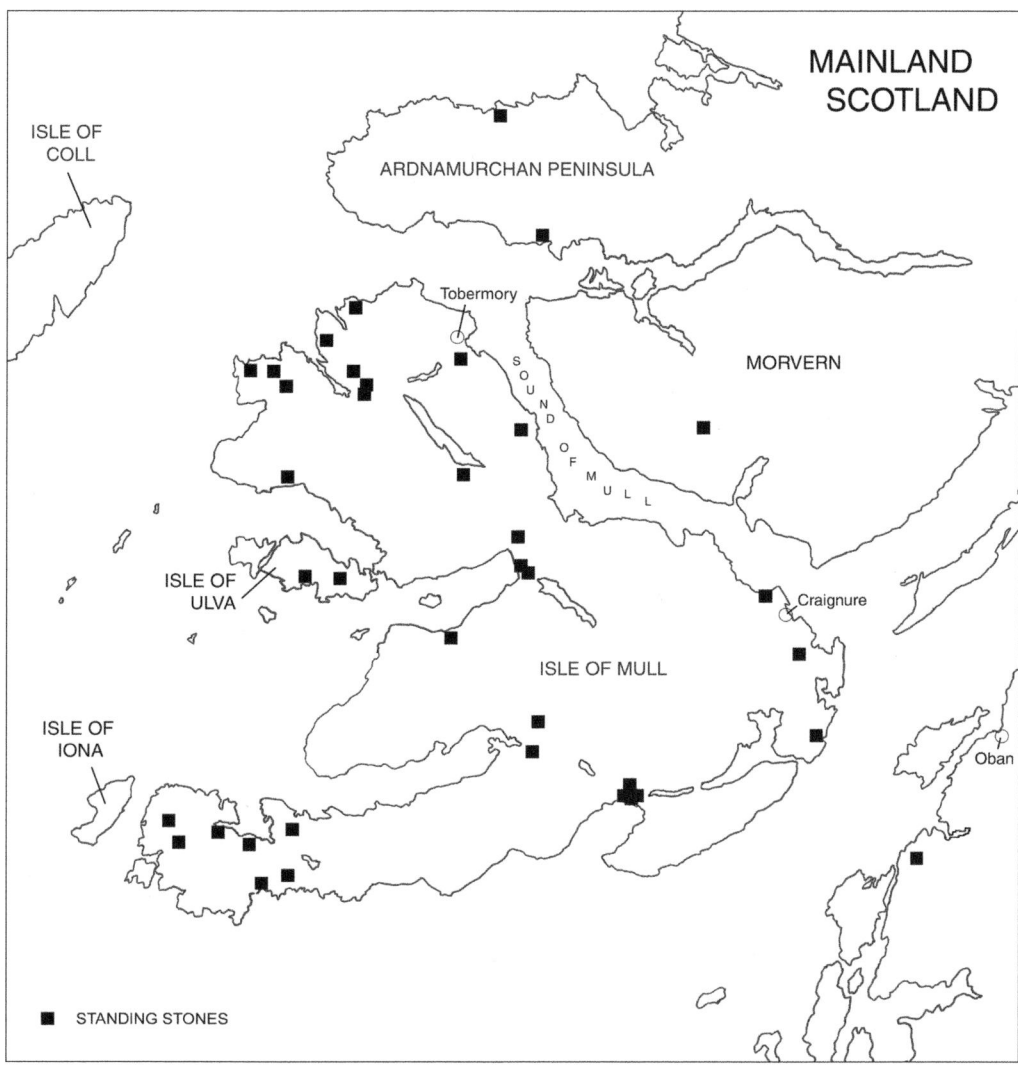

1 The distribution of standing stones on the Isle of Mull and surrounding area

or easily obtainable, but the differences in design are obviously a very deliberate choice.

Case Study: the Isle of Mull

Sometimes these patterns can be broken down even further and differences in design can be seen on different parts of the same island – the Isle of Mull provides a case study. Here, short stone rows are confined to the north-west of the island. The single standing stones can be found all across the island apart from the north-west. The pairs of stones are few and situated widely across the island, as are the stone circle and other possible circle. It may be suggested that these different groupings perhaps represented or commemorated something specific to the different people or kinship groups across the island. Although I can only speculate on their meaning, it is highly significant that in wide ranging but discrete parts of the same island, different monumental designs were utilised. These designs also differ from those on the nearest points of the adjacent mainland, where single standing stones are found in small numbers and isolated contexts. At the same time, as mentioned above, there are a number of similarities between the different sites.

The sites of single standing stones, pairs, or small groups such as the short stone rows on the Isle of Mull, almost without exception, have a view of a large body of water, either the sea or a loch, in at least one direction. Often, if the site chosen had been a few metres away, the watery view would be lost. Furthermore, standing stones are usually placed on flattish areas of land, often on a ridge or plateau, with a gentle slope upwards in one direction and a slope down on all other sides. Nearly always, higher ground rises in the distance on all sides except that which held the immediate slope upwards. Similar patterns exist on other islands; the stones almost always have views of the sea. Interestingly, in many cases, stone circles do not. The circles are often situated on flatter, inland areas of ground or in places where sea views are lost. Often, a movement of a few metres in one or any direction changes the view. Although it is impossible to say definitively that all stone circles were placed out of sight of the sea it seems that the trend was for this situation. This preference has also been noted by Fowler and Cummings (2003, 2-3), who stated that within the Irish Sea area '… stone circles … very rarely provide views of the sea'.

It is argued here that the similarities in the positioning of these monuments in the landscape cannot be fortuitous. The current argument lends itself to the theory that perhaps an underlying idea or premise existed regarding the setting of these sites. If the location was not so important, a greater variety in the placing of these sites might be expected. For example, standing stones on the islands are, with a few very rare exceptions, never placed on the tops of ridges or outcrops, but are always slightly downslope. They are rarely found in very hilly or very low ground, such as along a valley floor. The parallels between these locations show evidence of the very careful forethought that went into the positioning of standing stones. What was seen from them, or where they could be seen from, was important. The surrounding landscape and views from and of these sites were clearly important to the people who erected or visited them.

However, the differences in design lead to the conclusion that regional differences relating to space, belonging and knowledge of different areas of land or the heavens (if astronomical explanations are taken into account) were expressed through the monuments. The differences in monumental design between both islands and mainland, and islands with other islands suggest that the people who erected these stones may have possessed an island-wide sense of difference which transcended local or kinship identity. I would like to argue that in the past islanders could have portrayed their knowledge and experience of being somewhere 'other' through the monuments. Whilst there were underlying 'rules' relating to landscape setting, an islandscape- or area-based sense of difference could be expressed through design. This sense or need to be differentiated from the mainland, other islands or different parts of the same island is still recognisable today.

This point brings me back to the questions asked at the beginning of this paper regarding the differences between islands and the mainland. I have argued that the overview given by modern maps, the media and our own experiences of islands have all shaped our perceptions of them as isolated, bounded units. I have also tried to stress that I do not believe islands can be studied in isolation from the surrounding or adjacent mainland and other nearby islands, as patterns such as these can easily be overlooked. Yet I have argued that islanders may, under specific circumstances, feel they are different from other islanders and that there is also something intrinsically different about being on an island as a visitor. Returning to an earlier point, the fundamental aspect of islands is that they are surrounded by the sea and this may be the reason why we are drawn to their study so strongly.

ISLANDS AND THE SEA

The situation is indeed more complex than islands being physically separate from the mainland. The geography does not easily define what is happening in different places at different times. So why is it that islands somehow remain different from the mainland? Perhaps today it has a lot to do with modern transport, ferry times, airport schedules and the weather, all of which affect our accessibility to these places. Our experiences of navigating the sea are very different from those in the past. We are far more detached from it. On board a large ferry or flying high above the ocean, we are disengaged from the sea. We no longer know the sea we are crossing. We do not have to worry about currents or tides or falling overboard from the ferry in bad weather.

I believe that this disengagement from the sea has led to a change in our attitudes towards it; consciously or unconsciously the sea will always be a barrier. Crossing this barrier can perhaps be compared to a 'rite of passage'. Indeed, 'To cross rivers and water could be seen as a liminal, and important, experience' (Brophy 2000, 66). The act of negotiating a large body of water is something that the majority of people are not used to on a daily basis. The experience of crossing the sea can stimulate a combination of unusual feelings, both physical and emotional; excitement, nervousness, anticipation, giddiness and seasickness. These feelings intensify on a small vessel, but even from the relative safety and removed situation of a large ferry, crossing the sea still invokes a feeling of going to a profoundly different place. When visiting an island it can feel like you are leaving another world behind when you begin to cross the water.

The sea is an uncertain place. To the everyday passenger it is very hard to pinpoint your position and distance when you are at sea. Land that appears very close can take a long time to reach, and unseen currents or underwater rocks and reefs mean that taking a direct line towards a certain point is not always possible. The ebb and flow of the tides and currents can be seen and studied, but remain unpredictable. For example, on a calm day grand swells in the Atlantic can suddenly appear to come out of nowhere because they are a product of storms hundreds of miles out to sea (Cornish 1910). The sea is an ambiguous resource; it has the power to provide subsistence and the power to take it away. It is an unusual substance; it has a surface, but can be penetrated – on it we can float or sink and it is full of hidden depths and mysteries. It is inhabited by strange wildlife, large fish, huge mammals and beautiful jellyfish that most of us would be totally unaware of without the aid of television. When on the sea you never know when you may see a porpoise or a whale, and if you are lucky enough to catch a glimpse of one it inspires a certain feeling of wonder.

Watery depths have long given rise to myths and legends, from the Kraken of Greek mythology to stories of mermaids and mermen and, of course, the good old Loch Ness Monster. On the Hebridean Islands themselves, perceptions of the strangeness and 'otherworldliness' of the sea is expressed through the many tales of mysterious sea creatures or monsters that inhabit large lakes or rivers. For example, Loch na Meal, just south of Tobermory on Mull translates as 'loch of the monster' (Macnab 1998, 15). A stretch of water in the Minch, separating Lewis from the Shiant Isles, is called 'The Sound of the Blue Men'; after men supposedly human in size, but blue in colour, who spend their time swimming round and round the Isles (Robertson 1995, 169-70). Tales abound on the islands of mermaids and mermen; a number of inhabitants of Benbecula reported seeing a mermaid close to the seashore in about 1830 whose lower body was described like that of a salmon without scales (*ibid*, 151-3).

It is interesting that variations of these stories are not just confined to the Western Isles but appear in all cultures and continents around the world, and mythology concerning water is connected with all types of water from small ponds to great oceans. As Richards (1996, 316) has noted, 'Water represents a fundamental element in virtually all non-Western cosmological schemes,' and a common recurring theme is that of the sea as a passage or doorway to the underworld (see Bradley 2000, 10-12).

The unpredictability of the sea has meant that fishermen and sailors are traditionally very superstitious, often saying prayers or carrying out rituals before embarking upon a sea mission. For example, in the 1690s, during a voyage around the Western Isles, Martin Martin (Martin 1999 [*c.*1695], 76) noted that it was an ancient custom among the inhabitants of the Outer Hebrides to hang a male goat on the boat's mast to procure a favourable wind. Another custom was to row the boat around sunways when first setting out to sea to ensure a fortunate voyage (*ibid*,

81). In more recent times figureheads were placed on ships as guardians of the vessels they adorned and even today a bottle of champagne is traditionally smashed against the hull of a ship on its maiden voyage to ensure a safe journey.

Like the ancient mariner or islander, the feelings evoked by crossing the sea today can remain with the visitor once they are on the island, even if these emotions are for different reasons. The islands themselves seem mysterious and unusual; they can appear and disappear in the fog or the rain. Legends of floating mysterious islands prevail even today and there are many believers in the story of the mythical island of Atlantis. It is easy to see why. The weather systems surrounding islands can change in an instant and even the light has a different quality on islands. The awareness of being somewhere different is very strong. I believe this is largely because of the experience of crossing the unpredictable, unknown watery plain.

CONCLUSIONS

In conclusion, the experience of crossing that visual and mental barrier of the sea may have been vastly different for many different people at different times, but crossing it may nonetheless have triggered a similar sense of going to an otherworldly place. The properties and nature of the sea itself are often overlooked and underplayed in island studies, the focus being on the land. This paper has focused mainly on the Western Isles and their relationship to the western coast of Scotland, and has not looked west to the Atlantic Ocean at all. The difference between islands and areas of mainland coast goes far deeper than the visual overview. It is about experience and knowledge of these places. To residents it is about a sense of identity and belonging to a particular place. To visitors, it is about knowing that an island is surrounded by water, and crossing that water involves a different type of physical and emotional journey. Most importantly, to those who choose to study the archaeology of these places, it is about knowing that islands are places which can be experienced as both connected and disconnected.

ACKNOWLEDGEMENTS

I would like to thank both Colin Richards and Julian Thomas for their comments on earlier versions of this paper.

REFERENCES

Beveridge, E. 2001 [1911], *North Uist*, Edinburgh
Bradley, R. 2000, *An Archaeology of Natural Places*, London

Brophy, K. 2000, 'Water coincidence? cursus monuments and rivers', in Ritchie, A. (ed.), *Neolithic Orkney in its European Context*, 59-70, Cambridge

Burl, A. 1976, *The Stone Circles of the British Isles*, London

Burl, A. 2000, *The Stone Circles of Britain, Ireland and Brittany*, London

Cornish, V. 1910, *Waves of the Sea and Other Water Waves,* London

Defoe, D. 1993 [1719], *Robinson Crusoe*, Hertfordshire

Evans, J.D. 1973, 'Islands as laboratories for the study of culture process', in Renfrew, C. (ed.), *The Explanation of Culture Change: Models in Prehistory*, 517-520, London

Fowler, C. & Cummings, V. 2003 'Places of transformation: building monuments from water and stone in the Neolithic of the Irish Sea', *J Royal Anthropol Inst* 9, 1-20

Golding, W. 1954, *Lord of the Flies*, London

Martin, M. 1999 [c.1695], *A Description of the Western Islands of Scotland*, Edinburgh

Macnab, P. 1998, *Traditional Tales of Mull*, Tobermory

Mewett, P.G. 1986, 'Boundaries and discourse in a Lewis crofting community', in Cohen, A.P. (ed.), *Symbolising Boundaries: Identity and Diversity in British Cultures*, 71-87, Manchester

Rainbird, P. 1999, 'Islands out of time: towards a critique of island archaeology', *J Med Archaeol* 12, 216-234

Richards, C. 1996, 'Henges and water: towards an elemental understanding of monumentality and landscape in Late Neolithic Britain', *J Material Culture* 1, 313-336

Ritchie, A. 1997, *Shetland*, Edinburgh

Ritchie, G. & Harman M. 1996, *Argyll and the Western Isles*, Edinburgh

Robertson, R.M. 1995, *Selected Highland Folktales*, Isle of Colonsay, Argyll

Stevenson, R.L. 1994 [1883], *Treasure Island*, London

Stevenson, R.L. 1994 [1886], *Kidnapped*, London

Wainwright, F.T. 1962, *The Northern Isles*, London

5

PEELING BACK THE LAYERS: RECONSTRUCTING A VANISHED IRON AGE LANDSCAPE

Deborah Lamb

INTRODUCTION

The diversity of Iron Age structures in the north and west of Scotland suggests an underlying complexity in the organisation of society. In this paper, I employ an inter-disciplinary approach to examine a specific location in Shetland, with the goal of constructing a socio-economic model of how it might have functioned in the Iron Age. An assessment can then be made as to how far local society was responding to local conditions as well as regional influences. This paper examines how evidence from historical documentation and place-names amplifies the archaeological field evidence for Iron Age settlement. This is done in three stages. Firstly, the historical evidence is examined in order to understand how the landscape has developed since the Iron Age. Next, the archaeological evidence for the landscape which pre-dated the Iron Age is considered. Finally these are compared with the field evidence for the Iron Age, to see if there are elements present in both the inherited landscape and the legacy landscape, which might cast new light on the Iron Age. In this locality, the evidence from before and after the Iron Age suggests an apparent continuity of patterns of land use, which in turn has implications for interpreting developments in local society.

This paper is part of a wider research project designed to assess how far the influence of local factors may have contributed to the organisation of Iron Age society in north and west Scotland. It was suggested in the early 1990s that a series of locally-based studies should be carried out in Atlantic Scotland, dealing with changes in patterns of settlement through time as well as through space (Hingley 1992, 25). The main work, of which this paper represents part, is one such locally-based study. The core objective of the main study is to generate a socio-economic model of how three small islands (Burra, Houss and Trondra in Shetland) may have functioned in the Iron Age. The foundation of the model is the archaeological evidence in the field, but a multi-disciplinary approach is used to predict other areas of probable activity during the Iron Age and to identify additional local issues, which are significant to interpreting the study area. This paper draws on historical documents and place-name analysis as well as archaeological evidence in order to construct a possible model of Iron Age settlement in one of the three islands.

THE IRON AGE IN SHETLAND

Shetland lies at a natural crossroads between the Atlantic Ocean and the northern North Sea, and between Scotland and Scandinavia (*1*). Its Iron Age lasted approximately from 500 BC to AD 625 (Owen & Lowe 1999, 269; Foster 1989, 40). In seeking to classify Iron Age Scotland, Piggott (1966, 4-5) placed Shetland in the Atlantic Province which he defined as stretching from Argyll and the Firth of Clyde in the south-west of Scotland, through Wester Ross and western Invernesshire up to Sutherland and Caithness, including both the western and the northern isles. The influence of the ocean, and the presence of monumental drystone buildings, suggested a common heritage for these regions. Given their geographical spread, however, a significant measure of regional diversity might be expected (Harding 1990, 5).

One aspect of this regional diversity is the complex typology of massive drystone circular houses found in the province, with regions usually showing a clear preference for a particular type. In Shetland, this is the broch (Fojut 1985, 81-4). There are some 120 Iron Age sites in Shetland, of which around 80 have now been identified as broch sites (Fojut 1985, 81-2; 2005, 169-170). Study has traditionally been concentrated on the broch (Fojut 1982; MacKie 2002), but reflecting on the relationship of the non-broch sites to their surroundings and to neighbouring broch communities may shed a different light on the organisation of Iron Age society.

The locally-based study of which this paper forms a part, takes the landscape as its starting point rather than any particular monuments lying within it. The location being considered is a group of three Shetland Islands: Burra (now known as West Burra), Houss (now known as East Burra) and Trondra. With a combined area of 16 km², the three islands form a geographical unity, lying adjacent to the south-west coast of mainland Shetland (*2*). In terms of known Iron Age monuments, they contain two poorly preserved broch sites, one at Brough on Burra and one at Burland on Trondra. There is also a midden at House on Houss, from which Iron

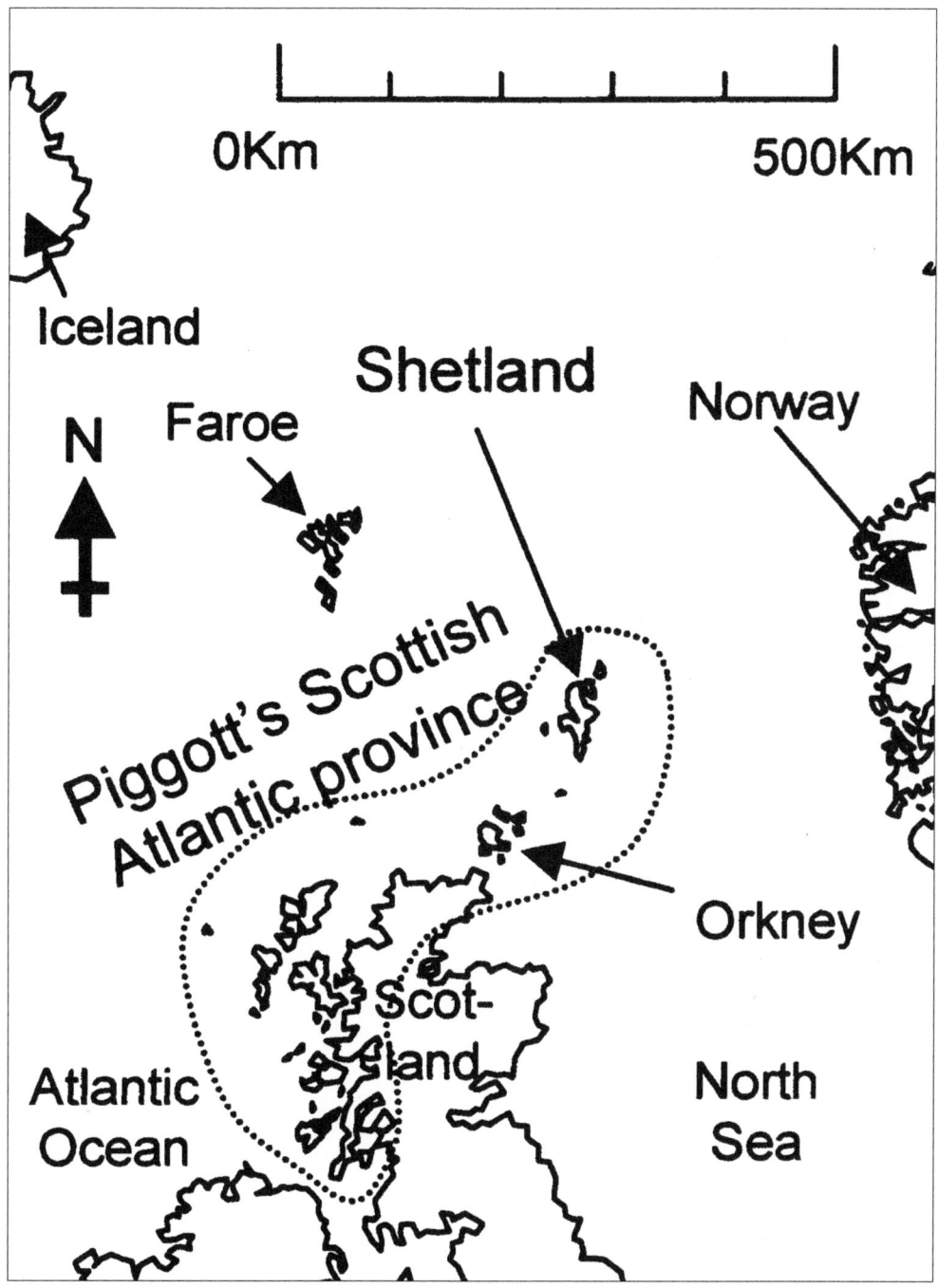

1 Location of Shetland *(D. Lamb)*

Scottish Odysseys: The Archaeology of Islands

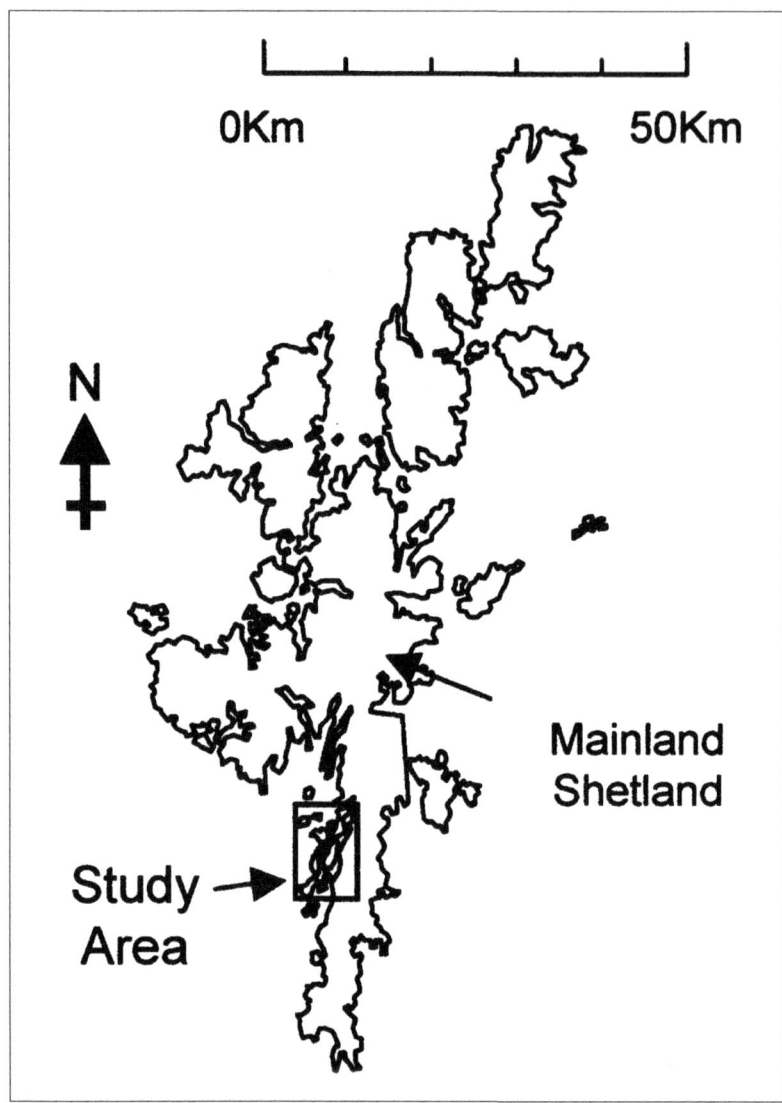

2 The Shetland Islands *(D. Lamb)*

Age material has been recovered (Fojut 1985, 83). In general, the islands enjoy an unusually high state of archaeological preservation (Hedges 1984, 45-7). This paper is particularly concerned with the island of Houss (*3*).

The island of Houss is divided almost into two parts, being joined at its narrowest point only by a shingle ayre some 50m wide (*4*). In the northern part of the island the land slopes more gently to the sea on the west coast, particularly along the south-west shore and in the north-west corner. The rest of the coast is mostly rocky and low cliff, with the exception of a small area on the north-east coast, at Hogaland. The part of the island south of the ayre is known as Symbister Ness. The coast here is almost entirely rocky low cliff. The main exception is a small area halfway down

Peeling Back the Layers: reconstructing a vanished Iron Age landscape

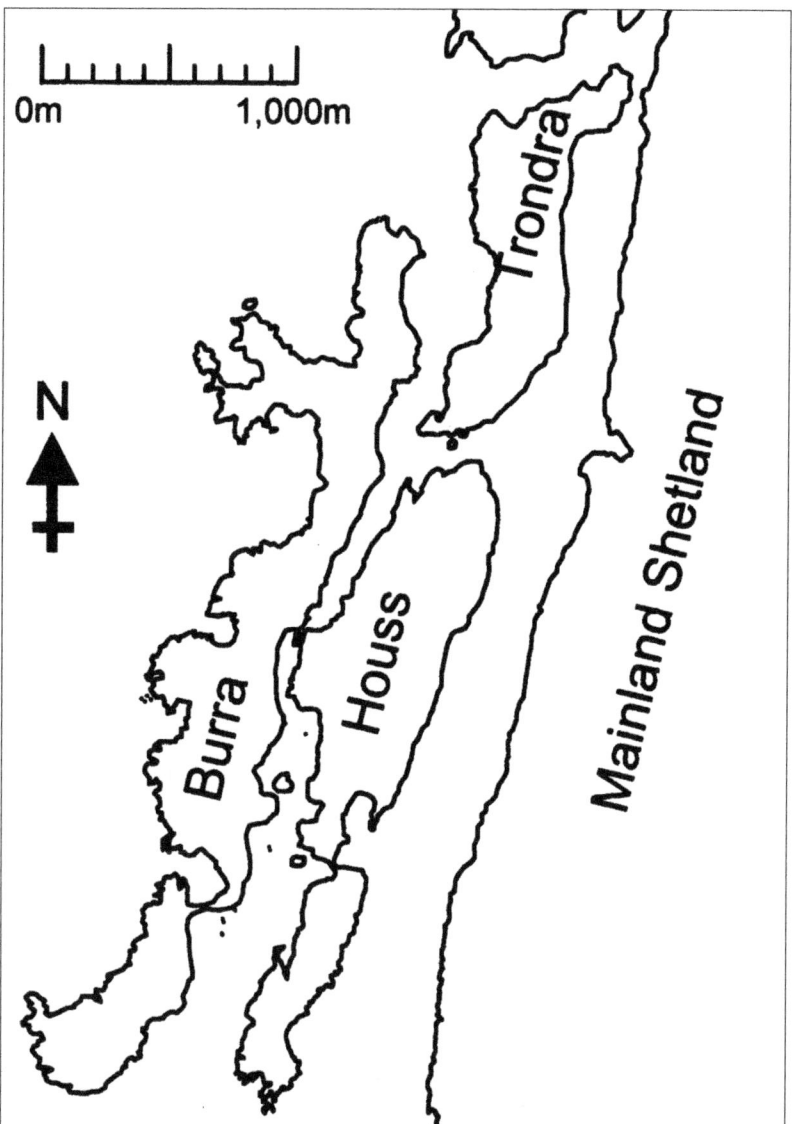

3 Map of study area *(D. Lamb)*

the western shore of the ness, where the land slopes easily to the sea. This area contains the now-deserted settlement of Symbister.

CONSTRUCTING THE MODEL

My broader research examines a defined archaeological landscape with the goal of constructing a socio-economic model of the area during the Iron Age. Two important factors in understanding this relationship are settlements and resources.

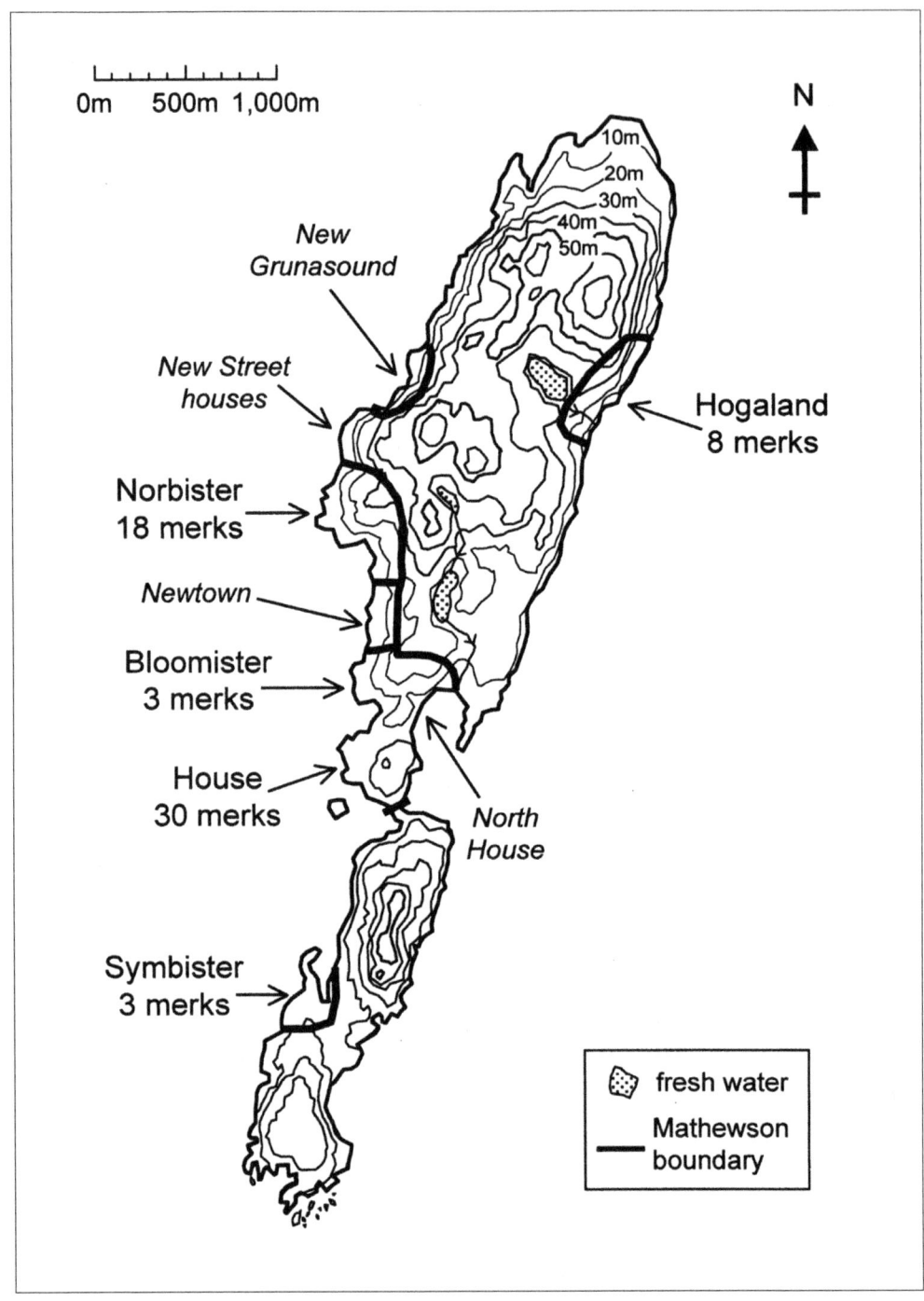

4 Nineteenth-century settlements on Houss (D. Lamb)

This paper constructs one possible model of the Iron Age landscape on the island of Houss. The approach taken is to consider in depth the use of the landscape before and after the Iron Age, and then look at the known Iron Age evidence.

Iron Age settlement had a lasting influence on the subsequent evolution of the medieval and post-medieval agricultural landscape, and its impact remains visible in the record. One of the problems with constructing a model based solely on the archaeological record, is that the longest-lived and most successful Shetland settlements are likely to have the least visible prehistoric evidence (Crawford 1987, 151). Later occupation may have removed all traces of earlier activity (Hunter 1996, 58-60 *passim*). From medieval times onwards, however, an increasing amount of documentary and place-name evidence is available about the landscape. This can be used to analyse and interpret developments which took place after the Iron Age and which, by process of elimination, may have existed during the Iron Age. Where different approaches come to consistent conclusions, the probability of the suggested reconstruction must increase, even though the data exploited in each area may be relatively weak (Paterson 1999, 261). As the roots of the modern landscape lie in the Iron Age, so do the roots of the Iron Age environment lie in the Neolithic and Bronze Age. The landscape which preceded the Iron Age is therefore an important contributory factor in knowing how the Iron Age landscape might have looked and functioned.

In this case, when taken together, the evidence from before and after the Iron Age suggests an apparent continuity of patterns of land use which in turn has implications for interpreting developments in local society.

THE SHETLAND LANDSCAPE

In Shetland, areas of naturally occurring soil are few and small. Typically, soils are shallow, stony and low in fertility (Dry & Robertson 1982, 62). The effects of cultivation, combined with the addition of materials such as ash, turves, dung, midden material, sand and seaweed, can result in the gradual increase of topsoil depth (Davidson & Simpson 1984, 75). Through centuries of manuring, thick topsoils can evolve and may provide a cogent reason for continuity in settlement focus, lasting in some cases from the Bronze Age into the twentieth century (Dockrill 2002, 156). Not all settlements, however, were occupied continuously, or for long. A generally well-populated Neolithic landscape of dispersed but loosely clustered settlements is believed to have contracted in the Bronze Age, when coastal areas were more favoured for settlement (Fojut 1999, 10; Whittle *et al* 1986, 148). The Iron Age is thought to have been a period of further retrenchment, marking the evolution of nucleated settlements close to the shore (Owen & Lowe 1999, 269).

Following a period of Pictish influence, the arrival of the Norse in the eighth century AD marked the beginning of Norse Shetland. Over 99 per cent of Shetland place names are derived from Old Norse (Fojut 1994, 69). In historical times before agricultural improvement and crofting tenure (Knox 1985, 6), the Shetland landscape had two types of land use: townships and the open rough hill land. Townships consisted of small farming settlements situated near the coast and were enclosed by a hill-dyke of turf and stone. Characteristically, the dyke started and finished at the shoreline (Tait 2000, 20-1). This distinctive layout persisted for centuries and marked the limit of a township (Crawford 1987, 150; Morris 1985, 230). A right to part of the township was accompanied by a right to use a proportional amount of the common land beyond the hill-dyke (Smith 2000, 40), but Shetlanders bought, sold and paid rent on arable land, i.e. only on land within the township. The value of a township was historically measured in merks. In medieval times, a merk was a piece of land that cost a set weight of silver. A piece of land was valued only on its arable area, within the township. The exact extent of the area involved varied considerably, according to the quality of the soil, for the same merk would buy either a large area of poor land, or a small area of good land.

Taxation was also based on the value of the township. Two important taxes were *scat* and *wattle*. These are both of Scandinavian origin and take a particular form in Shetland. *Scat* is a tax payable to the Crown from all lands within townships, probably dating from the late thirteenth century. *Wattle* is a later tax paid in 'nights', providing hospitality to the sheriff as he travelled round administering justice. A document of *c.*1612 indicates that this service was commuted to goods by Earl Robert Stewart, some time after 1565 (NAS RH9/15/169).

By the sixteenth and seventeenth centuries, when documents describing the sale and purchase of property first appear, all land outside townships was attributed to one township or another. Recorded property transactions referred to land in the townships only; the associated rights to the hill land were included implicitly.

During times of population expansion, additional smallholdings were created by enclosing parts of the hill land beyond the hill dyke. These were known as outsets (Smith 1984, 337). Historically younger than the townships, the outsets were not regarded as having any share in the resources or responsibilities of the adjacent township. They were not measured in merks, neither were they liable for tax. From the early eighteenth century until the middle of the nineteenth, many Shetland landowners created new outsets and parcelled out small units of land in order to increase the number of fishermen tenants. There were thought to be about 380 outsets in Shetland by 1770 (Smith 2000, 46).

PEELING BACK THE HISTORICAL LAYERS

Townships and Outsets
The oldest townships on Houss may be expected to have the deepest soils, and to have been occupied continuously over an extended period, possibly since the

Neolithic. They are likely to have been taxed early and to appear in the earliest known Shetland documents. Their very names may be indicative of long occupation. If they can be identified, they provide a starting point for considering the pattern of Iron Age settlement. Figure 4 shows the location of the settlements discussed in this paper.

Outsets are the most recent layer of occupation. They may be identified in one of two ways. The first is by documentary reference. Outsets which were recently occupied in the nineteenth century tend to be identified as such in contemporary documents. Secondly, outsets will not be measured in merks, for only established townships are valued in this way. Four nineteenth century documents list property on Houss and describe its value (4). The rental records for Burra and Houss for the year 1855 (SA Uncatalogued) list all the properties on Houss, indicating against each its value in merks, or the fact that it is an outset. These records treat Bloomister and North House as one property, worth three merks.

In 1832, a teacher from Yell named Mathewson was engaged by the then landowner to review the rental capacity of Burra and Houss. He produced a detailed survey of the dwellings and inhabitants of the two islands, and a well-drawn sketch map showing the boundaries of the then-cultivated land (SA D.1/385). The map shows the main division between arable land and rough grazing, and some boundaries between properties. Mathewson noted on his survey either the value of the property in merks, or the fact that it was an outset.

The sale of the whole islands of Burra and Houss in 1921 recorded that the property was being passed to the purchaser subject to the contents of documents listed in an attached Inventory of Writs (NAS RS111/213/48-50). The Inventory lists various bonds, deeds, will, charters, grants of wayleave etc., the earliest of which dates from 1830. It follows that the main description of the property must have been in use for property transactions from 1830 or earlier. The description identifies the value in merks of the individual townships, and identifies other properties as outsets. This description is the first item in the 'Search for Incumbrances' still used today by solicitors involved in buying and selling property on the two islands.

Lastly, in the early 1820s, the landowners of Shetland set about drawing up an official valuation roll, with a view to establishing their voting rights in parliamentary elections (SA CO.1/3/1). They gathered information by means of sending a questionnaire to every known landowner in Shetland. The roll lists every place in Shetland which was measured in merks of land. If it was not measured in merks, then it did not appear in this document. It follows that outsets were excluded. The Roll does, however, contain one anomaly. It shows House as valued at 36 merks. The property actually paid *cess* (a type of land-tax) on only 30 merks, and tax records, by their nature, tend not to underestimate the value of property to be taxed. Taking this into account along with the consistency of the other documents, it is likely that the correct figure for House is 30 merks.

From these documents, it is possible to identify the settlements on Houss in the nineteenth century (see *4*). These are listed below together with a summary of information about their status drawn from the above documents (Table 1).

Settlement	Crop of 1855	Mathewson, 1832-3	Pre-1830 disposition	Valuation Roll, 1825
Hogaland	8 merks	8 merks	8 merks	8 merks
New Grunasound	Outset	Outset	(no mention)	(no mention)
New Street	Outsets	Outsets	(no mention)	(no mention)
Norbister	18 merks	18 merks	18 merks	18 merks
New Town	Outset	Outset	Outset	(no mention)
Bloomister	3 merks	2 merks	3 merks	3 merks
North House		1 merk	Outset	(no mention)
House	30 merks	30 merks	30 merks	36 merks
Symbister	3 merks	3 merks	3 merks	3 merks

TABLE 1 SETTLEMENTS ON HOUSS IN THE NINETEENTH CENTURY AND THEIR VALUATIONS

From this analysis, it seems that New Grunasound, New Street and New Town were all fairly recently established at the time the documents were drawn up. This is already suggested by the presence of the element 'New' in each of their names. Interestingly, none of the three names is in local use. New Grunasound is known locally as 'Crö'. A *crö* is the local term for a sheep-fold, and may suggest what the area was used for, before it became a permanent habitation. The properties on New Street are known only by their individual names. New Town is known as Guttery Toun, because the land is full of mud, mire and puddles. Its poorly drained nature confirms that it has not been as intensively worked over as long a period, as adjacent properties in the area. These three settlements may therefore be regarded as less likely to have been occupied in the Iron Age.

Mathewson marks the individual houses at Bloomister, North House and House, but does not show any clear boundaries between their respective holdings. Bloomister and North House appear to have been treated as a single property in the Rental of 1855. Mathewson explains in his survey that 'by a late division one Merk was taken from Bloomister and given to Northhouse' (SA D.1/385). He also notes that North House 'was originally an outset'. Originally, therefore Bloomister was worth three merks and North House was an outset. The status of North House is, however, unusual.

As stated above, townships were valued in merks but outsets were not. Mathewson writes of North House that 'As an outset it was rated as 3 Merks to the Tenants' but did not form part of 'the old Rental land' (SA D.1/385). The term 'rated as' is a curious phrase, not otherwise found in descriptions of Shetland property. It suggests that the status of this outset was unusual, and may mean that North House was established at a time when the distinction between township and outset was recognised but not yet critical in terms of rights and responsibilities. This being so, the period before 1600 is suggested as likely for the expansion of settlement at North House.

Most townships have only one centre of population, but Mathewson's map shows two in Norbister. He refers to the smaller of these as 'Norbister Houlls', but does not identify it either as a separate township or as an outset. It is treated consistently throughout all historical documentation as part of Norbister, and may represent an expansion from Norbister before the distinction between township and outset was fixed. Since the documentary evidence is consistent in including both parts of the settlement in the same township, this expansion is likely to have taken place well before 1600. The oldest townships on Houss at this stage are listed in Table 2.

Settlement	Value
Hogaland	8 merks
Norbister	18 merks
Bloomister	3 merks
House	30 merks
Symbister	3 merks

TABLE 2 THE OLDEST TOWNSHIPS ON HOUSS AND THEIR VALUE

Documentary Evidence

The individual strands of evidence are tenuous, but taken together evidence from agricultural quality, taxation records and early Shetland documents, suggests a possible sequence of settlement for the five oldest settlements.

Agricultural quality

In Shetland, deep soils indicate long occupation. If a small property is worth the same as a large property, it must be because the smaller piece of ground has better soil and in Shetland that usually means deeper soil. In theory, therefore, comparing area with value over known properties ought to generate an indication of the comparative quality of their soil, and therefore potentially of the length of time that piece of land has been cultivated.

In the census of 1851, householders were required to state the extent of land they farmed in acres. By comparing the acreage of townships with their value in merks shown in other documents, the list in Table 3 is generated.

Settlement	Value	Area	Merks/acre
Hogaland	8 merks	10 acres	0.80
Norbister	18 merks	25 acres	0.72
Bloomister	3 merks	3 acres	1.00
House	30 merks	27¼ acres	1.32
Symbister	3 merks	5 acres	0.60

TABLE 3 ACREAGE OF TOWNSHIPS AND THEIR VALUE IN MERKS

This would suggest that House is by far the best land on the island, and therefore potentially the settlement which has been occupied longest, whilst Symbister is the poorest. However, there are problems with using this analysis too simplistically. Firstly, the numbers of merks may not be strictly comparable. Although originally a merk represented a set weight of silver, from the late Middle Ages merks of land paid rent at different rates. These varied between four and twelve pennies per merk, sometimes within a single township. This variability may be a consideration here. Secondly, it has already been pointed out that Norbister may have expanded at an early date, before township boundaries became fixed. The two centres of occupation and cultivation within Norbister are separated by an uncultivated area. By calculating merks per acre over the whole township, this may have unfairly depressed the average score, understating the actual agricultural productivity of the cultivated areas.

Taxation
High value land will be taxed more thoroughly and at an earlier date than poorer places. Potentially, tax records provide a source of comparative value and therefore comparative longevity. Of the two main taxes paid in Shetland, *scat* probably dates from the late thirteenth century, whilst it is known that *wattle* was in existence around 1565. It follows that townships which pay *wattle* but not *scat* came into existence between 1300 and the late sixteenth century (Smith, forthcoming). Various documents list *scat* and *wattle* payments. One of the most reliable was drawn up by Thomas Gifford in 1716. It is a very accurate and careful work; Table 4 shows the entries for the island of Houss.

Hogaland, Norbister and House clearly date from before the thirteenth century. Bloomister and Symbister are not identified as separate payers of tax, although there is the possibility that for tax purposes they are regarded as part of another township.

General documentary evidence
There are only around 125 documents extant concerning Shetland for the whole period from 1200 to 1560, so much can be attributed to accident of survival. Four of the five settlements, however, are mentioned specifically (Table 5).

Peeling Back the Layers: reconstructing a vanished Iron Age landscape

Settlement	Scat	Wattle
Hogaland	Hugaland	Hugaland
Norbister	Norbuster	Norbuster
Bloomister	(no mention)	(no mention)
House	Houss	Houss
Symbister	(no mention)	(no mention)

TABLE 4 SCAT AND WATTLE PAYMENTS ON THE ISLAND OF HOUSS, AS RECORDED BY THOMAS GIFFORD

Settlement	Documents dated
Hogaland	1587
Norbister	1577, 1578
Bloomister	(none)
House	c.1510, 1560, 1575, 1578, 1580, 1584, 1587, 1588 (twice), 1589 (twice)
Symbister	1577

TABLE 5 THE DATES OF DOCUMENTS REFERRING TO THE OLDEST TOWNSHIPS ON HOUSS

The Hogaland reference is in a long list of lands owned by the archdeaconry of Shetland. It is quite a common place-name, and although the context suggests that this is Hogaland on Houss, it might in fact be a settlement of the same name on Burra. The mention of Symbister is, however, specific, and occurs in a document which lists by name over 750 Shetland men by parish, including 'Erasmus & Thomas in Sinbustar'. The same document mentions James and Dandie, both of Norbister. House emerges as a significant settlement and home to an important branch of the Sinclair family, who were prominent in Shetland history between the late fifteenth and the late sixteenth century. The notable absence is Bloomister. Bloomister is good quality land, contiguous with the House settlement area, and therefore a likely area for early expansion. From AD 1300 onwards, it does not appear to have been taxed in its own right, although by the nineteenth century it was valued at three merks. It is not mentioned in any documents between 1195 and 1611. Even though the quality of the land is good, it may only have been established post-1600. From documentary evidence, therefore, the four oldest settlements on Houss appear to be:

Hogaland: Scatted and therefore founded pre-1300, it is small in size but contains quite good quality land suggesting long occupation.
Norbister: Also scatted and therefore pre-1300, this settlement appears to have been expanded at least once, suggesting some success. It is extensive in area and

contains on average good land which can be very good in the cultivated areas.

House: Dating from before 1300, this settlement contains the best quality land on the island. It appears to have expanded twice, once towards Bloomister and later towards North House. Its early appearance in documents attests to the settlement's early importance.

Symbister: This is the only settlement on Symbister Ness. It was not scatted, suggesting that it was not established until after 1300. Documentary evidence indicates that it was, however, in existence by 1577. The settlement is small, and the quality of the land is poor. This reinforces the impression that it was not intensively worked over a long period.

Place-Name Evidence

Place-name analysis potentially provides a bridge between historical documents and events and conditions prior to recorded history. The place-names of Shetland are overwhelmingly Norse, and some may possibly reach back to the period when the Norse arrived, at the end of the Late Iron Age. This exciting possibility needs to be approached with caution, however, for written evidence is mostly late. Over the centuries, older names have been lost and replaced, and whilst place-names may appear Norse, both later and earlier names can be misidentified as such. Bearing these limitations in mind, the names of the four core settlements identified so far, are derived as follows:

Norbister: the name is derived from two Norse elements, *norðr-* meaning north and *bólstaðr* meaning farm (Jakobsen 1936, 130; Stewart 1987, 58).

Symbister: similarly, this name is derived from *sunn-* meaning south and *bólstaðr* meaning farm (Jakobsen 1936, 130; Stewart 1987, 58).

Hogaland: the *–land* element denotes farmland (Jakobsen 1936, 76; Stewart 1987, 191) but the first element of the name is variously explained as *haugr* meaning cairn or mound (Jakobsen 1936, 51-2; Stewart 1987, 193) or *hagi* meaning pasture (Jakobsen 1936, 50). The Shetland term hjog can also denote a hill (Jakobsen 1936, 51).

House: this is derived from *hús* meaning house (Jakobsen 1936, 62; Stewart 1987, 150).

Old Norse is rich in words indicating habitation; examples are listed in Table 6.

It is difficult to recover the connotations of the different designations. They may reflect change through time, analysis of which might indicate a chronology of settlement expansion. They may indicate differences in size or location of farm, or specify the relationship between a group of farms. Indeed, these explanations need not be mutually exclusive. It is also the case that the original connotations may have become irrelevant over time. Situations change, and historical records do not always confirm the early low status initially implied by the generic name. Large, central, high-status farms will often be the oldest, but outlying settlements sometimes

Old Norse	Surviving name element
boer, býr	-by
bólstaðr	-bister
garðr	-garth, -gar
hús	-house
land	-land
sætr, setr	-setter
skáli	-skaill
staðr	-sta, -ster, -ston

TABLE 6 OLD NORSE WORDS SUGGESTING HABITATION

become as productive as the original ones, especially if the area was well-manured before the farm was established. Bearing this in mind, the term *bólstaðr* seems to carry some meaning as regards age, size and situation. In Orkney, farms with this name are often large and fairly low-lying, being well-established at an early period. In Shetland, on the other hand, they are often half the size of *staðr* farms, and have a closer connection to the sea. In both Orkney and Shetland, they often occur in pairs or groups.

The north/south pair on Houss may have come into being as the result of dividing an existing farm, but there are difficulties with this. Norbister and Symbister both appear in the written record for the first time in the late 1570s, but there are apparently large differences in status in terms of physical size, value and quality of soil. Also, Norbister was taxed in its own right at an early period. If this was a formal division, it was not an equal one. In this case, therefore, the names could simply be geographical indicators. The term 'land' also seems to carry some meaning as regards age, size and situation. These farms are definitely lesser. In Norway, they occur on more marginal sites susceptible to crop failure and they are apparently secondary in relation to *staðr* farms (Andersen 1995, 19). In Orkney, they tend to be on less advantageous sites and among the smaller farms (Thomson 1995, 59). In terms of chronology, smaller and poorer means potentially later in historical terms, with such places occupied only later, when the better sites were already taken.

The first element in the name Hogaland is subject to different interpretations. In this case, the name could refer to the Neolithic cairn on the hill behind Hogaland, but not necessarily as Hogaland is a common farm-name in Shetland. It is possible that the name derives from *hagi* meaning 'pasture' (Jakobsen 1936, 50), which may denote the kind of farming carried out on the site. There is little evidence for a shieling system in Shetland, but grazing was important and pasture areas were obvious choices for expansion because the soil was well-manured. Some early secondary settlements did begin as pasturage farms in the outfield or between the main settlements, but these usually include the element *setter* (Stewart 1965, 229-44) rather than *haga* (Stewart 1965, 125).

The most important settlement on the island appears to have been House. The *hús* element is common in Shetland place-names, but seldom stands alone. Uncompounded, it occurs only three times in Shetland (Stewart 1987, 173), but two of these occur for the first time on nineteenth-century maps. House on Houss is the exception.

As shown by the early documentary evidence, a major branch of the powerful Sinclair family was based here. The ruins of a haa house still stand at House, the only example of the type on Burra, Houss or Trondra. Haa houses developed after the seventeenth century (Finnie 1996). At a time when most Shetland houses were single storey, they made a statement by being two or three stories high, and prominently situated. In the grounds of the haa house at House, there are the foundations of an earlier large building, known locally as Da Galleries. House has therefore been the setting for a major dwelling for an extended period of time.

House could simply be a comparatively modern and obvious name for the place, because it was the location of a succession of prestige dwellings. There is no hard evidence for the settlement having been called anything else, but I suggest that it may have been called Huseby. Change over time means sometimes the *-by* element of names is not important enough to be retained (Crawford 1987, 112), and the presence of a great house would add rationalisation to the name change. There are other indications that Huseby is a possible name.

Huseby farms are important farms, usually large, old and central, reflecting their high status as the original settlement. They often show signs of subsequent division, whilst the original farm retains its status (Thomson 1995, 53-4). House shows signs of all of these prerequisites. A further key point may also be present. Huseby farms have been associated with estates. In this sense, the word 'estate' is used to indicate operational management linking the constituent parts. It is not used to describe simple ownership of a range of land holdings.

The situation regarding estates differs between Orkney and Shetland. In Orkney, a hierarchical structure for farms has been proposed (Fenton 1997, 29) and even a regular administrative system centred on huseby farms (Steinnes 1959). Whilst the differential status of the farms on Houss might suggest a hierarchy, the actual evidence for estates on Shetland is only slight (Smith 1995, 35). There may have been estates at Strom in Whiteness and Brow in Dunrossness, but neither Strom nor Brow is connected with a huseby name. It is also the case that the histories of Orkney and of Shetland are different, particularly after 1195. Shetland was a much less aristocratic society than Orkney.

Overall, therefore, looking at the historical and place-name evidence, one possibility might be that Norbister, Symbister and Hogaland are the remaining component parts of a single large Norse estate which covered the island of Houss, and was centred on the settlement at House. If this was the situation not long after the end of the Iron Age, the question arises as to whether it represented a progression from the Iron Age or a break with what had gone immediately before.

Having considered the legacy landscape of the Iron Age, it is necessary also to look at the landscape which it inherited from the Neolithic and Bronze Age, before drawing any conclusions about how the Iron Age landscape itself might have looked and functioned. Here, the evidence is from archaeology.

The Archaeological Evidence

Because of the nature of the Shetland landscape, with its pockets of largely anthropogenic agricultural soils, archaeological sites are more likely to be found on uncultivated land which has been used as grazing in historical times, or where cultivation has been abandoned. Long-lived settlements, where continued agriculture has produced the deepest soil, have the least visible archaeological remains. Successful settlements occupied in historical times may well have been occupied in the Neolithic, the Bronze Age or the Iron Age, but the archaeological evidence of that occupation is likely to have been long cleared or rebuilt.

Even allowing for this difficulty of interpretation, the difference between the north and south parts of Houss, is marked (5). The north part of the island contains Neolithic cairns and several sites either positively identified as oval houses or recognised as areas of potential settlement. Oval houses are traditionally treated as Neolithic, but they were a very long-lived design, continuing into the Early Iron Age (Fojut 2006, 18). The house sites are on uncultivated land, or on recently developed outsets like Guttery Toun, and many are associated with prehistoric field systems. Still others may lie under the core historical settlements. Of particular interest is a dense area of boundary walls, consisting of discontinuous lines of earthfast stones disappearing in some cases under the peat. These boundaries are found all over the grazing land outside the modern crofts, but particularly in the northernmost third of the island.

The north part of the island also contains a standing stone on the common grazing close to cultivated land and around eight burnt mounds which are all located along the western coast among the core historical settlements. This pattern of Bronze Age monuments shows the pattern of retrenchment which has often been predicted, with an apparent preference for the west coast where the terrain is easiest because it gently slopes down to the sea.

The Iron Age might be expected to show evidence of further retrenchment, and appears to do so, with the two recorded Iron Age sites all being sited at House. They comprise a midden (with an associated structure) and a souterrain. The archaeological record on Symbister Ness provides a contrast. There are no oval houses or field boundaries, in spite of the ness being exactly the kind of terrain where they should be easy to locate. There is, however, a group of three

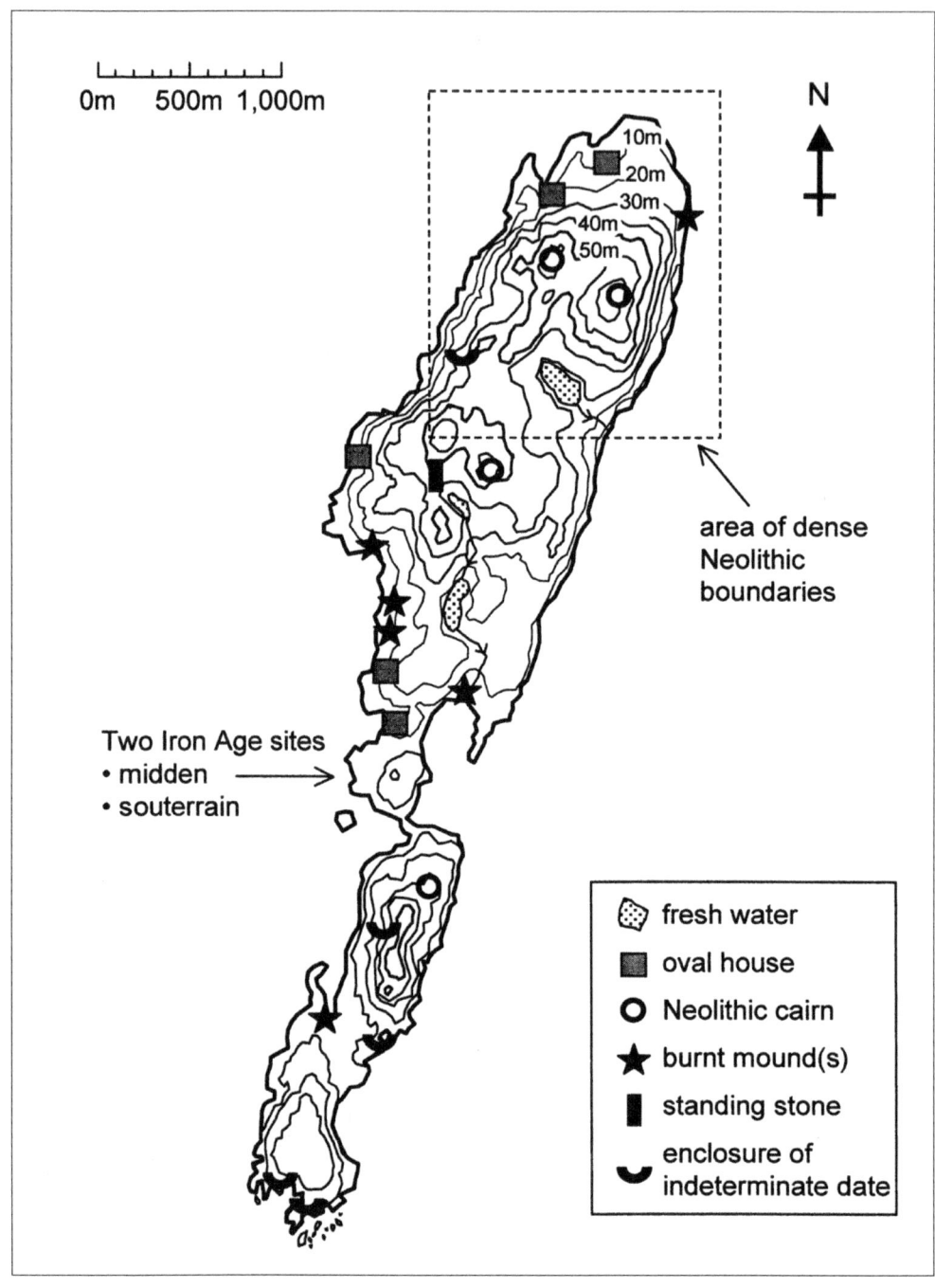

5 Pre-Iron Age sites and monuments on Houss *(D. Lamb)*

burnt mounds standing on the deserted croft of Symbister; these include one of the largest burnt mounds on Shetland, standing 2.2m high. The most numerous monuments on the ness are enclosures of indeterminate date. These are of turf or turf and stone construction, and are mostly coastal although too insubstantial to be, say, promontory forts. There appears to be a clear distinction between the two parts of the island. To the north of the ayre, the boundaries dividing the landscape suggest early intensive agricultural activity on what is now the common grazing land. To the south, there is no evidence to suggest that Symbister Ness was occupied domestically at all in Neolithic times. Only the presence of burnt mounds at one location suggests Bronze Age activity. The only archaeological evidence for Iron Age activity is at House.

A MODEL FOR THE IRON AGE ON HOUSS

One common thread which potentially unites the pre-Iron Age archaeological and the post-Iron Age historical evidence is whole island management. If the oldest settlements are the remaining component parts of a single large estate which covered the island of Houss, this could have functioned in several ways. With the original farm at House retaining its status, the two satellite farms at the settlements later known as Norbister and Hogaland might have been arable. Livestock could have been confined to Symbister Ness south of the ayre, with initially seasonal occupation of the later settlement of Symbister. The farm at House would have been located centrally between the two areas of farming activity, and the north and south farms could have been not so much names, as a description of location. Population pressure would lead to expansion of the initial settlements, and later to occupation of the pasturage farm. Alternatively, the Hogaland farm may have been used in Norse times initially as a pasturage farm, as its name possibly suggests.

A distinction of land-use north and south of the ayre may have existed before the Iron Age. The natural neck of land makes it easy to turn the whole of Symbister Ness into grazing for stock, and there is no evidence to suggest Neolithic habitation on the ness, and only the presence of burnt mounds at one location to suggest Bronze Age activity. Given the low score of Symbister when merks are compared to acreage, it appears that the land has not been worked agriculturally for long. On the contrary, the evidence for early intensive agricultural activity seems to lie on the common grazing land in the north part of the island, where boundaries divide the landscape.

Without survey and examination of the soil, it is not possible to say for certain that these were arable fields, but as climate became more changeable towards the end of the Neolithic period, it would have been prudent for the population to use a range of east-facing and west-facing arable areas in order to optimise grain-growing conditions in different years. The settlement later known as Hogaland may have been cultivated for crops at this time.

One model for Iron-Age Houss is that it was run as an integrated unit in line with pre-existing land-use division, using arable areas facing different aspects in the north of the island for raising crops, and the natural peninsula to the south for grazing and dairying.

This raises questions about the role of the brochs on neighbouring Burra and Trondra, for Houss does not contain a broch site. There are implications for the later Norse settlement too, depending on how the social conditions of the Iron Age are interpreted. Perhaps the Norse found individual freehold farmers working cooperatively, and planted their own tenants, creating a new estate. Alternatively, if the island was a Pictish estate in the Late Iron Age, then it may have been simply taken over in its entirety. In looking at the situation on Houss, however, it is important to remember the geographical unity it shares with Burra and Trondra, and how it may have related to these close neighbours, easily reached by boat over a shallow sea. The suggested model can be no more than that. There is no hard proof for whole island management on Iron Age Houss. Each single strand of evidence is weak on its own, but taken together they build a cable of argument that is worthy of consideration.

REFERENCES

Andersen, P.S. 1995, 'The Norwegian background', in Crawford, B.E. (ed.), *Scandinavian Settlement in Northern Britain*, 16-25, London

Crawford, B.E. 1987, *Scandinavian Scotland*, Leicester

Davidson, D.A. & Simpson, I.A. 1984, 'The formation of deep topsoils in Orkney', *Earth Surface Processes and Landforms* 9, 75-81

Dockrill, S.J. 2002, 'Brochs, economy and power', in Ballin Smith, B. & Banks, I. (eds), *In the Shadow of the Brochs, the Iron Age in Scotland*, 153-62, Stroud

Dry, F.T. & Robertson, J.S. 1982, *Soil and Land Capability for Agriculture: Orkney and Shetland*, Aberdeen

Fenton, A. 1997, *The Northern Isles: Orkney and Shetland*, East Linton

Finnie, G.M. 1996, 'An introduction to the haa houses of Shetland', *Vernacular Building* 20, 39-55

Fojut, N. 1982, 'Towards a geography of Shetland brochs', *Glasgow Archaeol J* 9, 38-59

Fojut, N. 1985, 'Some thoughts on the Shetland Iron Age', in Smith, B. (ed.), *Shetland Archaeology*, 47-84

Fojut, N. 1994, *A Guide to Prehistoric and Viking Shetland*, Lerwick

Fojut, N. 1999, 'The archaeological background', in Owen, O. & Lowe, C. (eds), *Kebister, the Four-thousand-year-old Story of One Shetland Township*, 7-13, Edinburgh

Fojut, N. 2005, 'Any closer towards a geography of Shetland brochs', in Turner, V.E., Nicholson, R.A., Dockrill, S.J. & Bond, J.M. (eds), *Tall Stories? 2 Millennia of Brochs*, 166-71, Lerwick

Fojut, N. 2006, *Prehistoric and Viking Shetland*, Lerwick

Foster, S.M. 1989, 'Transformation in social space: the Iron Age of Orkney and Caithness', *Scottish Archaeological Review* 6, 34-51

Harding, D.W. 1990, 'Changing perspectives in the Atlantic Iron Age', in Armit, I. (ed.), *Beyond the Brochs, Changing Perspectives on the Later Iron Age in Atlantic Scotland*, 5-16, Edinburgh

Hedges, J.W. 1984, 'Gordon Parry's West Burra survey', *Glasgow Archaeol J* 11, 41-59

Hingley, R. 1992, 'Society in Scotland from 700 BC to AD 200', *Proc Soc Antiq Scot* 122, 7-53

Hunter, J.R. 1996, *Fair Isle: the Archaeology of an Island Community*, Edinburgh

Jakobsen, J. 1936, *The Place-Names of Shetland*, Copenhagen

Knox, S.A. 1985, *The Making of the Shetland Landscape*, Edinburgh

MacKie, E.W. 2002, *The Roundhouses, Brochs and Wheelhouses of Atlantic Scotland c. 700BC-AD500*, Oxford

Morris, C.D. 1985, 'Viking Orkney: a survey', in Renfrew, C. (ed.), *The Prehistory of Orkney*, 210-42, Edinburgh

Owen, O. & Lowe, C. 1999, *Kebister, the Four-thousand-year-old Story of One Shetland Township*, Edinburgh

Paterson, J. 1999, 'Counting heads: an overview', in Bintliff, J. & Sbonias, K. (eds) *Reconstructing Past Population Trends in Mediterranean Europe (3000 BC - AD 1800)*, 259-61, Oxford

Piggott, S. 1966, 'A scheme for the Scottish Iron Age', in Rivet, A.L.F. (ed.), *The Iron Age in Northern Britain*, 1-15, Edinburgh

Smith, B. 1995, 'Scandinavian place-names in Shetland with a study of the district of Whiteness', in Crawford, B.E. (ed.), *Scandinavian Settlement in Northern Britain*, 26-41, London

Smith, B. 2000, *Toons and Tenants: settlement and society in Shetland, 1299-1899*, Lerwick

Smith, B. (forthcoming), 'Andro Smyth's database of Shetland farm names 1628-43'

Smith, H.D. 1984, *Shetland Life and Trade 1550-1914*, Edinburgh

Steinnes, A. 1959, 'The 'Huseby' system in Orkney', *Scott Hist Rev* 38, 36-46

Stewart, J. 1965, 'Shetland Farm Names', in Small, A. (ed.) *The Fourth Viking Congress*, 247-66, Edinburgh

Stewart, J. 1987, *Shetland Place-Names*, Lerwick

Tait, I. 2000, *Rural Life in Shetland & Guidebook to the Croft House Museum*, Lerwick

Thomson, W.P.L. 1995, 'Orkney farm-names: a re-assessment of their chronology', in Crawford, B.E. (ed.) *Scandinavian Settlement in Northern Britain*, 42-63, London

Whittle, A., Keith-Lucas, M., Milles, A., Noddle, B., Rees, S. & Romans, J.C.C. 1986, *Scord of Brouster, An Early Agricultural Settlement on Shetland, Excavations 1977-1979*, Oxford

PRIMARY SOURCES

National Archives of Scotland (NAS)

NAS RH9/15/169 Abbreviation of rental of duties and landmaills of lordship of Yetland, paid to chamberlain thereof, Miscellaneous Papers/Papers relating to Orkney and Shetland.

NAS RS111/213/48-50 Disposition of East and West Burra by William Ewing Gilmour in favour of John Percy Henderson registered 12 September 1921, General Register of Sasines applicable to the Counties of Orkney and Zetland.

Shetland Archives (SA)

SA CO.1/3/1 Valuation Roll

SA D.1/385 Rental of Burra and House Islands

SA Uncatalogued Rental of the Burra Isles – Crop of 1855

6

SPLENDID ISOLATION? CHANGING PERCEPTIONS OF DÙN ÈISTEAN, AN ISLAND ON THE NORTH COAST OF THE ISLE OF LEWIS

Rachel C. Barrowman

GEOLOGY AND GEOGRAPHY

Dùn Èistean is a fortified inter-tidal sea stack in the township of Cnoc Ard in Ness, on the north-east coast of the Isle of Lewis (NGR: NB 5355 6501) (*1*). The landward sides of the stack are enclosed by a low turf and stone wall and partially enclosed by this are the turfed-over footings of seven different groups of structures and an artificial pond dug to collect rainwater. The most prominent structure on the site is a large circular mound of rubble situated on the highest point at the seaward edge of the stack.

The basement geology at Dùn Èistean is comprised of meta-sediment and metamorphic Lewisian Gneiss, with jointing along lines of structural weakness (Burgess & Church 1997, 281 & 283). This jointing has resulted in an incised profile along this part of the north-east Lewis coastline, and the high cliffs in this area display signs of erosion, with block removal and areas of slumping, and the formation of promontories and stacks, e.g. Dùn Èistean, Dùn Eorodale and Luchruban.

HISTORICAL AND ARCHAEOLOGICAL BACKGROUND

The stack is separated from the mainland cliffs by a gap up to 15m wide and 16m deep which until three years ago could only be crossed at low tide by scrambling

Scottish Odysseys: The Archaeology of Islands

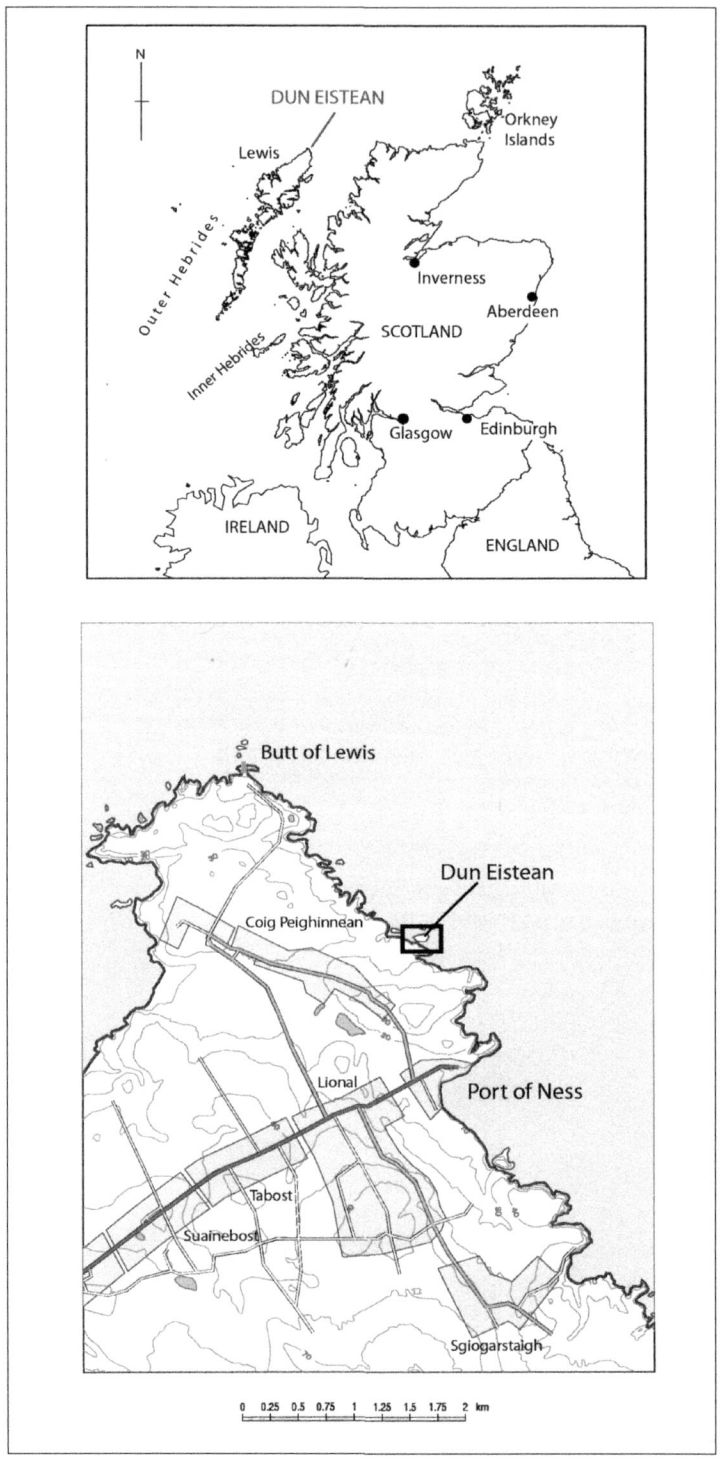

1 Location of Dùn Èistean, Ness. *GUARD*

Splendid Isolation? Changing perceptions of Dùn Èistean

across the rocks and climbing the steep rock face on the other side, or by specialist rope access techniques. It can be a romantic and deserted setting, especially on a wild and stormy day. Although not practised much today, many local Cnoc Ard men remember the excellent rock fishing from the foot of the seaward cliffs, the quality of the location no doubt enhanced by the difficult access. Dùn Èistean is also part of the common grazings for Cnoc Ard and rams were put onto the stack during the months when they weren't running with the ewes – a convenient place to keep them separated from the flock, where no fencing was necessary and the grass was lush. An unsourced oblique aerial photograph now in the Lewis and Harris Museum Collection, taken of the site when it was still being regularly grazed (*2*), shows the structures and walling around the Dùn in amazing clarity. With the decline of the intricacies of crofting life over the past 20 years however, the site has become covered in thick grassy tussocks and even in winter the footings of the structures are much harder to discern.

Dùn Èistean is not specifically referred to in any of the scant surviving primary documentation of Lewis. In local tradition it is identified as the stronghold of the

2 Aerial photograph, oblique from the east. *Lewis Museum Trust*

Clan Morrison of Ness and since 1967 has been owned by the Clan Morrison Society. Local traditions are strong in Ness, whereas documentary sources are few and far between. In his *The Early History of Ness: An Interpretation*, Dr Domhnall Uilleam Stiùbhart, director of the Dùn Èistean History Project, discusses the historical sources relating to Ness during the medieval era. He concludes that

> Any historian wishing to research the area during this period ... immediately runs up against a fundamental obstacle, namely, that conventional primary sources, the contemporary written documents that are grist to the historical mill, are to say the least rather thin on the ground. Indeed, they do not really exist at all.

Stiùbhart 2006a, 1

Instead it is the oral traditions that preserve the stories of Ness, and whilst these are far from ideal as a historical source, as Stiùbhart points out

> supposedly 'trustworthy' contemporary documents ... themselves involve manifold difficulties of interpretation ... We can either concede defeat and maintain that Ness and its people have no history to speak of before written records began, or else we can attempt to make use of what material we possess.

Stiùbhart 2006a, 2

The first surviving mention of the Dùn by name is by Martin Martin from his excursions in 1695 (Donald Munro, High Dean of the Isles, who visited Lewis in 1549, does not write of Dùn Èistean at all). Martin writes that:

> There are several natural and artificial Forts in the Coast of this Island, which are call'd Dun, from the Irish word Dain, which signifies a Fort: The natural Forts here are Dun-owle, Dun-eoradil, Dun-eisten

Martin 1703, 8

One of Martin Martin's informants was the Reverend Donald Morrison from Lewis who was a descendent of the Morrison brieves of Ness, traditionally thought to be the hereditary judges of Lewis. Despite this connection, however, he does not seem to have furnished Martin with any particular stories concerning the site and indeed Martin describes the site as being a 'natural fort' rather than an artificial one. Presumably Martin is distinguishing here between Dùn sites that utilise a natural island and those that are built structures, such as the broch, Dùn Chàrlabhaigh. However, by implication, his description may suggest that his local informants also had no knowledge of Dùn Èistean as an artificially-enhanced fort, and certainly no mention is made of ruins on the Dùn. Could it be that the Dùn's history was of little significance locally at the time?

One hundred and fifty years later, in 1852, the Ordnance Survey visited Cnoc Ard and recorded Dùn Èistean in their Name Books. Their local informant for this township was a John Morrison. They record Dùn Èistean as follows:

> This is a small round Island which is arable on the Sea Shore and Isolated only at high water. There is the ruins of some kind of building on the highest point of it which appears more at present like a heap of stones thrown together than the ruin of a castle as the name Signifies. Nothing regarding it can be collected from the neighbouring people. There are other ruins on the Island beside that considered as the castle.
>
> OS Name Book 3A, 18

There appears to be a significant disinterest or lack of knowledge regarding the historical significance of the site by both local inhabitants and visitors during this period. However, this was all to change 20 years later when Captain F.W.L. Thomas was the first person to recognise and record Dùn Èistean archaeologically, reporting observations made by the Lewis minister and antiquarian Malcolm MacPhail in his 1878 article, 'Traditions of the Morrisons' (Thomas 1878, 516).

> Towards the north-east corner of the island is a dun or castle, sometimes called Tigh nam Arm; or the House of the Arms, now but 4½ feet high. The outside of the dun is an oblong square, 23 by 18 feet; and this basement is nearly solid, for the central area, which is of an oval shape, is only 6½ by 4½ feet, and there is no appearance of a doorway. The entrance or doorway was no doubt at the height of the first floor, similar to a dun in Taransay. The walls are of dry-stone masonry, but that is no proof of age in this part of the country. When exploring the ruins, the Rev M Macphail, who made the above measurements, found a small piece of flint, fragments of charcoal, and a strip of leather such as was used for making brogues.
>
> Thomas 1878, 516

Thomas was also the first to record a Morrison connection to the site, noting that 'Dun Eystein is a natural stronghold ... to which the Morrisons were wont to retire when hard pressed or in times of war' and that there were once 'squints or loopholes' in the wall that encloses the site on the landward side. He also writes that 'There are the remains of huts upon the island; and on the south sides is a flat ledge, called Palla na Biorlinn, or the Ledge of the Galley or Birlin, wheron tradition tells that the Morrisons used to haul up their boat' (*ibid*).

Later, in an article '*On the Duns of the Outer Hebrides*' published after Thomas' death in 1890, the same information was reiterated, but with no mention of the 'basement', and MacPhail's small find of flint was identified as 'probably a strike-a-light' (Thomas 1890, 365-369). In this article, Thomas describes the tigh as having the appearance of 'an incipient peel', probably from the twelfth century, by comparison with Cubbie Roo's castle in Orkney (Thomas 1890, 366).

It is unknown where Thomas got his information concerning the Morrison connection, but it presumably originated in oral tradition, either contemporary with Thomas' life or recorded in earlier documents. As mentioned above, traditionally the Morrisons functioned as the *britheamhan* (brieves or judges) of Ness in the Late Medieval period. Recent assertions by Michael Robson suggest that Thomas may have taken Dùn Èistean as being the unnamed fort connected with the brieves and described in a 1630s account of 'The ewill trowbles of the Lewes, and how the Mackleoid of the Lewes was with his whol tribe destroyed and put from the Possesion of the Lewes' which recounts the replacement of the MacLeods by the MacKenzies (NLS Advocates Manuscript 22.7.11 ff.9-10, cited by Robson in 2004, 41). In one passage in the *ewill trowbles* it is stated that '... the breiwe and his kinn ... strengthened themselfe within a fort in the Iland called Ness' (*ibid*). This account relates to a turbulent time in Lewis' history (see for instance MacCoinnich 2002) and was written only 20 years or so after the MacKenzies succeeded.

A more extensive archaeological description of the Dùn was made by the Royal Commission in 1928, who described the foundations of various 'small huts' and enclosures, an 'artificial pond' to the south of the tigh 'banked on the E and excavated on the W, still showing moisture' (RCAHMS 1928, 7, no.15). Forty years later, the site was again visited by the Ordnance Survey and described as a settlement, 'probably medieval, comprising a complex of small rectangular stone built huts with rounded corners, now heavily turfed'. The artificial pond on this occasion was described as being dry, the tigh is described as oval, but with 'no trace of built walling' and overall the OS found this structure 'impossible to classify' (NMRS; visited by OS (RL) 16 June 1969). These surveys led to the site being scheduled as a monument of national importance in 1992, at the same time as many others in the Western Isles, and in 1997 it was recognised as being under threat from coastal erosion during the Lewis Coastal Erosion Survey (Burgess & Church 1997, 281-2).

None of these archaeological descriptions record any local traditions, however, and Thomas' article of 100 years earlier remains the first account to name Dùn Èistean in connection with the Morrisons. The earlier perception of the site as being empty, 'natural' and 'ruinous', from the descriptions by Martin Martin and the OS surveyors, changes with Thomas' account. His description of Dùn Èistean furnishes the stack with great significance and importance – the picture of the Morrisons hauling their boats up Palla nan Biorlinn and defending their home is vivid and immediately populates the site (*3*). His words create a strong imagery of the activities that may have occurred on the island in the past, an imagery that

3 Postcard of Dùn Èistean. *Reproduced with kind permission of Mr Tony Morrison*

has been embraced by many Morrisons since, the world over, especially those overseas whose ancestors originate from Lewis. When the Clan Morrison society was founded in 1909, an image of a castle on Dùn Èistean was used as the Clan crest, with a defiant fist extended from the castellated wall heads, and the war cry of the Clan is said to be 'Dùn Èistean!'.

The launching of the Clan's website in 1999 has meant that the tiny island of Dùn Èistean has met an international audience of Morrisons. This far north-west corner of the British Isles, considered remote and marginal by many British mainlanders, has become at the same time internationally renowned and a familiar friend to many individuals living thousands of miles away, most of whom have never stepped on the turf of Dùn Èistean.

The Morrisons' enthusiasm for the island and its history, and frustration at the lack of physical proof to support the vivid traditions associated with it, led to the creation of a project committee in 1999, with representatives from the Comunn Eachdraidh Nis (the Ness Historical Society), the Clan Morrison Society and the Western Isles regional archaeologist, Dr Mary Macleod. The committee initiated the investigation of the site with a view to its interpretation and presentation to the public, and its protection, if possible, from further deterioration. The Clan Morrison Society was convinced that their castle, as depicted on their crest, was waiting to be uncovered.

CURRENT ARCHAEOLOGICAL INVESTIGATIONS

Glasgow University Archaeological Research Division (GUARD) was commissioned by the Dùn Èistean committee to start archaeological investigation of the site in 2000, and topographical survey was carried out in April and May of that year (Barrowman & Driscoll 2000). The results of the survey work revealed more extensive structural remains than had previously been described. The topographic survey and structure-by-structure account of the site produced by Barrowman and Driscoll in 2000 demonstrated that 'Dùn Èistean is exceptional for both its complex form and its fine state of preservation, but its structures are unusual and not easily paralleled in the archaeological record'. Despite the unusual nature of the site, it was presumed that it had probably been utilised in the Iron Age with later reuse in the medieval and later periods. This same assumption had been the predominant hypothesis made for the many other Iron Age promontory and island Dùn sites in Lewis (see for instance Armit 1996, 217-8).

It was also thought possible that the site may be Early Medieval, comparable in form to others identified in Celtic Britain and Ireland. These sites are typically situated on a promontory or coastal stack site and consist of a group or groups of buildings, often enclosed by a wall or bank (e.g. Barrowman *et al* forthcoming; Morris 1996); coastal settlements surveyed by Dr Raymond Lamb in the Northern Isles and Sutherland and published in the *Scottish Archaeological Forum* (Lamb 1973) are particularly relevant. There are few examples of comparable sites that have been surveyed in Lewis, although two may be found at the coastal chapel-sites of Rubha Chirc and, possibly, Cunndal (Barrowman 2005a, 66-69 & 75).

Seven groups of features were recorded on Dùn Èistean (*4*): Structures A to G, protected on the north, west and south sides of the island by the perimeter wall, Structure H. Structure A consists of two rectangular conjoining buildings set into a triangular-shaped enclosure joined on to the perimeter wall. Structures B and D, two groups of interconnecting cellular structures, are also each set against the perimeter wall. Structure C, an upstanding sub-rectangular building, stands between Structures D and A. A man-made lochan, Structure E, sits at the lowest point of the stack, on the east side. Structure F, two hollows, possibly buildings, are situated at the top of Palla na Biorlinn and Structure G, the Dùn, on the highest point of the stack is situated beneath the mound of rubble (Barrowman & Driscoll 2000).

The topographic survey was followed in 2001 by geophysical surveys and evaluation excavations (Barrowman 2002). The geophysical survey revealed a strong series of linear positive and negative anomalies around Structure G in particular, suggesting a possible rock-cut ditch on the west side of the structure. Strong positive magnetic anomalies to the north of Structure A also suggested that burning might have been present. High resistance features were also interpreted as the possible remains of further buildings below the turf (MacGuire in Barrowman 2002).

During the trial trench evaluation in 2001, four small trenches were opened. Trench 1 through the south side of the circular mound, Structure G, confirmed, to everyone's surprise, Thomas' identification of an 'incipient peel'. Beneath the layers of collapsed rubble the wall of a significant clay-bonded stone building was uncovered. Finds from the topsoil and collapse from this structure included a perforated schist roof tile and sherds of local coarse pottery, of a type found

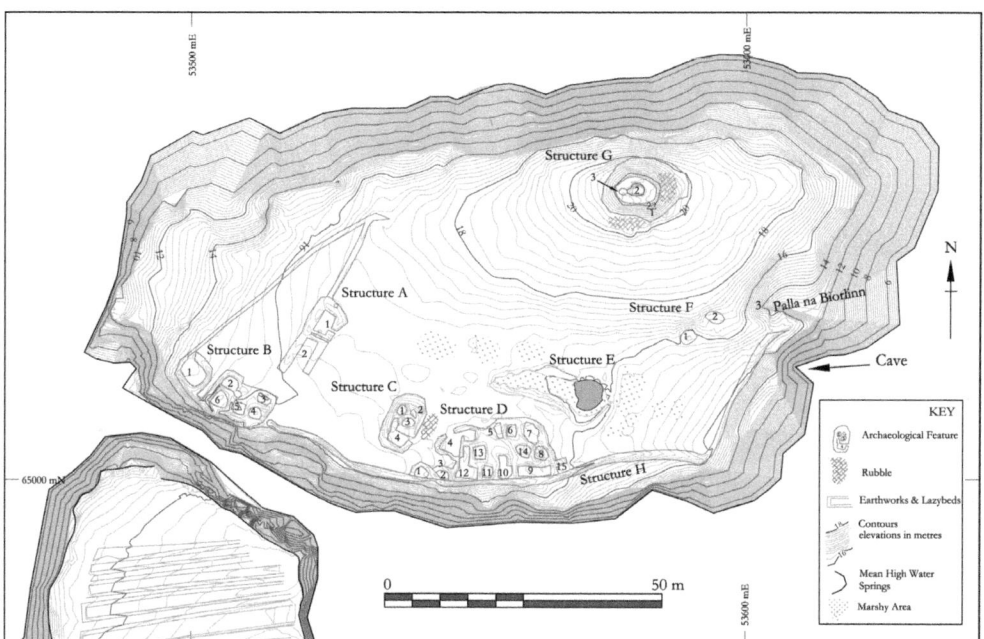

4 GUARD topographic survey 2000

throughout the Western Isles (see Campbell 2002; 2005; Cheape 1993). Trench 2 was excavated over one of the geophysical anomalies of high resistance but uncovered only bedrock. Trench 3 was excavated through part of one of the buildings in the Structure D cellular complex, where it joined the perimeter wall (Structure H) around the site. It revealed that the structure was built of turf whilst the perimeter wall was built of turf with a stone facing. The finds from this small trench were particularly rich, comprising of over a hundred sherds of local handmade pottery (or craggan), burnt bone, flint and quartz flakes, and small pieces of iron. A rim sherd of Scottish post-medieval Reduced Ware and a neck sherd from a German stoneware vessel, decorated with applied circular decoration, give a date for the occupation of the building between the fifteenth and seventeenth centuries. Trench 4 through the east wall of Structure A uncovered only the layers of collapse from the building and several sherds of craggan.

All the trenches, apart from Trench 2, confirmed the depth, survival and complexity of the archaeological deposits (Barrowman 2002). No evidence of an earlier Iron Age dun was uncovered under the rubble in Trench 1, and what was thought to have been an earlier, possibly circular, structure below later adaptations, was in fact the collapsed remains of an earlier rectangular building. The artefactual assemblage recovered from the trial excavations also pointed to a Late Medieval date for the buildings. Thomas' identification of the stone mound as 'Tigh nan Arm', an 'incipient keep', and the Morrison depiction of a castle on their crest, seemed much more likely than before. The perception of the site for those working on it changed considerably with this interpretative shift and occurred at the same time as a more subtle change in perception experienced whilst working on and accessing the site.

Access to the site was difficult during the topographic survey in 2000 – it was only possible to approach the island for a couple of hours at a low tide, and then there was a scramble across steep and slippery rocks using climbing gear and ropes. In May 2000 the team had climbed the cliff onto the site at a suitable low tide and then camped overnight on the island in order to complete the survey. Working on the site during this time gave them a unique opportunity to experience the site in complete isolation, as people had experienced it in history, truly cut off from the mainland of Lewis if only for a short time. The geophysical survey and trial trench evaluation, which took place the following year, required a longer season of three weeks' work and also more equipment. Camping on the island was no longer a practical solution and moving equipment backwards and forwards would have been very time consuming under the previous year's set up. Ropes and climbing harnesses had already been used as a back-up when accessing the site in previous years, but in 2001 this was taken one step further with the designing of a 'Tyrolean traverse', which was set up to allow unrestricted movement to and from the site regardless of tides. Personnel were able to clip a rope harness onto the traverse and pull themselves and equipment or soil samples backwards and forwards across the gap. As a result, normal working hours were now possible and staying overnight on the island was no longer necessary. Also, although physically the site still had the feeling of being exclusive and isolated, the work itself became less exclusively the preserve of the archaeologist when the interim reports for 2000 and 2001 were made available to a wider audience through the GUARD and Comunn Eachdraidh Nis websites, and could be read worldwide by anyone with access to a computer.

The experience of accessing and working on Dùn Èistean changed more dramatically for the archaeology team in 2002 due to the growing interest in the site from the international Morrison community. Following a publicity drive over the internet, fund-raising by the Clan Morrison Society in the USA, UK and further afield succeeded in raising enough money to commission the building of a steel footbridge across the ravine to the island from the mainland side. This was to be completed in time for the Clan Morrison Gathering on the Isle of Lewis planned for July 2002 so that members of the Clan Morrison community could step foot on their ancestral home. In June 2002, the rope traverse was used for the last time when the excavation of two trenches in advance of the construction of the footings of the bridge was undertaken, jointly funded with Historic Scotland. The evaluation in 2002 of the areas on the island and mainland sides to be affected by the footings revealed interesting results. Trench 1 was placed over the portion of the perimeter wall that was to be affected by the bridge, and also an area to the north of that, from which several worked pieces of flint and a piece of lead pistol shot were recovered. Trench 2 covered the mainland side and an area of *feannagan* (lazybeds). Sherds of craggan and a gun flint were recovered from this trench, but no remains of structures (Barrowman 2004).

Just in time for the clan gathering, the Clan Morrison Society succeeded in getting the bridge finished and in place. For years visitors to the site, many of whom had travelled miles to see it, had been unable to access the stack and could only gaze upon it from a distance or gain virtual access via the web. Now it was possible for them to walk on the site and at the opening of the bridge over 100 Morrisons and local visitors from Ness did just that. For the archaeologists who had undertaken the work so far, however, the romance and unique feeling of isolation on Dùn Èistean had now disappeared – access had become easier over two years to the point where it was not a problem at all (see Barrowman in prep). The site was no longer the exclusive preserve of the academic or specialist – it had been handed back to its rightful owners.

Yet who really owns Dùn Èistean? The Morrisons have a legal right to the land itself, and feel they have a right to its history, but is it not also a part of the history of Ness, the Western Isles, Scotland? The initial three years' work on the island for the Clan Morrison Society had culminated with the construction of the bridge. Although this access improvement came about largely due to the perseverance of the Morrisons, it means that almost anyone can now access the island and make it their own for an hour or two. Indeed, it has become a place to which people are drawn even if they have no interest in the Morrisons or archaeology – a new section of the Ness coast has been opened to all with Dùn Èistean included as a point of interest on a coastal path. The demonstrated archaeological potential of the site (e.g. Barrowman & Driscoll 2000, 7) and renewed local support led Dr Mary Macleod to make a successful bid to place Dùn Èistean at the centre of a Heritage Lottery Fund and Historic Scotland funded project across Ness.

In March 2005, GUARD were commissioned by a steering committee to undertake and manage the Dùn Èistean Archaeology Project (Atkinson *et al* 2004). DEAP is a multi-disciplinary field project running for three years and draws on the previous work by GUARD at the site. It also incorporates the results of a series of separately funded projects, which include documentary research, place-name analysis (Cox, forthcoming) and the collection of oral traditions (Stiùbhart 2006a; Stiùbhart 2006b). It is funded by a partnership between the Heritage Lottery Fund (HLF), Historic Scotland, the Clan Morrison Society, Comunn Eachdraidh Nis and the Comhairle nan Eilean Siar (Western Isles Council). The project includes an ambitious archaeological survey of the north of Ness (the Ness Archaeological Landscape Survey, NALS (see Barrowman 2006)) as well as the excavations and post-excavation work at Dùn Èistean.

The DEAP fieldwork started in 2005 and includes three seasons of survey and excavation followed by two seasons of post-excavation and analysis. The first season of excavation on Dùn Èistean was completed at the end of August 2005 and incorporated local and student volunteers. Post-excavation processing and other back-up, such as leaflet production and web-site maintenance, were all undertaken locally in Ness at the Comunn Eachdraidh. Comunn na Gaidhlig also funds a Gaelic student placement for the project each year, who works with the archaeology team, giving Gaelic tours of the site, writing Gaelic text for leaflets and the website, and working with other groups visiting the site, such as the Ness Sgoil Shamhraidh, through the medium of Gaelic.

The first season of the DEAP excavations by GUARD opened larger trenches over Structures A and G, with successful results (Barrowman 2005b). The ruined turf walls and stone footings of the large Structure A appeared, from the 2000 topographic survey, to be divided into two buildings, aligned south-west to north-east and possibly representing a dwelling and an outbuilding built side-by-side with a gap between them (Barrowman & Driscoll 2000, 14). Results from the 2005 excavation trench in Structure A (Trench A) bore out many of the conclusions from the topographic survey, although they also demonstrated that both buildings were domestic in nature, each with a central peat hearth. Below an abandonment layer of peat ash and broken pottery, each building had a compact clay floor utilising the surface of the natural clay above the bedrock. Both dwellings were aligned with the prevailing wind and built from drystone clad wall footings, packed with a dense clay and peat mix, with turf on top – features reminiscent of the more recent (nineteenth-century) black houses, the ruins of which can still be seen in Ness. The building at the north end (5) was more solid in its construction than that to the south and the hearth deposits suggested that it had been used more frequently.

Environmental samples were taken from all contexts, and flotation was undertaken at the Comunn Eachdraidh whilst the excavation was ongoing. Analysis of the samples overall produced only occasional carbonised plant macrofossils, with the majority of samples containing none. However, nine of the samples, all originating from Structure A hearth contexts or dumps/sweepings from hearth places, were rich in cereal grains, the larger hearth in the north room being particularly rich. These samples all suggest waste from cooking or other domestic activities such as cereal drying, and the cereal grain has been identified as oats and barley, although occasional six row hulled barley was also noted (work ongoing).

Finds were limited to sherds of locally handmade pottery, flakes of flint, corroded pieces of iron, a pistol shot and a small sherd of glass, and all suggest a sixteenth- to eighteenth-century date. At the end of the excavation, part of the abutting earth and stone walls of each structure was dismantled and traces of a third, earlier, structure were uncovered directly below. These included the hearth and some adjacent paving with a possible post-slot, the remainder of the building was presumably destroyed during the construction of the two more recent structures. Following the cessation of primary use and the abandonment of the structures, the walls slumped and a temporary shelter was built into the rubble at the north end of Room 1.

In the second structure investigated (Structure G) the topographic survey in 2000 and small evaluation trench dug in 2001 had revealed that below the circular

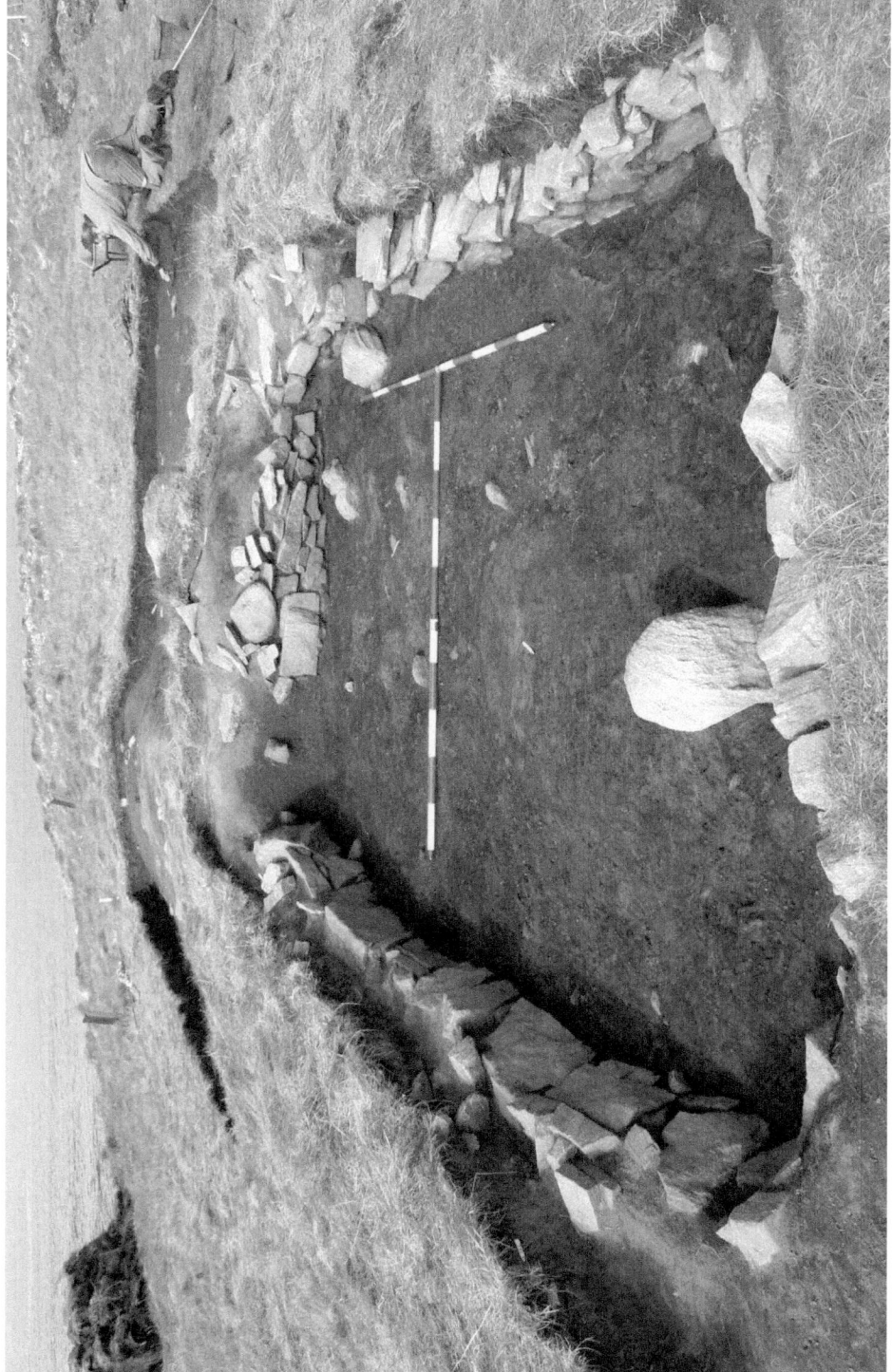

5 Structure A from the south-east, 2005, showing central hearth, stone and clay walls, and turf and clay perimeter wall Structure H to the north

rubble mound lay the remains of a square tower (Barrowman 2002, 26). In 2005 a large trench (Trench G) was opened across the mound, measuring 30m by 9m maximum to investigate not only the tower, but also the area around it where geophysical survey had suggested there are the remains of a circular structure, possibly a rock-cut ditch. Only the removal of turf, topsoil and the upper layers of rubble and modern disturbance was possible over this large trench within the first short season in 2005.

An early twentieth-century marker cairn that had been constructed on top of the mound first had to be removed for health and safety reasons, and the stone from this was quantified and stacked separately to allow for possible reconstruction in the future. The removal of the turf and the latest layer of collapsed soil and rubble from the trench revealed that the circular raised area upon which the tower was built is a natural rock platform, and not an earlier structure as first thought. By the end of the first season of excavation, part of the collapse around the tower had been completely removed to reveal a wall of well-built stonework, bonded with clay, and apparently utilising a core of specially-mixed clay and peat. At first the interior face of the wall remained elusive, having been damaged during the nineteenth-century investigations by MacPhail described above (Thomas 1878, 516) and later by re-working of the resulting hollow in the top of the mound into a temporary shelter. By the end of the excavation, the first indications of an interior face were uncovered giving a possible overall thickness of up to 2m for the base of the tower wall. The wall incorporates around 1m of core material, and was clearly built to carry a considerable load, and therefore height, of masonry. This structure will be investigated over the next two years, with the interior of the tower being the focus of the project next year. First indications are that it was built in one phase, and finds of a musket ball, flakes of flint and sherds of craggan within the rubble indicate that, like Structure A, the final use of the tower may date to between the sixteenth and eighteenth centuries AD.

CONCLUSIONS

The results of the first year of large-scale excavation have so far provided no evidence for an earlier use for the site and many of the signifiers which had previously been taken to suggest use in the Iron Age have not been found. No evidence has been uncovered as yet of an earlier structure below the tower, or for modification of a pre-existing building, and the finds assemblages from both structures also contain no residual earlier material, being all in keeping with a sixteenth- to eighteenth-century date. It seems more likely now that the structures on Dùn Èistean belong to one unified, contemporary site, not unlike the castle favoured by the ever-optimistic Clan Morrison Society. This high status site has been overlooked in the past, when Ness, and indeed Lewis, has been seen as a romantic and isolated region on the margins of Britain. It is an often stressed, but still very important point however, that before the eighteenth century the Western Isles were not out-of-the-way, they were just remote from some of the individuals who chose to write about them. For centuries the Minch has been a busy thoroughfare for shipping and Ness and the inhabitants of Lewis were right in the thick of things. They were far from being remote, isolated or marginal. For example, historian Aonghas MacCoinnich draws attention to the English traffic in the Minch en route to the Newfoundland and Arctic fishing grounds in the mid-1500s, and to the large Dutch fishing fleets and also Dutch traffic to and from the East and West Indies in the sixteenth and seventeenth centuries (MacCoinnich, forthcoming). It was not just goods that were being traded between these countries, but also news and information, which must surely have been one of the most powerful tools in any Clan's armoury.

Now we hope that we are reinvigorating and almost imitating this movement of information and ideas. Although in more recent times the site was forgotten, even by the people in Ness, the access improvements since 2000 have changed this. With a small number of local volunteers taking part in the project in its first year and visiting the site, many more have shown an interest in helping in 2006 and we hope that the site is slowly being adopted by Ness. Perceptions of the site have changed as access has improved, and they have changed mainly for the better. We hope that the perception of Dùn Èistean as the exclusive preserve of the Clan Morrison or the academic is slowly being altered through the work of the Dùn Èistean Archaeology Project.

ACKNOWLEDGEMENTS

I am indebted to the team who first worked on the site before I became involved in DEAP in 2003 – namely Dr Chris Barrowman (director of the survey and excavations from 2000 to 2002) and the teams: John Arthur, Gary Thomsett and John Duncan (2000 survey), Ian McHardy (rope access 2001 & 2002), Andrew Baines and Donna McGuire (2001 survey and excavation), and Alastair Becket, Ian McHardy and Scott Coulter (2002 excavation). Also to the 2005 excavation team, especially Chris Dalglish and Ian McHardy, and to Diane Aldritt who identified the palaeobotanical material. Thanks also to Professor Steve Driscoll and Robert Will (GUARD), Dr Mary Macleod (Western Isles Archaeologist, Comhairle nan Eilean Siar) and Comunn Eachdraidh Nis for their support.

REFERENCES

Armit, I. 1996, *The Archaeology of Skye and the Western Isles*, Edinburgh

Atkinson, J., Barrowman, C. & Barrowman, R. 2004, *Dùn Èistean Archaeology Project (DEAP)*, GUARD Project 2000, GUARD, Glasgow University

Barrowman, C. 2002, *Dun Eistean, Lewis: Geophysical Survey and Trial Excavation – Description of the Archaeological Structures*, with contributions from D. MacGuire, GUARD Projects 716.2 & 716.3, GUARD, Glasgow University

Barrowman, C. 2004, *Dun Eistean, Lewis*, GUARD Project 716.4, GUARD, Glasgow University

Barrowman, C.S. 2006, *Ness Archaeological Landscape Survey 2005*: Data Structure Report, GUARD Project 2000, GUARD, Glasgow University

Barrowman, C. (in prep) 'Breaching the defences of a clan stronghold – past work on a sea stack in Lewis', publication of the *Theoretical Archaeology Group conference session: Archaeology of the Inaccessible*, Dec. 2005

Barrowman, C. & Driscoll, S.T. 2000, *Dun Eistean, Lewis: Archaeological and Topographical Survey*, GUARD Project 716.1, GUARD, Glasgow University

Barrowman, R.C. 2005a, *Lewis Coastal Chapel-Sites Survey 2004/5*, Department of Archaeology, University of Glasgow

Barrowman, R.C. 2005b, *Dùn Èistean Archaeology Project Excavations 2005*: Data Structure Report, GUARD Project 2000, GUARD, Glasgow University

Barrowman, R.C., Batey, C.E. & Morris, C.D. (2007), *Excavations at Tintagel Castle, Cornwall, 1990-1999*, London (Society of Antiquaries of London)

Burgess, C. & Church, M. 1997, *Coastal Erosion Assessment, Lewis: A Report for Historic Scotland*, 2 vols, Edinburgh

Campbell, E. 2002, 'The Western Isles pottery sequence', in Ballin-Smith, B. & Banks, I. (eds), *In the Shadow of the Brochs: The Iron Age in Scotland*, 139-144, Stroud

Campbell, E. 2005, 'Pottery', in Branigan, K., *From Clan to Clearance: History and Archaeology on the Isle of Barra c. 850-1850 AD*, 53-4, Oxford

Cheape, H. 1993, 'Crogans and Barvas Ware: handmade pottery in the Hebrides', *Scottish Studies* 31(1992-3), 109-127

Cox, R.A.V. (forthcoming) *The Norse Element in the Place-names of Ness*, Project Dùn Èistean

Lamb, R.G. 1973, 'Coastal settlements of the North', *Scottish Archaeological Forum* 5, 76-98

Martin M. 1703, *A Description of the Western Isles of Scotland*, London

MacCoinnich, A. 2002 '"His spirit was given only to warre": conflict and identity in the Scottish gàidhhealtachd c. 1580 – c. 1630', in Murdoch, S. & MacKillop, A. (eds), *Fighting for Identity: Scottish Military Experience, c. 1550-1900*, 133-162, Leiden

MacCoinnich A. (forthcoming), 'Native, stranger and the fishing of the Isles, 1611-1637', in Macinnes, A.I. & Grosjean, A. (eds), *Pirates, Capitalists and Imperialists in the North Sea and Baltic States*

Morris, C.D. 1996, 'From Birsay to Tintagel: a personal view', in Crawford B.E. (ed.), *Scotland in Dark Age Britain*, 37-78, Aberdeen (St John's House Publications no. 6)

OS Name Books 3A, for Sheet 3 Barvas Parish, Index no 145, Ross County 1-8

RCAHMS 1928, *Ninth report with inventory of monuments and constructions in the Outer Hebrides, Skye and the Small Isles*, 7, no. 15, Edinburgh

Robson, M. 2004, *Forts and Fallen Walls: The duns of Northern Lewis*, 10 Callicvol, Port of Ness

Stiùbhart, D.U. 2006a, 'The early history of Ness: an interpretation', *Island Notes* 23 (English) and 24 (Gaelic)

Stiùbhart, D.U. 2006b, 'Some heathenish and superstitious rites: a letter from Lewis, 1700', *Scottish Studies* 34

Thomas, F.W.L. 1878, 'Traditions of the Morrisons (Clan MacGhillemhuire), hereditary judges of Lewis', *Proc Soc Antiq Scot* 12, 503-556

Thomas, F.W.L. 1890, 'On the duns of the Outer Hebrides', *Archaeologia Scotica* v, 365-415

7

ALL QUIET ON THE WESTERN FRONT? LANDSCAPE SURVEY ON FOULA, SHETLAND

Helen Bradley

INTRODUCTION

Foula (HT 954 387), westernmost island of the Shetland archipelago, is separated from Walls on Shetland Mainland by 14 miles of turbulent Atlantic Ocean (*1*). The island's lonely profile is a remarkable sight; its five peaks are some of the most dramatic on Shetland, with The Kame, at 1228ft, standing as one of the highest sea cliffs in the British Isles (*2*). Foula, which takes its name from the Old Norse (O.N.) *Fugløy*, meaning 'bird island,' can be seen on a clear day from Fair Isle and Westray, and sometimes even Rousay on Orkney. It measures 3 miles from north to south by 2.5 miles east to west, and has an underlying geology of Old Red Sandstone, shifting towards a band of mica-schist along the eastern coast (Mykura 1976). The relatively fertile land which frames the island's east coast is home to a population of around 30 people, who are mostly divided between the three main settlements of Hametoun (in the south), Ham (surrounding the island's only natural harbour at Ham Voe) and Harrier in the north. This low-lying improved ground slopes sharply upwards and westwards into the roughly grazed heather moorland of the western half of the island.

Foula's population has fluctuated from as little as three people in the aftermath of the *muckle fever* (smallpox) outbreaks of the eighteenth century, to as many as nearly 300 at the end of the nineteenth century (Page 1976). The population decreased somewhat rapidly in step with the creation of offshore Haaf fishing grounds after

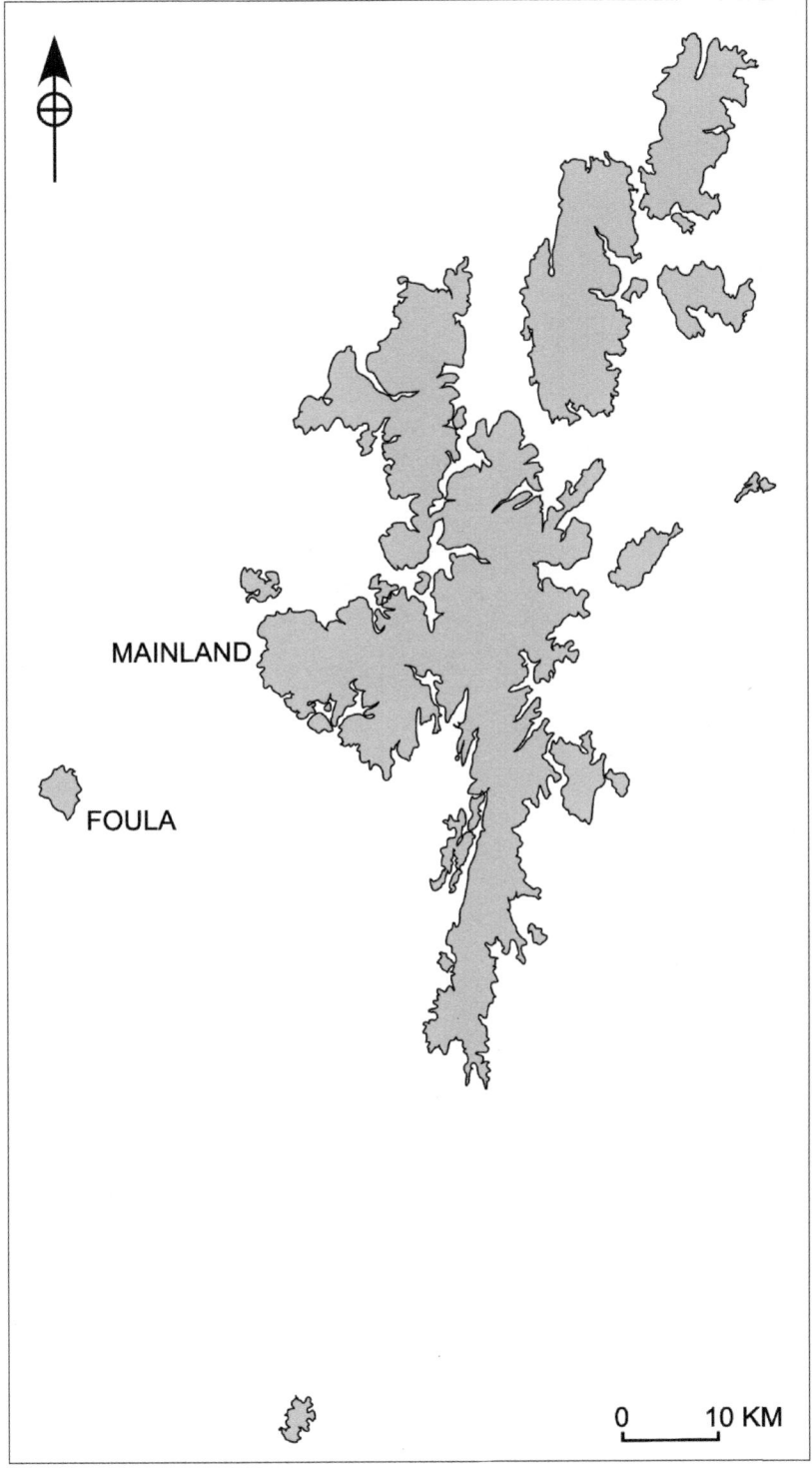

1 Location map

2 Hamnafield, the Sneug and the Kame (M. Ward)

this, which caused the depletion of fish in the waters surrounding the island. The ebb and flow of people is visible everywhere along the eastern coastal strip, where ruined farmsteads attest to the point at which population reached its high water mark and rolled back. Today, islanders possess a vast store of oral traditions referring back as far as the turn of the nineteenth century, and these stories serve to animate many of the island's visible remains, creating a superb dialogue between physical remains and living or inherited memory.

HISTORIOGRAPHY

> Foula; menacing in is solidarity, fascinating in its remoteness, like a gigantic ship anchored for countless ages. A little world outside the world, so near and yet so far.
>
> Svensson 1955, 45

A remote location, an enigmatic geography and a perceived sense of wilderness have all acted as a draw to a small number of writers over the last few hundred years. However, accounts from the nineteenth and twentieth century contain few references to antiquities or prehistoric remains, concentrating instead upon the various characteristics of Foula's landscape and the practices of its native inhabitants. On the methods employed to obtain wildfowl and their eggs, Lowe (1879, 317) writes

> I observed ... a stake stuck about six inches into the bank, and this is in many places so rotten as to fly all to pieces with a slight blow ...; they often strike the blade of a small dagger into the ground, and throwing a noose of a fishing chord over any of these, slip down without the least apprehension of danger.

The first records of antiquarian investigation are those of John Sands, who visited Foula on a number of occasions and took great interest in some of its more conspicuous remains, publishing his work in the form of letters and newspaper articles. He excavated three 'cairns of burned stones' (Sands 1885, 163) though he does not provide their location or an account of his findings. He also excavated two cist burials on the top of the Sneug, providing a somewhat unusual accompanying description:

> On one large slab I saw the impression of a human body, with the contents of the intestines about half an inch in depth. In the centre, what had been flesh had turned into vegetable fibres and there was a pool of dark grey liquid on the ground.
>
> Sands 1885, 163

Foula is mentioned briefly by the Royal Commission on the Ancient and Historical Monuments of Scotland in its inventory of 1946. Two possible burial cairns, four burnt mounds, a probable Norse dwelling and what is referred to as a 'chapel site and burial ground' were listed, although the report goes on to say that 'there are now no clear indications of the ground plan of the chapel, nor any traces of a burial ground' (RCAHMS 1946: 154). These sites were investigated again in 1968 when the Brathay Exploration Group produced a brief account of the archaeology of Foula (Simpson 1968).

Foula's Norse connections have been examined in depth by John Baldwin (1978, 1981, 1984, 1996), whose etymological studies have provided invaluable reconstructions of settlement expansion on the island. In terms of archaeology, any knowledge of sites other than those noted by the Royal Commission has accumulated as a result of the work of Foula Heritage and Shetland Amenity Trust. Sheila Gear and a number of other islanders established the Foula Heritage Group in 2001 as an offshoot of the Shetland Past Project, and have recorded over 200 sites throughout the island. The results presented below are the product of ongoing survey in partnership with Sheila, during the course of which we have recorded around 750 further sites. This research began as a dissertation for a Masters in Landscape Archaeology at the University of Sheffield, and has since developed into the Foula Landscape Project.

RESULTS

The many elements of Foula's landscape development are most evident in the settled areas of The Hametoun and Harrier, where both tunships have witnessed extensive settlement from early prehistory to the present day. These areas are by no means the only 'busy' landscapes on Foula; the island is replete with archaeology throughout its settled lands, ranging from burial cairns and burnt mounds to boat noosts and horizontal mills, sheep cruies and skeos (O.N *skjaa*; 'drying house'). For an account of this length, however, The Hametoun, Harrier and their surroundings are an appropriate focus, as they contain the most significant of those sites picked up by the survey.

THE HAMETOUN

The Hametoun lies in a relatively sheltered valley at the south end of the island. It is bounded to the west by the sharp slopes of the Noup and the broad sweep of the Daal Valley. To the north and east, the land rolls away gently towards Ham and downwards to the jagged eastern coastline. The tunship itself has witnessed heavy drainage and improvement for rig cultivation within the areas enclosed by the head dyke. In dramatic contrast, the nearby South Ness peninsula, lying beyond the head dyke to the south-east, is largely featureless in terms of recent historic remains. It was used mostly for rough grazing in recent centuries, and also as an ideal spot for scalping (the process of removing soil (*muild*) for improving arable soils within the tun). This has simultaneously revealed and undermined a number of earlier sites, which connect to form a relict prehistoric landscape composed of land divisions, dwellings and funerary remains.

PREHISTORY ON THE SOUTH NESS

A system of denuded but substantial earth and turf dykes cut across the southern headland (*3*), displaying sections where orthostats are exposed at the base of the bank suggesting a late Neolithic/early Bronze Age date. A quartz knapping floor placed hard-up against one side of one of these dykes has produced a number of late Neolithic thumbnail scrapers to further support this date (Simpson 1968). The ways in which these dykes cut off the headland bears similarities to examples on Fair Isle of a similar date (Hunter 1996). These are thought to have been deliberately placed along the coast in order to use the sea as a barrier for providing pounds for the stockading of cattle (*ibid*), an interpretation which fits well for some of the Foula examples. A few hundred yards further north, a linear spread of sunken oval features containing areas of stonework were observed, apparently demarcated by the

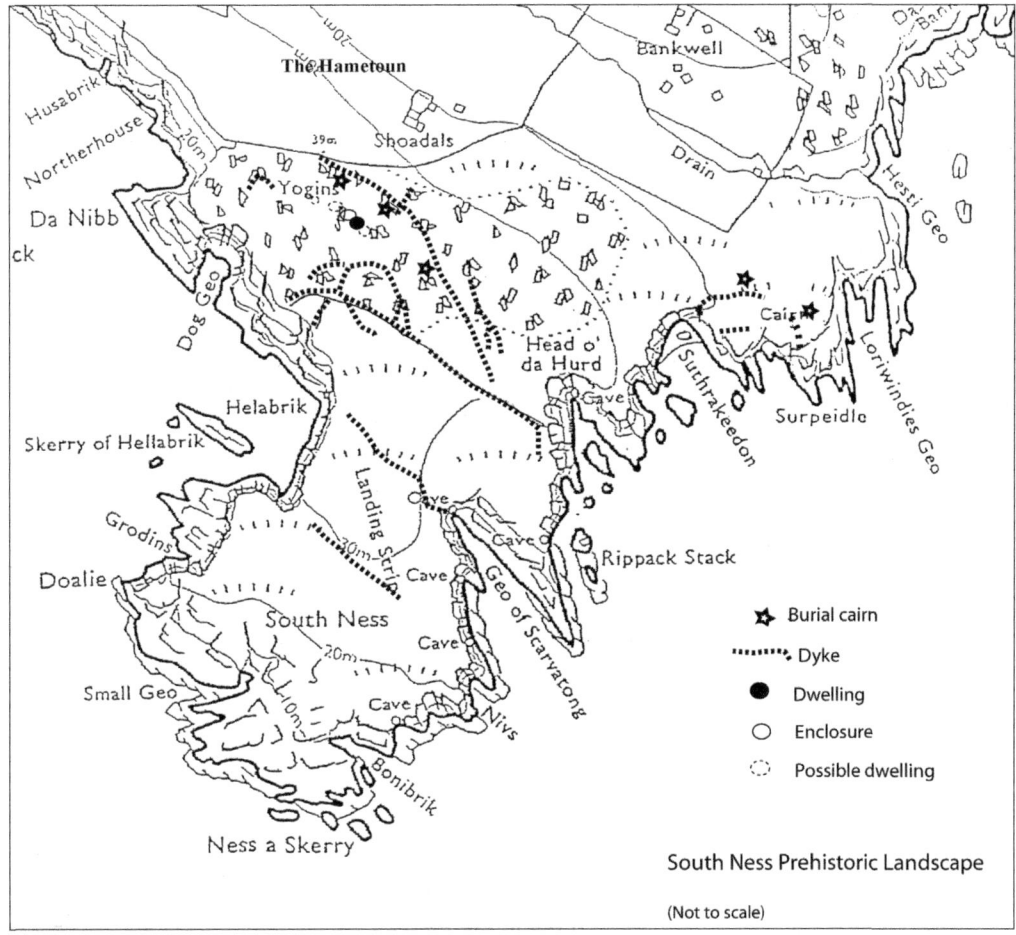

3 Sites mentioned in the text

stockade-type dykes to the south and by a large east-west aligned dyke to the north. Given the poor state of preservation for the neighbouring features, only one of these examples was identifiable as a ruined sub-oval dwelling. In places the walls are still intact and stand up to 1m high with upright orthostats used as facing slabs which line a recessed interior. The walls are of an inconsistent width throughout and lack any outer face, drawing parallels with similar Late Bronze Age examples at Mavis Grind (Cracknell & Smith 1985). No internal radial divisions are present on the South Ness dwelling, however, and the internal recesses may indicate an earlier date.

A hundred yards further north again, three burial cairns are placed evenly along a break of slope overlooking the Hametoun Valley. The most westerly of these, a low circular mound 8m in diameter, was highly denuded and lacked any internal structural features. These were possibly robbed for the construction of the nearby head dyke, making it difficult to date the cairn. Thirty metres further east, the second example was found to be better preserved and more substantial (10m in diameter) and displayed a large rectilinear chamber of edge-up orthostats, with two transverse slabs creating a central stall-like division, suggesting the possibility of a Neolithic construction date. The third cairn bore similarities to the second, with two upright in situ slabs at its centre, remnants of a rectilinear chamber or large cist. These are not the only funerary monuments in the area, as 200 yards eastwards towards the sea the survey noted another two cairns, both displaying well-preserved internal cists and external kerbing. It is a common feature for prehistoric burials on Shetland to be placed along the backbone of field-systems (Hunter 1996, Whittle *et al* 1986) and Foula's burials, placed along the margins of the South Ness dyke systems, follow this pattern of cairn field development.

It is no accident that the South Ness is witness to such a concentration of visible prehistoric remains, in contrast to the dearth of remains of a similar early date within the Hametoun settlement. This is a result of differences in land-use over more recent centuries. It takes us only a simple step across the Hametoun head dyke to encounter an entirely different environment. The effects of scalping are non-existent, and centuries of arable cultivation and land improvement are evident at every turn. Within this landscape, the only definitive traces of prehistory are to be found in those monuments less vulnerable to the delling spade. These are the two known burnt mounds within the settlement, one of which is practically destroyed where it lies amid the run-rig systems of the valley base. The larger example of the two, The Whirley Knowe, also lies at the heart of the settlement where the burn doglegs and heads east towards the sea. The impact of previous investigations is clear in the hollows in the surface of this mound, and it is almost certainly one of the 'mounds of burnt stones' excavated by Sands (1885). Fragments of Bronze Age steatite vessels and steatite-tempered Neolithic pottery were recovered from this mound at an unknown time (S. Gear *pers. comm.* 2005).

NORSE AND MEDIEVAL ROOTS

Whilst the prehistory of the Hametoun is somewhat compromised by later activity, the centuries of Norse and medieval occupation in this area have left us with some glimpses of how the landscape may have been organised during these periods. The modern Hametoun head dyke was constructed during the 1880s, over 40 years after the period of 'planking', when loose and dispersed land holdings were consolidated into fixed crofting boundaries (Baldwin 1984). The crofting settlements located at the upper northern half of the Hametoun represent a later stage in the process of land-taking, since they were constructed after the building of the modern head dyke and outside of its original path. A combination of documentary sources, local memory, building morphology, and landscape features have aided in the piecing

All quiet on the Western Front? Landscape survey on Foula, Shetland

together of the smaller and earlier settlement south of this, locating its medieval and Norse roots. This settlement takes in the buildings of Quinister, Grisigarth, Norderhaus, Guttren, and The Biggings (*4*).

One of the earliest documentary references to Foula is contained in the rentals acquired by King Frederick of Denmark from the 25 August 1582. This mentions 'Greesegaard' (Grisigarth) in Foula, which at this time consisted of 1½ marks of

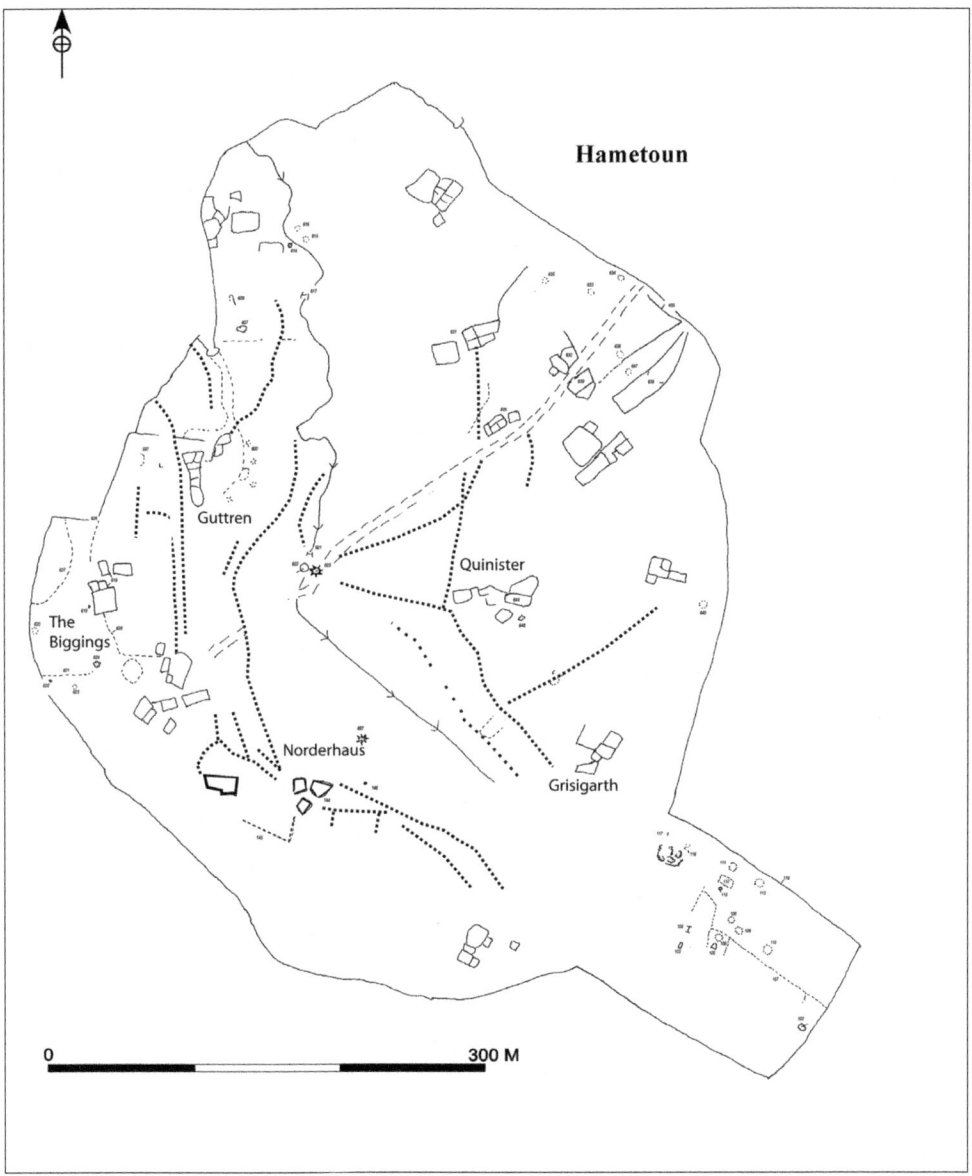

4 Sites mentioned in the text

5 Grisigarth looking west toward The Biggings and Guttren. *O Raybould*

land (Daae 1895) (5). This early date helps our reconstruction of the wider Hametoun settlement; Grisigarth sits high up on the slopes of the Hametoun valley near to the later crofthouses. Its modern ruins date only to the second decade of the nineteenth century (S. Gear *pers. comm.* 2005), but a number of partially buried fragments of walling are visible surrounding the building complex that hint towards earlier structures. The suffix 'Garth' or 'Gard' relates to the O.N. term for the enclosing of an area of land during the later stages of Norse land-taking, where an outset is created on the edges of improved and settled areas (Jackobsen 1936). Grisigarth was therefore broken out of the previously unimproved land at the margins of an existing settlement and was well established even as early as 1592.

Looking down into the heart of the valley, and to the settlement at The Biggings, may lead us towards earlier stages in Foula's occupation. A useful inroad into earlier settlement foci is to look for groupings of farm buildings that appear to have fragmented from an original core homestead (Crawford 1987). The Udal tenure system characteristic of the Norse period on Shetland is defined by a system of inheritance whereby property and land was divided equally between sons (with a half-share for daughters). This system partly explains the means through which the highly fragmented nature of medieval land holding began to take shape (*ibid*). The Biggings currently consists of occupied crofthouses, with both houses dating between 1870 and 1900 (J. Gear *pers. comm.* 2005). Bobby Isbister, the father of the current occupant of the South Biggings, recalled a further three houses in this locality known as Framhoose, Uphoose and Mews. The location of these houses is believed to be somewhere in the intermediate area between the modern crofthouses, but this area has seen a large amount of modern levelling and modification, and all that remains are a series of low amorphous earthworks. However, when these houses were occupied, this area would have represented a busy central Tun, characteristic of medieval and earlier settlement. The names afforded to these houses (north, south, up and fram) indicate a toponymical progression from an original holding, a pattern seen elsewhere on Shetland, for example at The Biggings, Papa Stour (Crawford 1985).

The Guttren crofthouse complex lies to the north of The Biggings, and is unique on Foula for its aspect, as its housing units are placed with their long axes facing downslope. The buildings are collapsed and soil accumulation has confused aspects of their construction, but where coursing remains, the walls are built using large facing stones infilled with smaller rubble. Many stories abide about the history of Guttren, so much so that it is difficult to dissociate myth from reality. Holbourn (1938), who bought the island from Ewing Gilmour in 1901, wrote that the name of this settlement originated from the name ('*Guttern*' or '*Guttorm*') of one of the first Norse settlers of the island, something which is less readily accepted by islanders today, who claim this name derives from a Norn[1] description for 'the house by the stream' (S. Gear. *pers. comm.* 2005). Bobby Isbister was able to recall an original Guttren house located nearer to the Hametoun burn, however no trace of any buildings were noted during our survey. We know that Guttren was occupied in 1774, as it is mentioned in the Kirk Sessions for this year. Whilst it would be tempting to ascribe an earlier Norse origin to the ruins visible today because of elements such as their orientation and wall construction, it is equally likely that these buildings belong to the medieval period at the earliest, in particular if these ruins represent a later range of buildings from the earlier burnside homestead. However, given its distinctive building style, it is worth considering that the construction of these dwellings involved the modification of an existing (perhaps ruined) settlement with its origins in the Norse period.

Another complex around which much Foula mythology is centred is the ruined buildings at Norderhaus. The complex consists of nine buildings surrounded by six partially visible enclosures. The buildings form a house with barn and byre placed parallel to one another across-slope, with associated small outbuildings. The visible remains were built sometime around the 1820s for a single family, and were occupied until the abandonment of the homestead around 1903 (S. Gear *pers. comm.* 2005). For a period of occupation of less than 100 years, and for a single household, there are an unusually large number of yards and enclosures associated with this site.

Holbourn (1938) again picked up on the name of this site and drew upon local folklore to suggest that this was a place where Scottish kings sent their sons to be trained in the Norse tongue. It seems likely that this somewhat fantastic story arose because of a desire to explain the existence of a 'north house' placed at the very southerly extreme of the settlement. It is not apparently 'north' of anything other than a precipitous cliff-edge. A closer look reveals a series of stone-lined banks 50 yards to the south of the complex which may represent examples of relict enclosures. If these do represent yards older than those relating to the present ruins, we could be in the vicinity of a 'south house'. However, aside from the occurrence of a small area of low earthworks accompanying the relict enclosures, no hint exists of earlier dwellings. Another possibility is that the construction of the Norderhaus buildings involved the reuse of earlier ruins; the name may have been adopted or created by the new settlers and considered fitting for a place believed or known to be of Norse origins.

These large croft complexes, which we consider to be the earliest in the Hametoun, are linked by a series of earthen terraces snaking across the valley sides. These earthen banks are substantial, as high as 2.5m on their lee side and are as wide as 2m. They draw impressive lines across the Hametoun landscape, connecting farmsteads to one another but petering out just before reaching each complex of buildings. It is not possible to establish whether croft houses have been dug into these terraces or whether the terraces post-date the houses, where cultivators have simply avoided working the land immediately above the houses (at least without undertaking the laborious process of carrying soil back upslope in order prevent the gathering soil from undermining the buildings). Providing a date for these terraces using landscape-based sources of evidence is complex. The traditional form of arable cultivation in the Hametoun has relied upon the delling spade, and not the plough (Fenton 1978). The process of delling downslope in strips can produce substantial collections of soil at the base of a slope after only a few years. As a result, it is important to resist the temptation to postulate an early, perhaps prehistoric, origin for these impressive terraces. However, it is equally unsatisfactory to presuppose a later historic origin without first solving a number of problems with this interpretation. If these terraces represent the termination of disused rigs from the later historic period, we would expect to see the vertical indented lines created by furrows between each rig.

If these terraces do represent only the terminations of rigs, this presents a highly formalised and organised system of run-rig agriculture, terminating at a fixed point along specific lines, with no visible boundaries between rigs. The pre-planking landscape of the Hametoun is unlikely to have followed such an organised pattern; these terraces might rather point toward the termination of larger arable plots. The traces of historic run-rig cultivation within the Hametoun are still very prominent within the landscape, occupying the low-lying level ground surrounding the Hametoun burn. It is therefore possible that the terraces on the higher slopes are the relict remains of prehistoric or perhaps Norse field plots. As the climate prior to the Little Ice Age (*c.*1300) was considerably more favourable than during the medieval period (Fenton 1978) Norse-period agriculture on the higher slopes of the Hametoun valley would have been viable.

The question remains of the relationships between these terraces and the early crofts. The terrace itself indicates the point at which the process of arable cultivation has stopped at the end of a plot of land, i.e. the downslope termination of a field plot. Why did arable cultivation stop here, allowing these boundaries to develop? This may be in order to respect and maintain access routes between crofting settlements, allowing people to move from croft to croft between areas of cultivation. Little is currently known about the character of Norse farmed landscapes, and equally little is known when run-rig begins on Shetland, a system of agriculture which is otherwise well studied in later periods (Bond *pers. comm.* 2005). The Hametoun offers great research potential, therefore, for further in-depth investigation of pre-medieval arable landscapes.

HARRIER

Harrier (*6*) lies at the north of the island, bounded to the north by the tail of Soberlie, to the west by the sharp rise of the Barkhill, and to the east by the gentler slopes of Da Heights and Crougar. It lies on a gradual slope that becomes increasingly boggy towards the south. Mapping of this area has revealed systems of robbed-out dykes, likely of Bronze Age origin, traversing the landscape from their starting point at the summit of Da Heights to the north-east. The survey also marked the presence of three highly denuded burnt mounds, and one of the larger examples of prehistoric burial monuments on the island, which, although highly dilapidated, bears resemblance to the square cairns found in other parts of Shetland. The burnt mounds and burial cairn occupy the heart of the Harrier valley, sitting at the centre of the natural bowl created by the surrounding hills.

EXPLORING THE 'CHAPEL SITE'

This spot at the heart of Harrier is also home to an enigmatic site marked on earlier maps, and referred to by the Royal Commission (1946) as a chapel. At first glance this consists of a substantial artificial mound, extending northwards and westwards from the old North Harrier house and byre, and mostly enclosed by a cornyard associated with the croft (*7*). The surface of the mound is irregular and stony throughout, in particular in the area enclosed by the cornyard.

The original date for the old house is unknown, though it is believed to be one of the oldest roofed buildings on the island (S. Gear *pers. comm.* 2005). There is

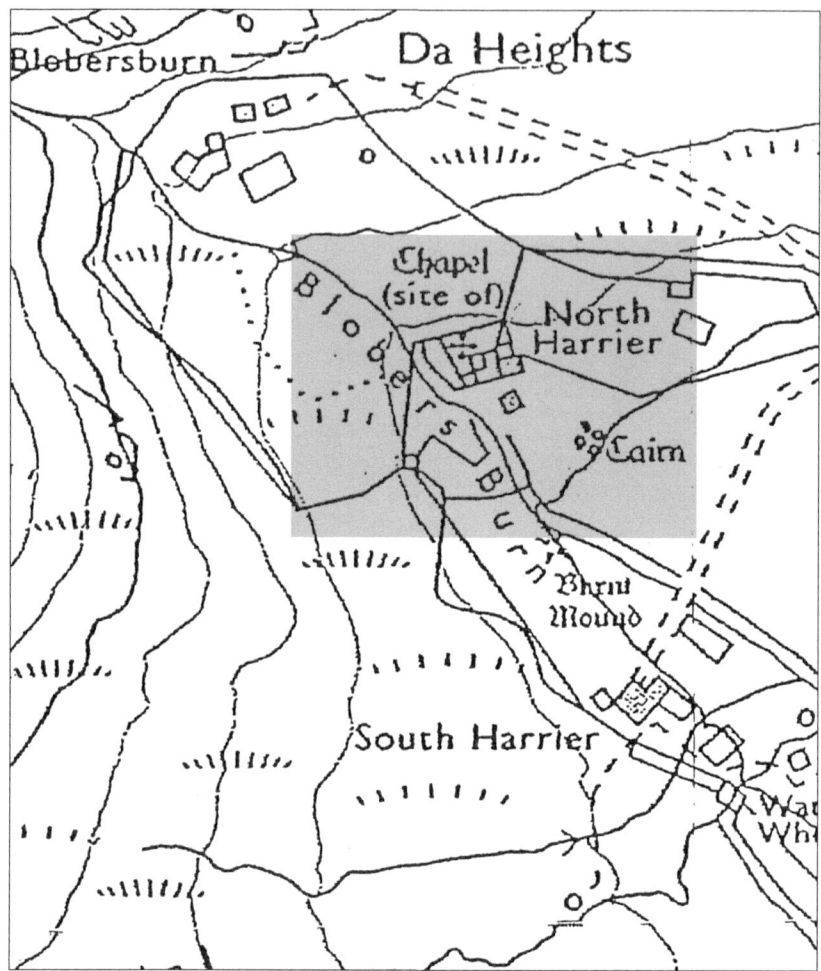

6 Harrier and the Chapel Site. From Ordnance Survey Map © Licence No.100041268

nothing distinctive about the construction of the house to separate it from other ruined crofts on Foula, although the lack of a chimney (*lum*) indicates that a central hearth was used until its abandonment. This is usually seen as a feature of an earlier crofthouse (Fenton 1978). The walls of the cornyard are more substantial than the usual yards belonging to Foula's crofts, as they are double-, rather than single-skinned, with smaller stone infilling. At the south-west corner of the enclosure are two small unroofed outbuildings sharing an unusually thick, 1.5m wide, central wall. Jutting westwards into the cornyard is another partially destroyed outbuilding. The upper courses of the one remaining gable wall share the same phase of construction as the repaired upper courses of the cornyard wall, but the lower courses indicate that the enclosure was built around this earlier building (likely to have been a

All quiet on the Western Front? Landscape survey on Foula, Shetland

7 Interior of the Cornyard enclosure, Chapel Site, (note large slabs in foreground) facing west

dwelling given the presence of a blocked *lum* and of small stone cupboards or wall presses in its construction).

The footings for three substantial parallel walls, constructed with massive sandstone blocks, are visible on an east-west alignment, partly revealed beneath the later buildings (*8*). In places, where they have been incorporated into the later structures, the walls stand as high as four or five courses. The phasing sequence suggests that an east-west aligned substantial rectilinear building (or perhaps two) were constructed, over which the later dwelling was constructed, reusing parts of the walls of the first phase. The outbuildings were also constructed by reusing these earlier walls. Although any relationship between the earlier walls and the unusually thick central wall of the later outbuildings is obscured, this may relate to a partition within the earlier buildings. Its substantial build matches well with the Phase One walls. Of particular interest is that the most northerly two of the parallel Phase One walls are only visible because substantial quantities of earth were excavated to create a level platform for the construction of the later dwelling house. These walls therefore pre-date the upper accumulations (on average a metre in depth) of the chapel.

Six substantial lintel-like stone slabs up to 2m long and 0.5m wide were noted within the cornyard. These were used within living memory as supports for corn

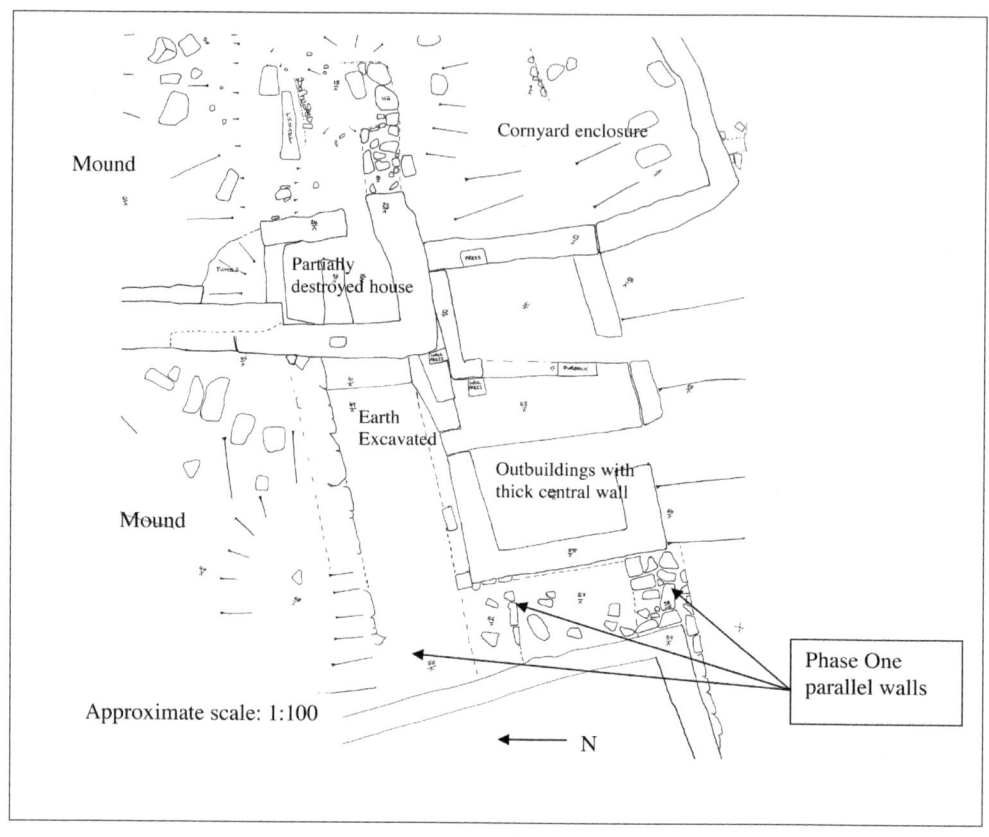

8 Plan of ruined outbuildings, south-west area of cornyard

stooks, though their origin is obscure (S. Gear *pers. comm.* 2005). It is possible that these were originally used as grave markers. Local memory recalls occasions where human bones were revealed in the upper levels of the mound (*ibid*) and, given the enduring oral tradition referring to the site as a chapel, it is possible that this is the case. A graveyard is not the only likely formation process for the mound, however, as the landowner has recovered a vast number of artefacts from it and the surrounding area over the years. This is predominantly pottery of Iron Age origin (*9*), with some sherds of Bronze Age date and also later sherds of medieval pottery.

In addition, substantial numbers of coarse stone tools lie strewn around the area, including small hand querns of Neolithic and Bronze Age date, rubbers, polishers, grinders, pounders, hammers and line-sinkers. Fragments of a round-sided steatite vessel were recovered from the topsoil below a dyke a few yards away, and other smaller fragments of steatite have originated from the area on and around the mound. The landowner has also recovered numerous small stone spindle whorls, one of which is beautifully crafted from pink-hued steatite. This material on the whole suggests prolonged activity with a domestic emphasis from early prehistory right through to

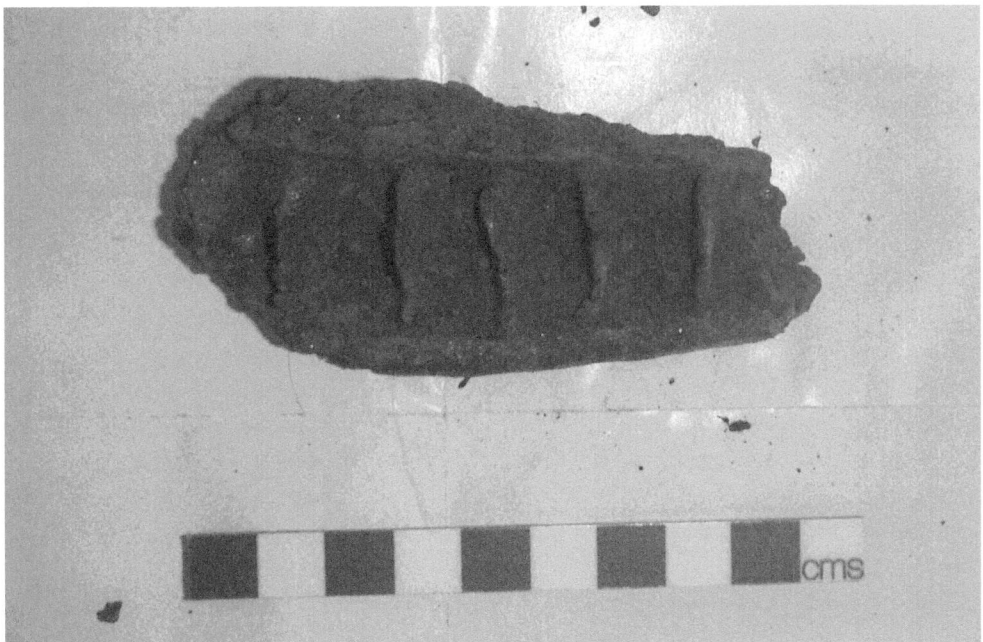

9 Iron Age sherd, Chapel Site mound

the Norse and medieval periods, but further work would be required to confidently establish sequence and character for all of the periods represented at the site.

RECONSTRUCTING HARRIER

If the site does conceal the remains of a chapel, how do we understand its placement in the sequence of settlement, in particular its relationship to Iron Age and Norse occupation at the site? An understanding of the *landnam* in Shetland is obfuscated by conflicting evidence for the interface between Pictish populations and incoming Viking settlers. In many cases Iron Age sites were reused, albeit a common hiatus in occupation is evident, varying from several hundred years (as at Underhoull, Unst) to apparently rapid succession (as with Brough of Birsay, Orkney) (Crawford 1987). Given the artefactual evidence, on an island as small as Foula, where ideal locations for settlement are more limited, it seems reasonable to suggest that a pre-existing settlement was considered ideal for new occupation, and possibly for the building of an early chapel.

Earl Thorfinn's chapel on the Brough of Birsay, a sophisticated and elaborate early church site, was the first seat of the Bishops of Orkney. Crawford (1987) has suggested that its construction may have instigated a widespread burst of private chapel building by individual families in all the areas of Norse settlement in

Scotland around the twelfth century. Furthermore, she considers the possibility that the chosen location for these chapels may have rested upon the adoption of an extant pre-Norse pattern. On Foula this process may have entailed the placement of a chapel, or the appropriation of one, within a pre-existing settlement focus at Harrier.

How likely is the presence of a pre-Norse ecclesiastic centre at the heart of the Harrier settlement? In contrast to medieval monastic settlement, which is typically characterised on Shetland by its isolated locations (Crawford 1987), pre-medieval ecclesiastic activity is more likely to be focused within main areas of settlement, where monks or priests took a more direct and parental concern over the lives of the wider community (Crawford 1987). If this is the case, we can perhaps envisage a religious site from this initial period of Christianisation on Shetland, placed at the heart of an occupied landscape. The dating of early chapels is a notorious problem, as the styles adopted are often uniformly simple, preventing the establishment of a chronology (*ibid*). The earliest sites are usually simple rectangular cells, such as that at Marwick in Birsay, Orkney. Other examples involved an elaboration upon this to create a separate nave and chancel, or a bicameral building (Fleming & Woolf 1992). These bicameral structures are usually thought to date to the twelfth century, and are found throughout the Northern and Western isles, with five examples on Shetland (four on Unst and one on Yell). Their simple arrangement of nave with square-sided chancel is one which might be represented by the lower courses or foundations of the Phase One walls at the Harrier site. However, further work is required to isolate the specific architectural characteristics of this chapel, and to more confidently date its origins.

SUMMARY

As is often the case with non-intrusive survey, the project has so far generated more questions than answers. The Hametoun landscape presents a useful tool for improving our understanding of the development of the Shetland Tun, and holds scope for further research into pre-medieval agricultural landscapes on Shetland. The work conducted at Harrier has served to better reveal a landscape (and specifically a locus at the heart of that landscape) of importance within the wider arena of Shetland archaeology. Future work on Foula will be centred in particular upon the chapel site, which may represent an integrated political and religious site of regional importance that, as yet, remains outside of general syntheses of Shetland archaeology. Geophysical (resistivity and magnetometry) survey on and around the chapel site is being carried out by members of the Bath and Camerton Archaeological Society during May 2006. These results will be used to inform the next stage of our investigation into the development of the chapel site, and of its surrounding landscape.

CONCLUSIONS: PUTTING FOULA IN ITS PLACE

Ultimately it is our aim to integrate Foula's archaeology into wider understandings of change in the Shetland Isles, and areas such as Harrier are an important vehicle for illustrating just how central Foula's past is, or should be, to our understanding of the islands as a whole. The project has highlighted the sheer quantity and diversity of archaeological remains on Foula, which has, itself, raised questions about why the island has remained conspicuous in its absence from archaeological literature. As archaeologists we have done away with many preconceptions about life in remote communities. Our discussions of islands and marginality have come a long way, but does the fact that some islands still await the same integration into wider studies as many of their neighbours relate to a sort of marginalisation? The reasons for such discrepancies are more often practical or financial than theoretical, and part of the gradual progress of archaeological research in the islands as a whole. However, the extent to which our research focuses upon certain areas at the expense of others may also have something to inform about our own motivations and about how we, as archaeologists, perceive islands.

To begin to draw lengthy comparisons between Foula and the St Kilda archipelago would undoubtedly open a 'can of worms' at this stage, and so must remain largely outside of the scope of this paper. However, I would like to sum up by considering a few points of contrast in the historiography of the two islands. In so many respects Foula might be regarded as the 'Hirta of the Shetland Islands' given the similarities, for example, in geographical aspect and terrifically dramatic landscapes. I don't intend this to be a sweeping generalised comparison, but these similarities do underline the question: why has Hirta been subject to such intensive study, while Foula has not? Andrew Fleming (2005) has dealt with the first half of this question at length, considering 'hirtaphilia' in its many manifestations – the iconic and exotic status the island has gained based on 'Celtic' romanticism, nineteenth-century fascination with the sublime and the island as microcosm for grand narratives of social evolution.

There's no single over-arching reason to explain Foula's lack of celebrity, aside from perhaps the one striking dissimilarity to the 'historical drama queen' of St Kilda (Fleming 2005, xii). No equivalent to Fleming's 'Hardrock consensus' has ever developed on Foula since there are no silent and melancholic villages of fallen stone upon which such ideas might have formed. Foula's muted voice, in comparison, is explained at least in part by the fact that an evacuation has never been a part of the island's history. Hirta has been drawn upon repeatedly as an allegory in philosophies centred upon the advent of modernity, the struggle of man against nature; and his inevitable doom, subsequently the island has suffered 'over-mythologised' (*ibid* xii) explanations for its evacuation. Foula, a little ironically, appears to have slipped by almost unnoticed simply because it is home to a successful community today, as in earlier times.

The historiographical contrast between the two islands is no great surprise given the different social and historical processes that they witnessed over the last few hundred years. Indeed, 'hirtaphilia' is no surprise in and of itself. However, the lack of much in the way of ethnographic or poetical enquiry on Foula has, by association, resulted in an ensuing vacuum in the study of its archaeology. One thing I have illustrated briefly in this paper is that any lack of historical interest about the island can certainly not be down to a matched lack in historical richness or complexity. It may well be the case that the world of archaeology is only big enough for one truly iconic peripheral community, and one stage for the playing out of grand allegorical themes. We may have established Hirta as the most romanticised island; it is now important we do not allow romanticism to cloud our commitment to creating fully inclusive syntheses of the development of the Northern and Western Isles.

ACKNOWLEDGEMENTS

Thanks are due to Sheila and Jim Gear, Foula Heritage, The Catherine Mackichan Trust, Hunter Archaeological Trust, Magnus Holbourn, Amy Ratter, Shetland Amenity Trust, Mark Ward, Hefin Meara, Owen Raybould, Camilla Priede, Anne Cowking, Antonia Thomas, Jule Bond, Beverly Ballin-Smith, David Scott-Langley, Isobel and John Holbourn, Steven Smith, John Baldwin, Katke MacDonald, Mark Edmonds, Nick Card and Colin Merrony.

NOTES

1 An old Shetland dialect; Old Scots combined with a strong Scandianavian influence spoken widely throughout the islands until the turn of the twentieth century and even later in some areas. Foula islanders are believed to have spoken Norn into the inter-war period (J. Gear *pers. comm* 2004).

REFERENCES

Baldwin, J.R. 1978, 'Norse influences in sheep husbandry on Foula, Shetland' in Baldwin, J.R. (ed.), *Scandinavian Shetland: An ongoing tradition?* 97-123, Lerwick

Baldwin, J.R. 1981, 'A hard won wilderness: man and environment on Foula, Shetland, and Western Faroes' *Proceedings of the Society of Antiquaries for Scotland* 118, 323-325

Baldwin J.R. 1984, 'Hogin and Hametoun: thoughts on the stratification of a Foula Tun', in Crawford, B.E. (ed.), *Essays in Shetland History*, PAGE Lerwick

Baldwin, J. 1996, 'Heaps, humps and bumps on the Foula Skattald', in Smith, B. and Waugh, D. (eds), *Shetland's Northern Links: Language and History*, 205-229, Edinburgh

Cracknell, S. & Smith, B. 1985, 'Excavation at Mavis Grind', in Smith, B. (ed.), *Shetland Archaeology: New Work in Shetland in the 1970s*, 86-94, Lerwick

Crawford, B.E. 1985, 'The Biggins, Papa Stour: a multidisciplinary investigation' in Smith, B. (ed.), *Shetland Archaeology: New Work in Shetland in the 1970s*, 128-158, Lerwick

Crawford, B.E. 1987, *Scandinavian Scotland*, Leicester

Daae, L. 1895, 'Om Fru Gorvel Fadersdatter og Hendes Norske Jordegods', *Historisk Tidsskrift* (Noreweigan) 3R, Vol 3, 264-8

Fenton, A. 1978, *The Northern Isles: Orkney and Shetland*, East Linton

Fleming, A. 2005, *St Kilda and The Wider World: Tales of an Iconic Island*, Macclesfield

Fleming, I. & Wolf, A. 1992, 'Cille Donnain: a Late Norse church in South Uist' *Proceedings of the Society of Antiquaries of Scotland* 122, 329-350

Gear, S. 1983, *Foula: Island West of the Sun*, London

Holbourn, I.S. 1938, *The Isle of Foula*, Edinburgh

Hunter, J.R. 1996, *Fair Isle: The Archaeology of an Island Community*, Edinburgh

Jackobsen, J. 1936, *The Place Names of Shetland*, London and Copenhagen

Lowe, G. 1879, *Tour Through the Orkneys and Shetland in 1774*, Kirkwall

Mykura, W. 1976, *British Regional Geology: Orkney and Shetland*, Edinburgh

Page, J.L. 1976, *The Isle of Foula. Observations on the Past, Present, and Future with their Implications for the Planner*. Unpublished PhD thesis, University of Aberdeen

RCAHMS 1946, *Inventory of the Ancient Monuments of Orkney and Shetland*, Edinburgh

Simpson, G. 1968, 'A Preliminary Survey of the Archaeology of Foula', in *Brathay Exploration Group Annual Report*, 313-323, Department of Archaeology, Queens University, Belfast

Svensson, R. 1955, *Lonely Isles*, London

Whittle, A., Lucas, M.K., Milles, A., Noddle, B., Rees, S. & Romans, J.C.C. 1986, *Scord of Brouster: An Early Agricultural Settlement on Shetland*, Oxford University Committee for Archaeology Monograph No 9

8

AT THE CROSSROADS: THE HISTORICAL ARCHAEOLOGY OF RATHLIN ISLAND

Wes Forsythe & Rosemary McConkey

INTRODUCTION

In 1617, a dispute over the ownership of Rathlin Island appeared before the courts. Crucial to the settlement of the case was the question of whether the island belonged to the Kingdom of Ireland or the Kingdom of Scotland. Defending his ownership of the island, Randal MacDonnell, Earl of Antrim, began his argument by pointing out that Rathlin was physically closer to Ireland than Scotland. It had a history since Norman times of being granted as a parcel of Irish territory and its ecclesiastical dues were paid to the Irish church. He also delved into early history to quote the definition of Irish Dalriada as including Rathlin, as set out by the sixth-century *Declaration of Druim Ceatt*. The governor of Carrickfergus, Sir Arthur Chichester, admitted 'If it be of Scotland, we have run into great error, for in the time of the rebellion we have often wasted it, and destroyed the inhabitants by the sword and by the halter as we did the rebels of Ireland' (Clark 1996, 112). In response, one Crawford of Lisnorris set out his case. Like MacDonnell, he began strongly. He had in his possession a grant of the island from James IV to one of his ancestors and he claimed Scots authorities regarded the island as part of the Sherifdom of Tarbert. He also strayed into early history by quoting Roman geographers including Solinus and Ptolemy's definition of the Hebrides as including Rathlin.

Finally the most infamous of arguments was produced – Rathlin has no snakes and as such must fall under the jurisdiction of St Patrick and therefore be Irish (Cal

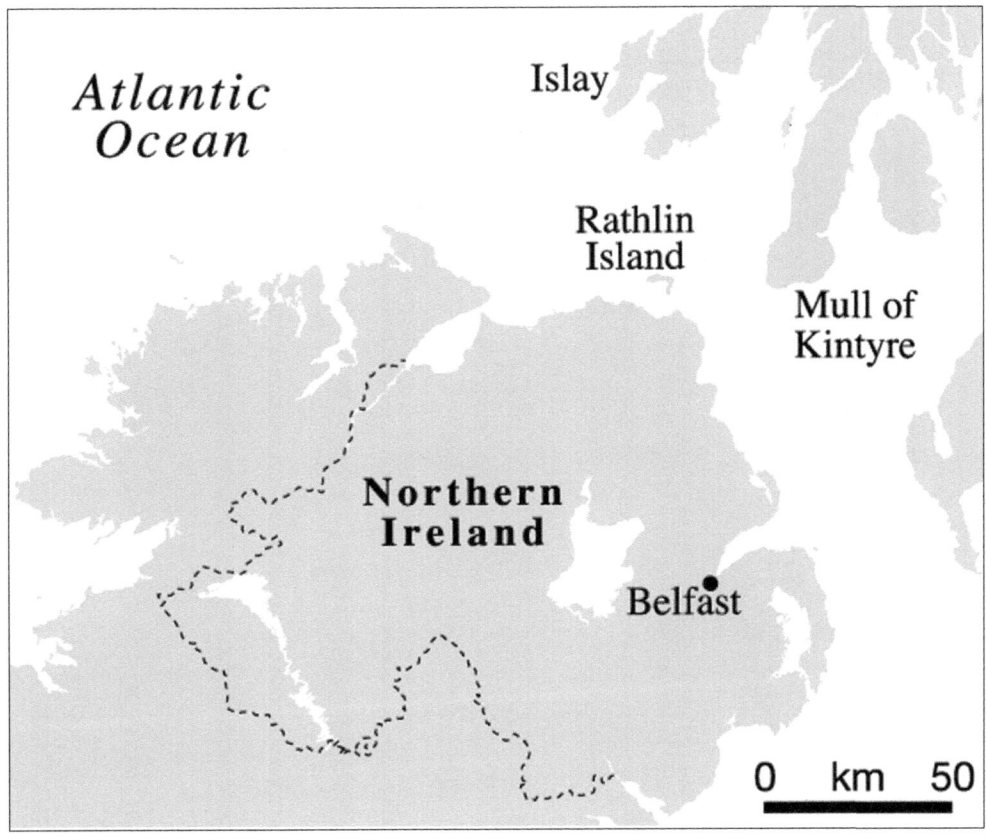

1 Location map of Rathlin in relation to the north of Ireland/south-west Scotland

Carew Mss 1617). The confusion surrounding the island's status is understandable after centuries of Scottish influence, culminating with the legal recognition of Randall MacDonnell, a descendant of the Lords of the Isles. The island, some five miles from the north Antrim coast and 13 from Kintyre, is sited at the northern entrance to the Irish Sea (*1*). As a result the island has been in a strategically advantageous position for both trade and conflict through the centuries.

Although Rathlin has been considered firmly Irish since the notable seventeenth-century court case, the island maintained its links to Scotland, these becoming increasingly economic in nature. In the post-medieval era, the established cultural links between the island and Scotland included the repopulating of the island after a number of particularly savage massacres in the sixteenth and seventeenth centuries. Kintyre and Islay people reputedly featured strongly in this new influx. The form of Irish spoken on Rathlin has strong Scots Gaelic influences and this linguistic contact is also expressed through some of the island's place-names. Taking a maritime focus, a recent archaeological survey of Rathlin has naturally sought to consider the island's relationship to both Ireland and Scotland. In this paper it is hoped to highlight the archaeology and historical evidence demonstrating in particular the longevity of the Scottish link.

EARLY SEA CONNECTIONS

Randal MacDonnell's reference to the Dalriadan connection was by no means unfounded, although the nature of this early Irish-Scottish kingdom has recently been disputed (Campbell 2001). The kingdom of Dál Riata, traditionally colonised by the Irish and centred around Argyll, had its counterpart in north-east Antrim. The connections are illustrated in the Preface of the *Amra Coluim Cille*, dating to the early eleventh century (Stokes 1899, 47; Herbert 1989, 68), which refers to a convention of kings held at Druim Ceatt (now known as Mullagh Hill, Limavady, County Derry) in the later sixth century. This is also mentioned in the *Annals of Ulster* (AU 575) and by Adomnan (Sharpe 1995, 151, I.49, 312-3). One of the primary reasons for the assembly was to reach a peaceful agreement between Irish and Scottish Dál Riata, and this appears to have been accomplished.

Numerous references in Adomnan's *Life of St Columba* convey the close connection between Iona and Ireland, and the frequency with which the saints made sea journeys in both directions (e.g. I.18, 30; II.5; see Sharpe 1995). During periods of settled weather, boats could have sailed directly across the open sea to their destinations, but during the winter, or when the weather was less predictable, they would have been more likely to 'island hop', shortening the duration of exposure to rough seas. On one occasion Columba instructed a monk, Berach, who was sailing from Iona to Tiree, not to cross the open sea, but to take the longer route via the Treshnish Islands because of the threat of 'a monster of the deep' (Sharpe 1995, 125, I. 19). If, as suggested by Marsden (1995, 75-76), the saints had sailed through the Sound of Islay on their journey from Iona to Ireland, then they would probably have passed close to, or perhaps stopped off on Rathlin.

Some confusion arises in the attempt to ascertain which of the early references pertain to ecclesiastical sites on Rathlin, as the name Rechru used in the various annals is also applied to several other islands including Lambay, County Dublin and an island in Lough Neagh. A number of sites, however, point to the existence of potentially early churches. Three graveyards, known as Kilvoruan, Kilbrida (O'Laverty 1887, 377 & 380) and Killeany (O'Boyle 1939, 51) are considered to be of antiquity and the 'Kill' element in the placename suggests early church foundations. Another enclosure, also named Kilvoruan, is traditionally regarded as monastic (O'Laverty 1887, 379). It lies on rough, partially overgrown upland, and apart from a prominent stone and low meandering bank, the remains are very difficult to trace. During the survey an attempt to map this enclosure was carried out using GPS equipment, probing for stone foundations among the thick vegetation. This revealed a roughly sub-oval enclosure in plan, bisected by a wall, with cell-like features around the internal perimeter. A further undefinable structure was identified in the interior. Additional elements may well exist beyond the limits of the surveyed area, but preliminary results suggest a monastic enclosure. There are also isolated artefactual finds of Early Medieval date. Souterrain ware was recovered during the excavation of an Early Bronze Age cemetery in Church Bay (Wiggins 2000, 59-61), and further possible sherds were found during the excavation of another prehistoric site in Knockans South (Conway 1995).

More impressive Early Medieval finds and sites are associated with Viking activity on the island. The initial phase of Viking activity in Ireland involved sporadic raiding mainly targeting coastal monasteries. The first of these took place on *Rechru*, probably Rathlin Island, in 795 (AU), the Isle of Skye being attacked in the same year. These earliest Vikings may have made voyages directly from Norway, but in the years between *c.*820 and 840, they are more likely to have conducted maritime activities from bases in the Northern and Western Isles of Scotland (Ó Corráin 2001, 18). After *c.*840 they established longphoirt within Ireland. Documentary sources are not helpful in identifying specific Viking settlements along the northern coast of Ireland, however, it is recorded that they did exist. The *Annals of Ulster* for the year 866 state that Aed, son of Niall plundered the Viking strongholds in the territory of the Cenél Eógain and Dál Araidi, and took their flocks and herds, implying that there must have been settled communities living in the area (AU 866).

Despite the lack of place-name evidence on Rathlin, archaeological material found there suggests that the Vikings had more than a passing interest in the island. Viking burials were discovered in Church Bay in the late eighteenth century (Hamilton 1839), identifiable from the artefacts accompanying the dead. A silver bossed penannular brooch dating to the early ninth century seems to reflect the work of a Viking craftsman heavily influenced by native Irish style (Armstrong 1915, 248; Warner 1973-4, 61). The grave in which it was found was marked by the only known standing stone on the island. Other Viking graves associated with standing stones occur in Scottish contexts, for example at Ballinaby in Islay, where the burial was accompanied by a pair of tortoise brooches, and Ardvonrig, Barra in the Hebrides (Shetelig 1954). Although the Rathlin graves are poorly documented, there is enough evidence to suggest the existence of a Viking cemetery there, as other finds include a handled bronze vessel and a sword (Warner 1973-74, 62). It would not be unreasonable to extrapolate an associated settlement at proximity. Apart from the well-known examples in Dublin, and those recently discovered at Cloghermore Cave, Co. Kerry (Connolly *et al* 2005), the Church Bay burials represent the only Viking cemetery yet found in Ireland (Harrison 2001, 66), the few other sites being isolated graves. Further Viking-Age material consists of a coin hoard interpreted by Dolley (1974, 39-40) as sub-Sihtric, dating to *c.*1040; it was recovered somewhere on Rathlin in 1916, but the circumstances surrounding its deposition are unknown.

An enigmatic 'boat-shaped' mound in Ballygill Middle townland lies on a natural, flat-topped eminence on generally low-lying damp land. The feature was pointed out as 'The Danes Burial Mound' by the landowner during the recent survey. It measures *c.*18.3m in length by 4.5m in maximum width, tapering to 2.2m at the south-east and 1.4m at the north-western end. It stands to a height of 0.85m. There are indications of some former intrusion in the interior at the south-eastern end. It is tempting to speculate that this is a boat burial, but of course it is impossible to be certain without further investigation. Two other possible Irish boat burials were both recorded from Ulster. One at Ballyholme, Co. Down, was discovered in 1903 (Cochrane 1906, 450-454), and the other, preserved in a mound in Ballywillin bog, Co. Antrim, was found in *c.*1813 (Briggs 1974, 158-160). More are known in the Scottish Isles (e.g. Scar, Sanday and Westness, Rousay in the Orkneys, and Kiloran Bay, Colonsay), although most were not covered by a mound (see Owen & Dalland 1999).

THE MEDIEVAL PERIOD

Despite the increasing Normanisation of twelfth-century Scotland under the Canmore dynasty, a number of peripheral kingdoms ruled by chiefs or petty 'kings', continued to wield considerable control. Those along the western seaboard and among the Isles were strongly maritime in character. By 1136, Fergus had emerged as ruler of Galloway – at that time essentially consisting of the modern counties of Wigtownshire and Kirkcudbrightshire (Brooke 1994, 78-79). His great-grandson, Alan, extended his power and influence beyond the confines of Galloway in the early thirteenth century. In addition to his title of Constable of Scotland, he had lands in Lauderdale and Cunningham, inherited through his Norman mother (Stringer 1993, 83), and his marriage to Margaret of Huntingdon also gave him greater access to the English royal court (Brooke 1994, 131). In *c.*1212 he was granted extensive holdings in north-east Ulster, including Rathlin Island, by King John of England, as a reward for his services in Ireland (Cal Doc Ireland 1171-1251). It has been argued that this grant was purely speculative, without much serious effort on Alan's part to establish his claim, on the basis that the grant was repeated under more favourable terms (as an incentive) in 1215 (McNeill 1980, 15). While it may be true that Alan's attention was focused in a number of directions, particularly during the 1220s when he was preoccupied with a power-struggle in the Isle of Man (Brooke 1994, 132), he did have good reason to develop his interests in Ulster, and on Rathlin in particular. The latter's position between the northern Irish mainland and Scotland was strategic in controlling the sea routes used in the frequent interchange of mercenaries from both sides of the Irish Sea. Aside from his own personal ambitions, as Constable of Scotland and commander of Scottish royal forces, he would have been keen to prevent the Scottish rebels' use of Irish support in their resistance to the Scottish Crown, not least the MacHeths and MacWilliams in Moray and Ross, (see MacDonald 1999; Stringer

2 The ruins of Bruce's Castle on a promontory overlooking the northern entrance to the Irish Sea

1993, 86-87; Duffy 1991, 63). According to Sturla Thordarsson, Alan had the independent capability to muster a fleet of 150 to 200 ships, which Stringer (1993, 84) estimated would have amounted to an army of up to 3000 men. It seems likely that he would have attempted to establish a monitoring post, at least, on Rathlin.

The remnant of a fortification, known as Bruce's Castle – so called because of its association with Robert Bruce in 1306-7 – lies on a promontory on the north-eastern corner of Rathlin (*2*). Its position was undoubtedly influenced by its commanding views across the northern gateway to the Irish Sea, as far as Islay to the north, Kintyre to the east and the Antrim coast to the south. The castle comprises an inner ward, within which are two portions of wall, and a larger outer ward cut off from the landward side by a ditch. At the southern end of the ditch is the fragment of what was probably one of a pair of circular angle towers, which McNeill postulated may date to the later fourteenth century (1980, 69; 1983, 104). John Barbour's late fourteenth-century poem *The Brus* states that after Robert Bruce's defeat at the Battle of Methven in 1306, he fled to Rathlin to escape his pursuers (McDiarmid & Stevenson 1980 vol II, 71-2). Barbour recounts that on his arrival there the fearful islanders retreated with their cattle to a 'rycht stalwart castell', implying that some kind of stronghold already existed there by the early fourteenth century. It may be that a fortification had been built during the thirteenth century – perhaps even by Alan of Galloway – and was modified and extended over the following centuries. A pottery sherd of High Medieval date was recovered from the base of a wall in the course of a test excavation in the outworks of the castle (see below).

At present the only other evidence for medieval occupation on the island comes from a hut site in Carravindoon townland, a short distance south of Bruce's Castle. It lies within a complex of huts and field system partially investigated during the survey (McConkey & Moore, forthcoming). A date of cal AD 1180-1274 (2 Sigma) was obtained from a hearth in one of the occupation layers, and the date range incorporates the time-frame corresponding to Alan of Galloway's ownership of the island. The hut probably represents a homestead occupied by members of the local population. Barbour's poem, describing events occurring some 40 years after the *terminus ante quem*, indicates that the people living on the island were practising animal husbandry. The narrative continues that they agreed to supply Bruce's entourage of 300 men with food during his sojourn on Rathlin, implying that they had access to additional resources, probably acquired through arable farming and fishing. Cereal grains retrieved from the excavated hearth consisted of hulled and naked barley (*Hordeum* var. *nudum*), possible oats (*Avena* spp.) and a single instance of wheat (*Triticum* sp.). Five seeds of cultivated flax (*Linum usitatissimum*) were also present (Plunkett in McConkey & Moore, forthcoming).

After Alan's death in 1234, Hugh de Lacy, the Anglo-Norman Earl of Ulster, granted much of his Ulster lands, including Rathlin Island, to Walter and John Bisset, members of a powerful Scottish family with land in both England and Scotland (MacDonnell 1987, 38). Through his marriage to Margery Bisset in 1399, Rathlin came into the possession of John Mór MacDonnell of the Isles (Hill 1978 [1873], 21-22). The MacDonnells built castles and successfully strengthened their hold on their Irish possessions throughout the fifteenth century. Rathlin continued to be a valuable asset during the following century, especially in light of the frequent communications between the Isles and the Antrim Glens. It was also an important staging post for Scottish Redshanks crossing to Ireland, much to the chagrin of the English in their attempts to subdue the Irish and increase their control in Ulster (Cal Carew Mss. 1575, 21, no. 23). The island rapidly became a pawn in the ongoing battle between the Antrim Scots and the English, and was the target in a number of attacks against the MacDonnells.

In the second half of the sixteenth century there were repeated attempts to oust the Scots from Rathlin. A reference to the island in 1566 demonstrates the English perception of the island as a crucial bridgehead and refuge for Scots activity on the north coast of Ireland:

> First for the quietness of Ulster and Connaught is to take away the Isle of Raghlins [Rathlin] from the Scots and there to place 25 soldiers in the castell that one Sorley Boy now keeps, for this Raghlins is the greatest enemy that Ireland hath, it is the only succour of the Scots for thither they bring their spoils out of Ireland, and there keep them until they can convey them into Scotland.

Clark 1996, 85

The prominent Scot referred to was Sorley Boy MacDonnell, whose iconic leadership was key to the MacDonnells' success until his death at the end of the century. During this period, the island changed hands a number of times as the English tried to break the Scots' foothold on the north coast, but provisioning a garrison in these hostile waters proved difficult (Hill 1978 [1873], 156). In 1573, the island was granted to Walter, the Earl of Essex (Cal Carew Mss 1573). Like the Normans before him, Essex found himself in possession of a territory which was far from obedience and stability. Essex attempted to secure the island in 1575. He drove the Scots into a castle 'of very great strength' (Cal Carew Mss 1575) and using two guns managed to breach the walls (CSPI 1575). The besieged inhabitants were given over to the English and put to death – 200 souls in all, although Essex reported that another 300-400 found hiding in sea caves were also killed (Cal Carew Mss 1575). Excavation carried out at Bruce's Castle showed the original rock-cut ditch had been fortified by placing sods to absorb artillery fire (Forsythe & McConkey forthcoming). This modification probably dates to the 1560s when Sorley Boy was noted to be fortifying the site, although by the 1580s the castle was described as half-ruined (CSPI 1568; 1585).

The Queen's response to Essex was enthusiastic:

> the taking of the island of the Raughlins, the common receipt and harbour of such Scots as do infest that realm of Ireland; and that your proceeding against Sarleboy has taken happy success ... In the meantime we think it very convenient ... that there be continued a ward of thirty soldiers in the fort lately taken in the said island
>
> Cal Carew Mss 1575

The Scots reacted swiftly – the following month Norreys reported that his hoy and small boat had been taken by the Scots and burnt (CSPI 1575). Six weeks after the massacre, Sorley Boy successfully stormed Carrickfergus castle and carried off cattle. By the early seventeenth century, the MacDonnells under Sorley Boy had managed to successfully hold on to the island in the face of English aggression. They would play a careful diplomatic game for much of the proceeding century, siding alternately with the English and Irish. Randal MacDonnell managed to obtain his Irish holdings from the Crown in 1603 whilst maintaining his Catholic faith – an almost unique feat in Ulster (Ir Pat Roll Jas I, 3; Rep Pat Roll Jas I, 8, 52).

THE MODERN PERIOD

The eighteenth century saw a prolonged period of political stability and economic expansion, especially after 1740. Nevertheless Alexander MacDonnell, fifth Earl of Antrim, was in financial difficulties and in 1746 sold the island to the Rev. John Gage.

The Gages were of Norman-English decent, and were granted land in Magilligan, County Derry, in the early seventeenth century (Young 1929, 282-4). Rathlin would remain in their possession until the early twentieth century. By the time the Gages acquired Rathlin, Irish landowners were being encouraged to improve their estates by the introduction of agricultural and infrastructural reforms aimed at developing the commercial prospects of their holdings (e.g. Busteed 2001; Barnard 1994; 1995). It was expected that such reform would also have a beneficial effect on the lives of tenants and the conditions they lived in. The expanding Irish economy freed up capital to allow landowners to invest in their properties, though notoriously few carried out reforms beyond the walls of their personal estates. Two major activities demonstrate the increasingly commercialised world of the islanders in the modern period – kelp production and smuggling. Both were intimately bound up with the economies of Ireland and Scotland, and demonstrate the islanders' participation in and manipulation of the emerging markets (Forsythe 2006a).

In the north of Ireland, linen production was a key industry and islanders were able to participate in the trade by growing flax, cottage weaving and kelp production (Forsythe 2006b). Kelp was used to bleach linen, but also had uses in glass and soap production. The production of kelp, the burnt ashes of seaweed, has seventeenth-century origins in Ireland, but it wasn't until the eighteenth century that it became widespread due to the demand for alkaline soda. The kelp production industry in Antrim was underway by the second decade of the eighteenth century, however the first record of Rathlin is 1746 when the *Belfast News-Letter* reports the arrival of Mary of Rathlin carrying a cargo of kelp (*Belfast News-Letter* 8/8/1746; McErlean 2002). The nearest mainland Irish town to Rathlin, Ballycastle, had a glassworks in operation in the 1740s and thus provided a further local application for kelp.

Kelp became an important cash crop for coastal and island communities in Ireland and Scotland, in particular for the payment of rents. Seaweed was collected from the shore, or by boat, dried and burnt in kilns over a period of 12-24 hours. The resulting gelatinous mass solidified into the heavy kelp, which was extracted from the kilns and carried to storehouses for export. The method of production in the Western Isles of Scotland was said to be introduced to Uist from Ireland by a returning highlander, a McLeod, around 1730 (Clow & Clow 1947, 298). Certainly there are parallels in the form of the main monuments of the industry, the kelp kilns (Forsythe, 2006b).

On Rathlin in the middle of the nineteenth century there were said to be 150 kilns in operation (Gage 1995); archaeological survey recorded 83. These were found on the rocky terraces below the cliffs and scarps. The fact that they are located away from current field systems undoubtedly led to their survival. The kilns are rectangular in form and built at ground level or around a shallow pit. Constructed with drystone boulders, sometimes with sods packed around the sides, they are often incomplete, as extracting the heavy, solid kelp required one of the sides to be broken open (3). Similar rectangular kilns have been noted from Argyll and these contrast with a

At the crossroads: the historical archaeology of Rathlin Island

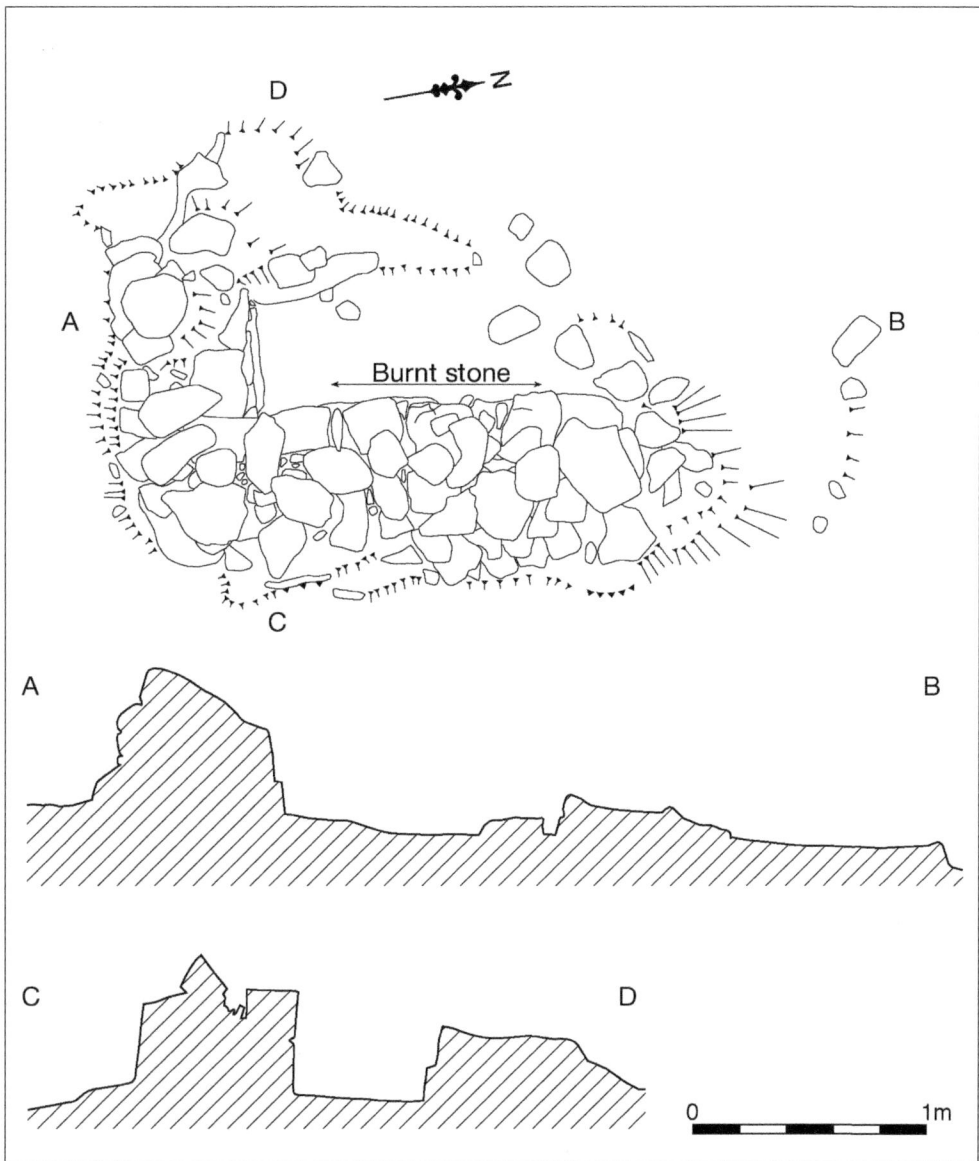

3 A kelp kiln in typically incomplete condition due to the necessity of breaking open the structure to extract the kelp

circular kiln tradition documented in the northern islands such as Orkney (Hay & Stell 1986, 163; Thomson 1983). In Ireland some have suggested that a circular kiln may represent the early phase of the industry, with the rectangular form adopted during the kelp revival of the 1840s (McErlean 2002). However, contemporary accounts show that both forms were in operation in the early phase of the industry and that the rectangular version was the favoured form (Beaton 1799). The arguments centred around the circulation of air being restricted in the circular kiln, inhibiting it from reaching the required temperature. Other monuments associated with the industry include roughly built seaweed-drying walls often in the vicinity of the kilns and three storehouses used to house the product prior to export.

In the eighteenth century much of the kelp went to the linen centres in Ireland, Scottish merchants were also present and came to dominate the market in the nineteenth century. Scottish kelp was held to be of superior quality to the Irish product. Later analysis would show that there was little to separate them, however canny Scots merchants took full advantage, buying Rathlin kelp at Irish prices and selling it in the markets of Liverpool as a Scottish product (Hamilton 1839). Production continued into the early nineteenth century when it faced extinction due to cheaper alternatives. However, the discovery of iodine and its applications in medicine and photography offered a lifeline to kelp-burners who concentrated on burning the iodine-rich laminaria species. By the mid-nineteenth century much of the kelp produced in Ireland was being shipped to Glasgow by merchants such as William Patterson (Booth 1979, 53). Although some areas of the coast seemed to let the now more limited and less profitable kelp industry decline, more marginal areas such as the islands, maintained the practice into the early twentieth century.

As well as benefiting from the legitimate business of kelp production, islanders were also involved in illegal pursuits. Smuggling was particularly prominent in the eighteenth and early nineteenth centuries. Coastal communities took advantage of the different tax regimes in Ireland and Britain to profit from black market trade in smuggled goods. Islands were excellent places to hide goods and Rathlin had been known as a storehouse for Scottish booty since the sixteenth century. In 1758 the new landlord, John Gage, presented a petition to Parliament in which he mentioned the 'vast numbers' engaged in smuggling (PRONI D/1011/15/11). The Isle of Man had an important role due to its anomalous constitutional position, but this was ended in 1765 and thereafter the smuggling intensified in North Antrim and Kintyre (Irvine 1976, 41). The Campbeltown customs records dating to the turn of the nineteenth century provide some fine insights into the trade (PRONI T/3082/7). They demonstrate that Rathlin and the small island of Sanda, off the southern tip of Kintyre, were vital to the trade and that the commodities involved included tobacco, spirits, salt, linen, wool, tea, herrings, oatmeal, soap and barley. Wider connections with Guersey and North America are also evident. In 1792, customs officers found 93 mats of unmanufactured tobacco leaf, three casks and 14 mats of rolled tobacco and two casks of muscovado sugar in Ushet Port at the southern tip of Rathlin. Although the smugglers' vessel got away, the revenue collector considered the damage done to the smuggling trade to be considerable. However, by 1805, Rathlin reappears in the records as 'a considerable depot of smuggling goods' (*ibid*). The first decade of the nineteenth century was a profitable one for smugglers. Gage was a minor when his father died in 1801 and an agent was in charge of Rathlin until 1811.

At the crossroads: the historical archaeology of Rathlin Island

The agent was heavily involved in smuggling and bribed a pliable customs officer to turn a blind eye (Gage 1995, 80). After Gage took over he arranged that the coastguard be permanently installed on the island (1821). Cottages were built for them on the south side of Church Bay and the small pier was erected. In addition, the entrance to Ushet port was blocked up to prevent its misuse and a coastguard house built in response to smuggling activity stands nearby (Clark 1996, 136).

All islands with demonstrable contact with the outside world by necessity required boats and places to launch and land them. Many of Rathlin's landing places may be considered as ancillary to both the kelp and smuggling trades. The landing places range from unmodified shores, to cleared beaches, to built harbour structures. Many were small in scale, reflecting the volume and size of the boats using them. Similarly, there is a range of sites reflecting the need to shelter boats from the elements, some relying on local topography and others on built structures. The boats used by islanders included skin-covered currachs in the eighteenth century, with the advantage of being easy to land and carry up the shore to safety. During the early nineteenth century these were superseded by wooden *drontheims* (the term a corruption of the Norwegian port of Trondheim where the boats originated). *Drontheims* were commonly 6-8.5m long and had to be dragged over a boulder shore to safety. Shelter for currachs in Irish islands is as simple as covering the upturned boats in sheets held down with weighted ropes. More formal facilities for skin and wooden boats are stone enclosures, often utilising the natural topography, e.g. gulleys, bedrock outcrops etc. A few are of naust-like construction, the top of the beach excavated and lined with stone. These provide a further link with Scandinavian and Scottish sites, although as noted in the Northern Isles, they are likely to be eighteenth and nineteenth century in date (e.g. Hunter 1992, 126).

One of the earliest detailed accounts of Rathlin in 1784 notes an interesting cultural division arising from the island's topography and the resulting economic effect (Hamilton 1839). The west end, being 300m above sea level, had less access to the shore, engaged less in the kelp trade and had few landing places. Agriculture was the main activity and Irish was universally spoken. The south end by contrast was more low-lying, with wider terraces and many small ports where kelp was made and exported. Here, by virtue of fishing and kelp trading contacts, the inhabitants were more versatile and English was well known. One of the research aims of the Rathlin survey project was to investigate how accurately this kind of environmental determinism would be reflected in the archaeological record. Most kelp monuments are indeed located on the southern limb of the island, unsurprisingly along accessible, seaweed-rich shores. However, there are a few outliers – mainly in Kebble townland at the western tip of the island; this area was cleared by the landlord for sheep in the nineteenth century and therefore activity here may represent a later additional drive for productivity by him. The other indicator of the claimed cultural division was the landing places. These are more widely spread than the kelp monuments although again most occur at the southern end to service kelp (and likely smuggling) requirements. The archaeology would tend to support the basis for the claimed cultural distinction in the island, albeit with a slightly more generous distribution of activities than that claimed in 1784.

SETTLEMENT AND IMPROVEMENT

In comparing Rathlin's emerging economy with some of the other islands off the north of Ireland in the modern period it is clear that it was relatively successful (Forsythe 2006a). It had varied agricultural land, engaged in some fishing, grew and processed flax for the linen industry, and had a well-regulated kelp industry. Its substantial role in smuggling would also have provided extra wealth. Irish landlords of the period generally have a very poor reputation, but the Gage family lived on Rathlin and actively participated in managing its economic life (smuggling excepted). It has been said that the mere presence of an Irish landlord on his estate for a significant part of the year was in itself an important aspect of improvement, so dire was their reputation for absenteeism (Busteed 2001, 19). Managing the resources of the island involved improvements to the island roads, enclosure of fields and division of the shore for seaweed gathering. Other expressions of improvement include the provision of facilities to support the island economy including the larger landing places, mills and a large corn-drying kiln. The process of controlling and centralising island production may also be seen in relation to kelp – Gage provided a storehouse for the product (*4*), weighed in the kelp and arranged for transfer to mainly Scottish merchant ships. A final aspect of improvement was the example set by the Gages in their own dwelling and fields. In the 1760s-1770s a row of weavers' cottages were built at Church Bay in the hope of stimulating the linen industry on the island. These attracted weavers from the mainland, but the newcomers eventually moved out and settled among the community. Gage rebuilt his Manor House (by 1790) on the site; only the east end of the new dwelling may contain the core of the original cottages (*5*). The Manor House reflected contemporary Georgian tastes in its form and façade and featured walled gardens for experimentation with new species that was fashionable among the gentry of the day. In addition, Gage enclosed his own fields with neat walls and large stone gateposts at the entrances.

The impact of the above reforms on the lives of ordinary islanders is harder to define. By the early nineteenth century large tracts of the island were converted to fields and the landlord had reformed the townland divisions on the island to reflect the distribution of settlement more accurately. The first edition Ordnance Survey map (1835) shows a mix of both dispersed and clachan-type dwellings. The island houses were firmly in the gable-ended byre tradition of much of the north and west of Ireland. They were in the process of change, becoming more sub-divided and incorporating features until then associated solely with houses of the rich. These included red brick fireplaces and window glass. Some changes were made for practical

4 The kelp storehouse in Church Bay

reasons – there was a lack of turf on the island and converting to coal (often traded for kelp) required burning in a grate and a flue to protect the thatch from hot sparks. Others, such as dummy chimneys, were cosmetic, showing the influence of Georgian preferences for symmetry on the island homes. Some buildings show parallels with Kintyre, in particular the range farmsteads or cottage ranges thought there to date to the 25 years either side of the turn of the nineteenth century (Dalglish 2003). These are characterised by linear buildings that have been heavily subdivided, combining the dwelling house, byre and store, but keeping livestock separate from human inhabitants (*6*). These dwellings have a wide distribution in Ireland (north of a line between Louth-Mayo) and while they may be associated with improvement it is clear that by the mid-nineteenth century they were out of favour with many reformers (Devon Commission 1847).

Whilst Rathlin undoubtedly benefited from its location on a busy shipping route, within easy distance of markets in Coleraine, Belfast, Glasgow and Liverpool, its development was in no small part due to its landlord. Although his system of allotting sections of land and shore to different tenants and charging additional shore rent was not without its disputes, it would seem that he knew the importance of

5 The Manor house, formerly cottages for mainland weavers and later the residence of the island's proprietors

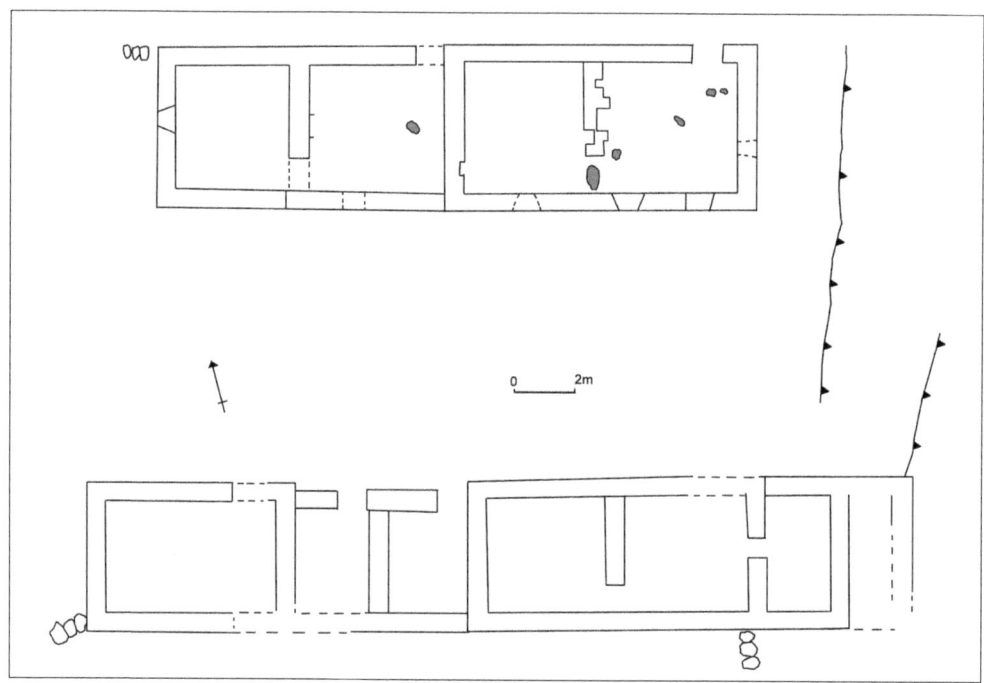

6 Vernacular cottages – the extended farmsteads at Ally Lower

making the island competitive and developing a successful process of production and export. It is also clear that he viewed his tenants not simply as labouring peasants for him and his family. This was best illustrated by his attitude in times of distress, the Great Famine (1847) caused him to cancel rents and buy corn for the islanders at his own expense, 'for I cannot forget that by their labour and industry in the time of their prosperity my family and myself derive all our support' (PRONI T/1883/65).

Rathlin Island has been affected by proximity to Scotland for centuries. Dynastic ambitions, trading opportunities and cultural connections have seen an exchange of goods, people and ideas. In the Early Medieval period the influence of the church and Irish dynasties extended into Scotland. By the thirteenth century Norman Scots reversed the trend, viewing the island as strategically central to their maritime power-base, this view would persist into the struggles for Gaelic or English dominance in the sixteenth century. As ties became more economic than political, Scotland and her expanding commercial centres continued to attract Rathlin produce and fashionable ideas on reform and improvement influenced both Scottish and Irish landowners.

REFERENCES

Armstrong, E.C.R. 1915, 'Four brooches preserved in the library of Trinity College Dublin', *Proc Roy Irish Acad* 32 C, no 15 & 16, 243-248

AU *Annals of Ulster* AD 431–1201, CELT: Corpus of Electronic Texts Edition (2003), University College Cork. Accessed by www.ucc.ie/celt/published/T100001A/index.html

Barnard, T.C. 1994, 'The Hartlib circle and the cult and culture of improvement in Ireland', in Greengrass, M., Leslie, M., & Raylor, T. (eds), *Samuel Hartlib and Universal Reformation*, 281-297, Cambridge

Barnard, T.C. 1995, 'Improving clergymen, 1660-1760', in Ford, A., McGuire, J. & Milne, K. (eds), *As by Law Established, The Church of Ireland Since the Reformation*, 136-151, Dublin

Beaton, A. 1799, 'On the art of making kelp, and of increasing the growth of marine plants from which it is made', *Trans Highland Soc* 1, 32-41

Booth, E. 1979, 'The history of the seaweed industry. Part 3: the iodine industry', *Chemistry and Industry*, 52-55

Briggs, S. 1974, 'A boat burial from County Antrim', *Med Archaeol* 18, 158-60

Brooke, D. 1994, *Wild Men and Holy Places*, Edinburgh

Busteed, M. 2001, 'Sir James Caldwell, c.1720-84: An Anglo-Irish landlord in an Age of Improvement', *Irish Stud Rev* 9 (3), 317-329

Campbell, E. 2001, 'Were the Scots Irish?', *Antiquity* 75 (288), 285-292

Clark, W. 1996, *Rathlin: its Island Story*, reprinted 1971, Coleraine

Clow, A. & Clow, N.L. 1947, 'The natural and economic history of kelp', *Annals of Science* 5 (4), 297-316

Cochrane, Dr. 1906, 'Exhibits', *J Roy Soc Antiq* 16, 450-454

Connolly, M., Coyne F. & Lynch L. 2005, *Underworld: Death and Burial in Cloghermore Cave, Co. Kerry*, Bray, Wordwell

Conway, M. 1995, 'Antrim 1994:008 'Shandragh', Knockans South, Rathlin Island', in Bennett, I. (ed.), *Archaeological Excavations in Ireland: Excavations in 1994*, Dublin

Dalglish, C. 2003, *Rural Society in the Age of Reason. An archaeology of the emergence of modern life in the southern Scottish highlands*, New York

Dolley, M. 1974, 'A forgotten Hiberno-Norse find from Rathlin Island', *Seaby's Coin and Medal Bulletin* (Feb), 39-40

Duffy, S. 1991, 'The Bruce Brothers and the Irish Sea world, 1306-29', *Cambr Med Celtic Stud* 21, 55-86

Forsythe, W. 2006a *Improving Insularity: An archaeology of the islands off the north coast of Ireland in the later historic period, 1700-1847*, unpublished PhD thesis, University of Ulster

Forsythe, W. 2006b, 'The archaeology of the kelp industry in northern Irish islands', *Internat J Nautical Archaeol* 35 (2), 218-229

Forsythe, W. & McConkey, R. (forthcoming), *An Archaeological Survey of Rathlin Island*

Gage, C. 1995 [1851], *A History of the Island of Rathlin Island*, Coleraine

Hamilton, W. 1839, *Letters Concerning the Northern Coast of the County of Antrim; containing observations on the antiquities, manners and customs of that country*, Coleraine

Harrison, S.H. 2001, 'Viking graves and grave-goods in Ireland', in Larsen, A.C. (ed.), *The Vikings in Ireland*, 61-75, Roskilde

Hay, G.D. & Stell, G.P. 1986, *Monuments of Industry an Illustrated Historical Record*, Edinburgh

Herbert, M. 1989, 'The preface to Amra Coluim Cille', in Ó. Corráin, D., Breatnach, L. & McCone, K. (eds), *Sages, Saints and Storytellers*, 67-75, Maynooth (Maynooth Monogr 2)

Hill, G. 1978 [1873], *An Historical Account of the MacDonnells of Antrim*, Ballycastle

Hunter, J.R. 1992, 'The survey and excavation of boat nausts at Hurnip's Point, Deerness, Orkney', *Internat J Nautical Archaeol* 21 (2), 125-133

Irvine, J. 1976, 'The Campbeltown customs records', *The Glynns* 4, 36-47

Larsen, A.C. 2001, *The Vikings in Ireland*, Roskilde

MacDonald, A. 1997, *The Kingdom of the Isles: Scotland's Western Seaboard, c.1100-c.1336*, East Linton

MacDonald, A. 1999, 'Treachery in the remotest territories of Scotland: northern resistance to the Canmore Dynasty, 1130-1230', *The Canadian J Hist* 33, 161-192

MacDonnell, H. 1987, 'Glenarm Friary and the Bissets', *The Glynns* 15, 34-49

Marsden, J. 1995, *Sea-Road of the Saints: Celtic Holy Men in the Hebrides*, Edinburgh

McConkey, R. & Moore, P. forthcoming, 'Carrivindoon huts' in Forsythe, W. & McConkey, R., *An Archaeological survey of Rathlin Island*

McDiarmid, M.P. & Stevenson, J.A.C. 1980, *Barbour's Bruce*, 3 vols, Edinburgh

McErlean, T. 2002, 'The archaeology of the eighteenth and early nineteenth century kelp industry in Strangford Lough', in McErlean, T., McConkey, R., & Forsythe, W. (eds), *Strangford Lough: an Archaeological Survey of the Maritime Cultural Landscape*, 334-58, Belfast

McNeill, T.E. 1980, *Anglo-Norman Ulster*, Edinburgh

McNeill, T.E. 1983, 'The stone castles of northern County Antrim', *Ulster J Archaeol* 46, 101-128

O'Boyle, M. 1939, 'Place names of Rathlin Island', *J Down & Connor Hist Soc* 10, 44-54

Ó Corráin, D. 2001, 'The Vikings in Ireland', in Larsen, A.C. (ed.), *The Vikings in Ireland*, 17-27, Roskilde

O'Laverty, J. 1887, *An Historical Account of the Diocese of Down and Connor, Ancient and Modern*, vol. IV, Dublin

Owen, O. & Dalland, M. 1999, *Scar: A Viking Boat Burial on Sanday, Orkney*, East Linton

Sharpe, R. 1995, *Adomnan of Iona: Life of St. Columba*, London

Shetelig, H. 1954, *Viking Antiquities in Great Britain and Ireland* Part, VI, Oslo

Stringer, K. 1993, 'Periphery and core in thirteenth century Scotland: Alan son of Roland, lord of Galloway and constable of Scotland', in Grant A. & Stringer K. (eds), *Medieval Scotland: Essays Presented to G.W.S. Barrow*, 82-113, Edinburgh

Stokes, W. 1899, 'The Bodleian Amra Choluimb Chille', *Revue Celtique* 20, 30-55, 132-83, 248-89, 400-37

Thomson, W.P.L. 1983, *Kelp-making in Orkney*, Orkney

Warner, R. 1973-74, 'The reprovenancing of two important penannular brooches of the Viking period', *Ulster Journal of Archaeology*, Vols 36 & 37, 58-70

Young, A.I. 1929, *Three Hundred Years in Innishowen*, Belfast

PRIMARY SOURCES

Cal Carew Mss: Calendar of the Carew Manuscripts 1575-1588, Brewer, J.S. & Bullen, W. (eds) 1868, London

Cal Carew Mss: Calendar of the Carew Manuscripts James I. Brewer, J S & Bullen, W. (eds) 1974, reprint 1873, London

Cal Doc Ireland: Calendar of Documents Relating to Ireland 1171-1251, Sweetman, H.S. (ed.) 1875, London

Devon Commission 1847 *Digest of evidence taken before Her Majesty's Commissioners of inquiry into the state of the law and practice in respect to the occupation of land in Ireland*, Dublin.

PUBLIC RECORD OFFICE OF NORTHERN IRELAND:

PRONI T/3082/7 Father Webb's copy of the Record books of Customs service of the Port of Campeltown (1739-1816).

PRONI D/1011/15/11 J Gage Petition to Irish Parliament (1758).

PRONI T/1883/65 R Gage correspondence on the impact of famine/emigration.

9

A FIFER IN THE NORTH: WILLIAM BRUCE AND THE LAIRD'S HOUSES OF EARLY MODERN SHETLAND

Sabina Strachan

INTRODUCTION

The enigmatic ruins at Sumburgh, Shetland, that Sir Walter Scott named 'Jarlshof' (NGR: HU 3982 0953) in 1821 (Scott 1871, 10), now form the most upstanding part of the complex of Late Bronze Age to early modern excavated remains on public view at the site (*1*). About 1m of overburden was cleared in the 1890s and areas of the south range were excavated to reveal part of the broch and a post-broch structure (now backfilled). Unfortunately, in these early interventions little evidence was recovered or analysed from the post-medieval occupation layers. Nevertheless, significant documentary sources survive and it is the link between the house and one lowland Scot, William Bruce, that intrigues the present writer.

William is first recorded in Shetland in the 1580s and the earliest part of the house appears to pre-date 1592. In Shetland terms this makes Jarlshof the earliest surviving laird's house presently identified, with the next examples dating to the mid-seventeenth century. Although there would have been comparatively significant landholders residing in Shetland before the close of the sixteenth century, the landholding pattern began to shift appreciably at that time, with the Stewart earls being accompanied by a greater influx of Scots. William Bruce represents one of these incomers, and with them came the prevailing house type of their peers: the laird's house.

1 Aerial view of Jarlshof. Crown Copyright, Historic Scotland

Shetland offered attractive opportunities to the sons of minor lairds or small proprietors who were more common in sheriffdoms such as Fife, Angus, Perth, Stirling and the Lothians 'in certain regions that were not dominated by great magnates' (Goodare 2001, 1104). The later impact of 'improvement' activities, however, was naturally far-reaching in east-central Scotland and thus few examples of laird's houses survive from the late sixteenth century in that area. Therefore, the survival of Jarlshof, an early, imported form of laird's house into Shetland, and the longevity of this type in the islands into the seventeenth and eighteenth centuries, presents us with a welcome insight into the form and function of the emergent early modern laird's house in Scotland as a whole.

SHETLAND LANDHOLDING AND SCOTTISH 'INCOMERS'

A medieval map of Shetland would have consisted of a patchwork of small landholdings. Most of the population would have been tenants and the elite would have held their lands under odal tenure, as opposed to feudal tenure. The odal estates were obliged in tenure with '*scat*' (a property tax) rather than tribute or service being owed by the odallers. Representatives managed the estates of the absentee landlords: primarily these were the lords of Norway (noble Scandinavian families), the bishops of Orkney, the canons of Kirkwall Cathedral and the archdeacon of Shetland (Smith

1978, 12; Sharples 1998, 203). The odal tenure system resulted in fragmentary estates as all heirs were entitled to portions. The eldest son inherited the 'heid buil', the principal landholding (Goudie 1878, 491), which is likely to have contained the most substantial dwelling. Unfortunately, none survive and the sixteenth-century references lack sufficient detail to help reconstruct the houses of odallers.

The earliest Scottish residents may well have been clerics, who first came to Shetland in the second half of the fourteenth century once the archdeaconry of Shetland and bishopric of Orkney were in Scottish hands. There seems to have been a further influx of Scots who acquired odal possessions after the annexation of the Northern Isles to the Scottish Crown in 1472. The Sinclair earls of Orkney (1379-1470) also held odal lands in Shetland, and their descendants remained active into the early modern period (Donaldson 1983, 9-10; Crawford 1985, 241 & 249). Orkney, as the seat of the earldom and the bishopric of Orkney, and with its superior fertility, was naturally a greater draw than Shetland. However, most Scots travelled to the far north after 1565 as connections and assistants of Earl Robert Stewart (Crawford 1999, 18 & 22). A survey of the register of testaments 1600-48 shows that 25-30 per cent of those registered had Scottish surnames (Donaldson 1983, 13). G. Donaldson (*ibid*, 15) goes on to suggest that the actual proportion of Shetland residents of Scots origin may in fact have been higher, as some, such as 'Anderson', already conformed to, or were changed to, the traditional patronymic system.

Inheritance by primogeniture allowed larger landholdings to develop after the introduction of feudal tenure in Shetland from 1588-9. Grants under the new form of tenure were often consolidated by acquisitions of odal land. Such policies resulted in individuals holding sizeable tracts, perhaps even controlling more than one estate, which supported significant numbers of sub-tenants. Many of these feuars were first-generation lowland Scots, often from landed families, who may be assumed to have brought with them to Shetland the characteristic early modern laird's house. The majority of surviving examples date to the eighteenth century, though there are a few, like the Old Haa of Brough, Yell (NGR: HU 5200 7948) and Tangwick Haa, Eshaness (NGR: HU 2324 7768), that were built before 1700. Sixteenth-century houses of lairds of Scottish origin are also known from the records, one example being the 1575 house of Bartholomew Strang in Unst (Shet Docs, no. 20), but little surviving fabric has been dated to this period.[1] The house of William Bruce at Sumburgh is the exception.

WILLIAM BRUCE, FROM FIFE TO SHETLAND

Earl Robert Stewart appointed his half-brother, Laurence Bruce of Cultmalindie (Perthshire), Great Foud (supreme law officer) of Shetland in 1571. Both Robert and Laurence were warded for two years from 1574/5; after their release Laurence was created admiral depute of Shetland and Robert's titles were confirmed. By 1585,

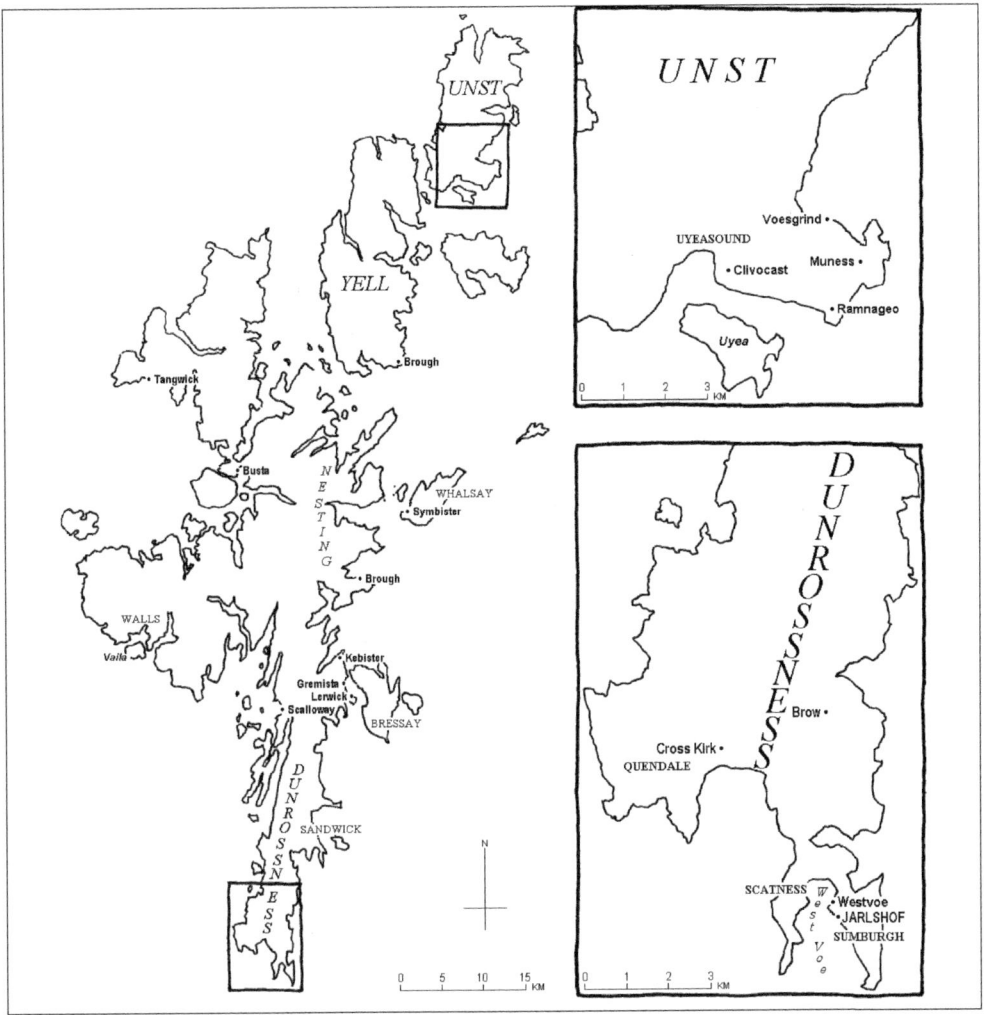

2 Shetland placenames mentioned in the text. *S Strachan*

Laurence's entourage included one William Bruce who is described as his 'weill belovit and trustie servitor' when Laurence set in tack to him 32 merks land in Symbister, Whalsay, that year (Shet Docs, no. 75). William is variously styled 'in' or 'of' Symbister in documents from 1586. He may have travelled to Shetland earlier, as a 'William Bruce' witnessed a document signed in Bressay in January 1581/2 (Shet Docs, no. 28); it seems reasonable to tie in William's relocation with Laurence's appointment as Principal Sheriff of Shetland in 1580/1. William apparently journeyed to the mainland often, at least initially, on behalf of his master. For example, 'William Bruce in Symbuster' or 'Simbister' is present at Cultmalindie and Edinburgh in January 1586/7 as 'bailie' for Laurence and within six months had returned north to ratify the transaction (Shet Docs, nos 89 & 98).

William was probably a younger son of a lairdly family and it has been suggested that he may have secured his position with Laurence through being close kin (Armstrong 1882, 6; Beveridge 1893, 175, fns 4 & 5). No record of William's birth or parentage is known, but as he retired to Crail and built up considerable business interests in that area, it is possible that he originated from Fife. W.B. Armstrong (1882, 13) hypothesised that his brother may have been Andrew Bruce, laird of Balfarg (Glenrothes, Fife), who is recorded as William's attorney in 1619, and in the same sasine one of the witnesses is 'Andrew Bruce', who is described as William's 'brother-german' (full- as opposed to half-brother).

We may presume that William built his own house in Symbister since the former proprietor, Colbein Ormesone, was still resident until at least the end of 1587 (Shet Docs, nos 38-9, 47 & 104). William's house is specifically referred to in 1592, and in 1608 an instrument of sasine is signed in 'the hall and dwelling house of William in Symbester' (Shet Docs, nos 209 & 445), but no trace of it survives near the present Symbister House of 1823. It seems likely that it was situated in the vicinity, however, as the lower courses of a *c.*1750 door jamb survive nearby and perhaps relate to a remodelling of the *c.*1585 house or courtyard (NGR: HU 5402 6233; RCAHMS 1946, vol. I, 88). By August 1589 William made a fortuitous marriage to Margaret Stewart, widow of William Sinclair of Underhoull or Uyea and niece of Earl Robert, by whom he acquired considerable landholdings in Unst (Shet Docs, no. 148). Laurence Bruce also built up a large estate in this northernmost island and built his seat, Muness Castle, here by 1598 (RCAHMS 1946, vol. III, 129). William may have also built a residence in Unst. Clivocast has been suggested as a possible site (Beveridge 1893, 177, fn 1) but later, a Gilbert Bruce of Clivocast of the Muness Bruces appears on the record (Armstrong 1882, 6) and he may be the rightful builder. Unfortunately, the masonry of the ruinous structure was reused in the later nineteenth century and the present writer has not been able to verify the suggested connection.

In March 1592 Earl Robert's heir, Patrick, issued a feu charter to the existing occupant, William Bruce of Symbister, of the 40 merks 'kingsland' (part of the lordship of Shetland which derived from the Norwegian royal estates) in Sumburgh and Scatness, Dunrossness parish, and four merks 'Provost's land' (lands which had belonged to the cathedral of Bergen) in Sumburgh (Shet Docs, no. 197). It is possible that William's tenancy began when he married Earl Robert's niece, as the 40 merks kingsland had been amongst those which Robert ordained 'salbe reservit to our selff to be usit and disponit upon be us at our plesor' in January 1588/9 (Shet Docs, no. 132). The most favourable land was to be found in Dunrossness, Shetland's southernmost parish and it was noted in the 1680s that its inhabitants were '(for the most part) Strangers from Scotland, and Orkney' (Kay 1711, 22). The first known record of William's designation 'of Sumburgh' dates to 1597 (Shet Docs, no. 257); this is interchangeable with 'of Symbister' in documents thereafter. The terms of the 1592 feu charter included the reservation to Patrick of right and

3 'Ruins of Jarlshoff', 1867 (Reid 1869, 45)

title to a house and yard lately established on the lands of Sumburgh to the south of 'the Newhall', and the use of pasturage there and in Scatness when he was in residence. The present author believes that 'the Newhall' is a house of the earls, of which no trace now survives, and the house to its south was the house built by William Bruce, Jarlshof. Unlike Symbister and Clivocast, considerable upstanding remains survive.

JARLSHOF: THE BUILDING SEQUENCE

Jarlshof was certainly in an advanced state of ruination by 1867, when it was depicted by John Reid (*3*). During the course of the 1897-1905 excavations of the Iron Age structures at the site, its walls were laid bare thus 'proving it to have been a much larger place than had been supposed, [though] the clearing of the debris yielded nothing of note' (Bruce 1906, 13). Its initial interpretation was left to the Royal Commission on the Ancient and Historical Monuments of Scotland (RCAHMS) investigators (1946, vol. III, 16-20) who visited in 1935. J.R.C. Hamilton (1956, 194-7) followed the RCAHMS interpretation in the Ministry of Works monograph of the 1930-52 excavations. The present author has reached different conclusions, however, on both the period over which Jarlshof was occupied, and the identities of its builders. On the latter point, the present author would question whether the Stewart earls were responsible for any part of Jarlshof, and this aspect will be discussed more fully elsewhere (Strachan, in preparation). The present contribution, however, looks particularly at the relationship between Jarlshof and lowland laird's houses and their influence on the subsequent development of such houses in Shetland.

The house consisted of four ranges around a courtyard until 1951, when the west range was demolished (*4*). If we first consider the likely building sequence, the north

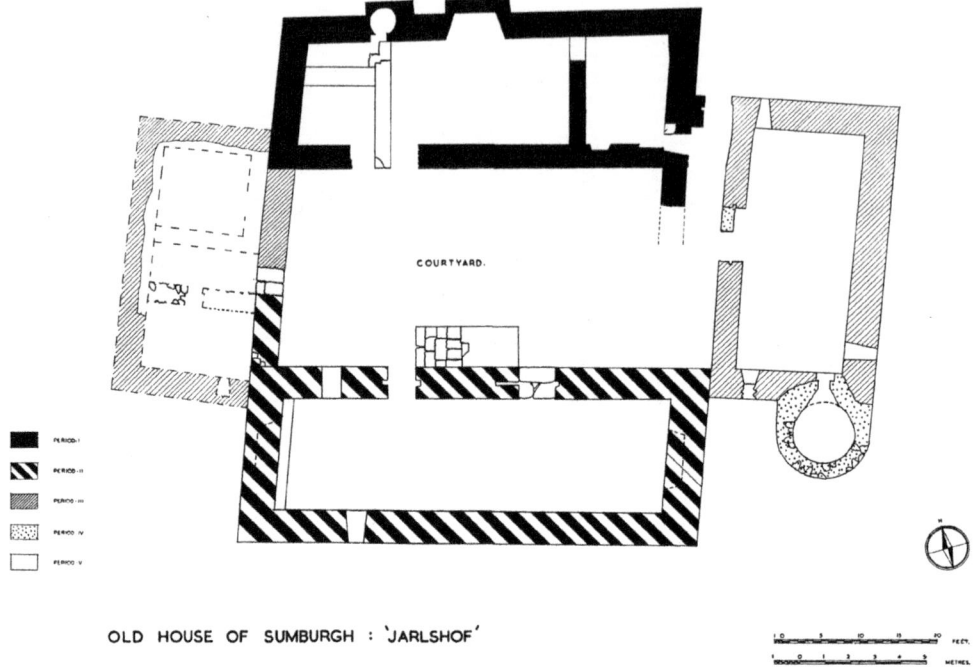

4 Plan of Jarlshof. Crown Copyright, Historic Scotland

range might be the earliest of the four, its floor being 0.4m below the level of the courtyard (RCAHMS 1946, vol. III, 18-19; Hamilton 1953, 35). Certainly it pre-dates the east and west wings, but its level may relate to a natural slope rather than indicating that it cannot be contemporaneous with either the courtyard or the south range. The supposition that it was built before the south range probably relates more to the RCAHMS (1946, vol. III, 20) interpretation of the documentary sources, that the north range must represent 'the Newhall' and thus the new house to its south must be the present south range. Returning to the building archaeology, short stubs of walling are bonded into the east and south walls of the north range suggesting that a building or an enclosure butted up against it. It is possible that the present south range replaced an earlier, but less permanent, building. It is likely that collapsed broch material would have provided a quarry for construction on the south side of the courtyard. The north range, perhaps an enclosure, and presumably other contemporary buildings (such as a south range) together constitute Phase I of the known sequence at Jarlshof.

An enclosure or an east range seems to have been reduced or abandoned before the present south range was built as the extant east gable wall projects into its presumed footprint. A length of wall, bonded with, and extending north from, the west end of the south range, suggests that the courtyard could have been entered from the west through a gateway in a screen wall. The east and west ranges post-date the building of both north and south blocks as they are not bonded into the latter's gable walls. The building of the west range would have necessitated the provision of an entrance to the courtyard from the east. The east side of the courtyard may initially have been open, or enclosed by no more than a screen wall. When a range was built here, however, it made provision for the present entrance arrangement at its junction with the north range (Hamilton 1956, 197; RCAHMS 1946, vol. III, 18). The addition of the east and west ranges may therefore have been conceived as part of a single remodelling.

Having considered the physical evidence, careful interpretation of documentary sources provides some parameters for dating its initial and subsequent phases of construction, though a date for its abandonment is more difficult to establish. The 1592 feu charter provides a secure date by which time a house to the south of the Newhall had been built. In August 1604 Earl Patrick forcibly exchanged 36 merks land in Sandwick (Dunrossness parish) for William Bruce's 44 merks land in Sumburgh and Scatness and 46 merks land in Underhoull (Shet Docs, no. 391). Patrick was persuaded to rescind this contract 15 months later, with William regaining entry on 25 November 1605. In the intervening period the occupiers were Patrick, together with his chamberlain, servants and tenants, and, specifically, his wife's nephew Malcolm Sinclair of Quendale (Shet Docs, no. 411; Grant 1907, 272 & 292). It is possible that Jarlshof was modified either during or immediately after William's absence, though we cannot assume that the earl himself would have occupied or remodelled William's house in Sumburgh over 1604-5. By that time Patrick's main residence in Shetland was Scalloway Castle (built 1599-1602).

The next incentive for modification may have been in response to the extensive damage caused by the illegal entry into the 'toun' of Sumburgh by Earl Patrick and followers on various days in June and July 1608. The perpetrators included William's stepsons Francis Sinclair of Uyea and Robert Sinclair of Ramnageo, their brother-in-law Richard Leask in Toft and their cousin Adam Sinclair of Brew (Brow) (Shet Docs, no. 472; Laing 1857, 390). The records show a catalogue of complaints by Bruce against the Sinclairs and vice versa since William had acquired Underhoull through William Sinclair's widow. The Brough Sinclairs (Nesting parish) had previously ransacked William's house in Symbister in 1592 (Shet Docs, no. 209) and in 1602 William had, successfully, laid claim to Francis and Robert Sinclair's lands.[2] It was shortly thereafter, however, that Patrick's influence began to wane. He last set foot in Shetland in 1608 and was held in ward in Edinburgh and Dumbarton from the summer of 1609. His earldom was confiscated two years later and he was executed for treason in 1615 (Thomson 1987, 172-8).

The decreet of the Lords of Council of February 1609 recorded that those found guilty of the illegal entry of 1608 had installed their followers, tenants and servants in the toun of Sumburgh. They had enclosed three Scots acres (1.54ha) of land with a 'great head dyke built of fail [turf], stone, earth and other materials' between the earl's house ('castle') and William's house in order to appropriate this land, said to be 'growing with green corn', for Patrick's use (Shet Docs, no. 473; Laing 1857, 391). The enclosure still existed at the beginning of 1609 as the guilty parties were ordained to demolish the dyke and restore it to its former condition and into William's possession. There followed a series of contracts between William and these men; first William discharged Patrick of his part and, in return, the earl consented that the house built by him on the shore of West Voe be either demolished or 'enjoyed and possessed' by William (Shet Docs, no. 480). Patrick's enforced absence from Shetland and Orkney was also soon to begin and a house at Sumburgh was not included amongst those which were to be handed over to Bishop Law in 1610 (RPC, vol. VIII, 444). Perhaps William did quarry from the earl's house beside the laird's 'baikhous' (Shet Docs, no. 480) for works at Jarlshof from 1609 and/or used it to supplement the ancillary buildings he had there. William's enhanced status is shown by the fact that he was also made a Commissioner of Peace for Shetland in 1610 (Grant 1907, 21).

The final phase of the occupation of Jarlshof is difficult to gauge from documentary sources. It is interesting to note that a sheriff court was held in 'the new house at Soundbrugh' in 1617, but it is not possible to say whether it was Bruce's house at Sumburgh that was used for the proceedings (Shet Ct Bk, 52). William himself is represented in land transferals in Shetland until 1622 (*ibid*, 94-95), but had conveyed his estates of Sumburgh and Symbister to his eldest son Robert (d.1636) the previous year. Shortly after his wife, Margaret Stewart's death in 1607, William remarried. His new wife, Isabella Spence, may have been a daughter of Sir James Spence of Wormiston in Fife (Beveridge 1893, 178-9; Grant 1907, 20-2). It is clear that William settled permanently in Fife with his second family in the early 1620s, consolidated his landholdings in the parishes of Crail, St Andrews and Kingsbarns, and died there in about 1630; his memorial survives in Crail churchyard (NGR: NO 6140 0799). Of William's Shetland estates, the principal holding was Sumburgh, as it was inherited by Robert's eldest son William (d.1675), with Symbister granted to his second son.

During John Bruce's excavations, plain head- and foot-stones in the courtyard were uncovered and the positions of the graves recorded; it was noted that the fact it had been used for burials 'appears to have been very much lost sight of' (Bruce 1906, 13-14 & fig. 1). The parish burial-ground was at Cross Kirk, Quendale and its deficiency was noted as early as the 1680s; 'if it blow but an ordinary gale, many of the Coffins are discovered, and sometimes naked Corpses' (Kay 1711, 17). A new church was built in 1790-1 at Brow and the masonry of the old church was quarried for Quendale House and its outbuildings (Mill *Diary* 1889, lxviii & lxxi). The Bruce Mausoleum (demolished 1936; see 5) was built to the immediate north-west of Jarlshof in 1867, next to an existing burial enclosure. Four unmarked burials were discovered in 1936-7 and the family papers were researched to discover their identities. The earliest of these interments belonged to John Bruce of Sumburgh (1764-1831), his wife and their children who died in infancy.[3] Jarlshof need not

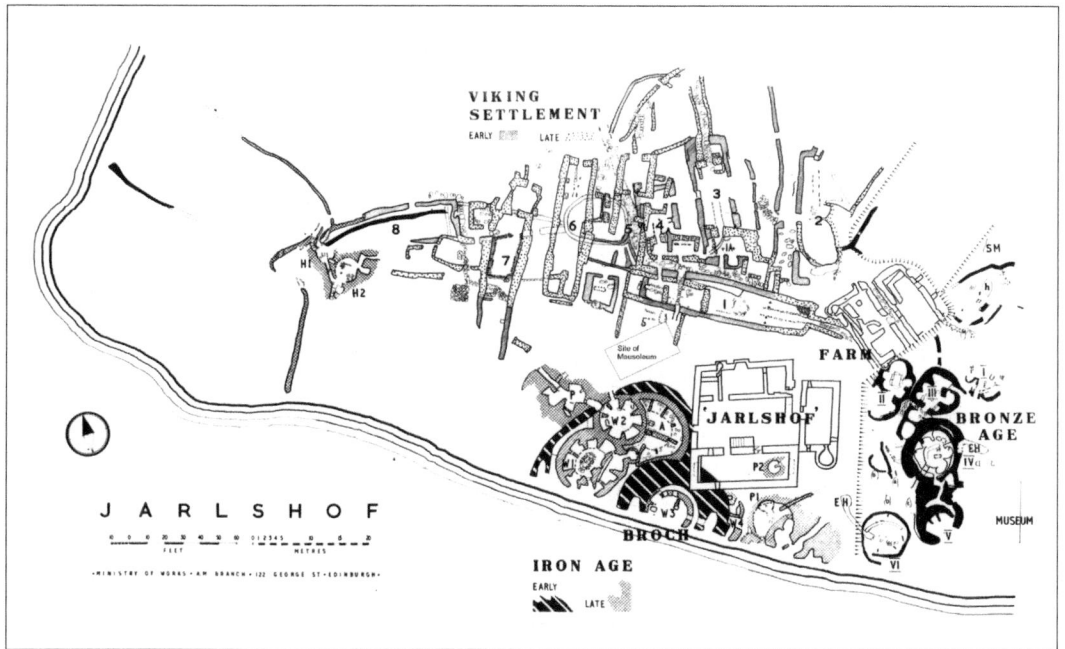

5 Plan of the complex at Jarlshof overmarked by S. Strachan to show position of mausoleum demolished in 1936. *Original plan is Crown Copyright, Historic Scotland*

necessarily have been abandoned before c.1800, since some landed families did build mausolea in the policies of their residences, however, the unusually close proximity between the two might suggest that the family's main residence was elsewhere by this date (R Fawcett *pers. comm.*). As many as 35 graves are indicated on the plan of the first excavations (Bruce 1906, fig. 1), in addition to the burial enclosures within west and north ranges of Jarlshof, the mausoleum, and its neighbouring enclosure. It seems possible, therefore, that Jarlshof could have been used as an alternative to Cross Kirk as a parish burial-ground at some point after the house was abandoned, either for a reasonably protracted period or as a result of a catastrophe such as an epidemic or shipwreck (Hamilton 1956, 196).[4]

A seawall was built to prevent further erosion of the broch and wheelhouses shortly after excavations began in 1897 (Bruce 1906, 12) and perhaps it was this progressive encroachment of the sea that had earlier spurred the Bruces of Sumburgh to build anew on a site further inland. When in the seventeenth or eighteenth centuries this may have taken place is not clear but its successor could have been Sumburgh Farmhouse (NGR: HU 4031 0936), which was built on higher ground 1.5km to the east. It has been suggested that Jarlshof was superseded by a new house on the site of the present day Sumburgh Hotel (NGR: HU 4001 0956) by the 1680s (RCAHMS 1946, vol. III, 20), but there is no corroborating evidence that the hotel, built as 'The Hall' in 1866-7, was constructed on the site of an earlier house.

JARLSHOF: LOWLAND PARALLELS

It is therefore worth making comparisons with lairds' houses from mainland Scotland in an attempt to suggest a more secure dating and to trace their influences in surviving Shetland examples. Hamilton (1956, 196) surmised that the north range at Jarlshof originally functioned as a single-room dwelling, with a masonry partition wall inserted at an early date to create a smaller room at the east end accessed from the truncated main room. The entrance is at the west end of the south wall and a recess indicates the likely position of a window. A fireplace was contained within a projection in the middle of the north wall and the projection to its west has been interpreted as a garderobe. Of the east room, Hamilton (1953, 35) wrote: 'burnt and cracked stones on the inner face of the gable shows that fires had been kindled in the room, but whether these were an original arrangement it is difficult to determine'. Its walls only survive to a maximum height of 1.5m, so the original number of storeys is a matter of conjecture. Evidence for open halls on the ground floor survive in a few mainland laird's houses such as Balsarroch in western Galloway (NGR: NW 9935 6913; Smith 1985) and Pitcastle in highland Perthshire (NGR: NN 9731 5546; Dunbar 1960). They probably date to the first half of the seventeenth century. In both cases the hall was ceiled over at a later date. Originally, parts of the roofspace probably contained lofts reached by ladders.

Under odal tenure, and then as a feuar under Earl Patrick from 1592, William Bruce's tenancy of his holdings in Dunrossness would have been reasonably secure and he was already a fairly substantial landholder. The north range could have been the kitchen range from the outset, perhaps with a contemporary house on the site of the present south range. Alternatively, and upon comparison with other examples, it could have had two storeys with the principal room or hall on the ground floor and sleeping accommodation above, supported by ancillary buildings. A close parallel may have been Graemeshall in Orkney (*6*) (NGR: HY 4876 0170), first built by Bishop George Graham who hailed from Dunblane, and dating from *c*.1615 to 1644 (Schrank 1995, 12 & 102). As it was demolished before 1874, the actual arrangement of rooms is unknown, but the one-and-a-half storey south range is particularly significant if this can be used as a model for Jarlshof. Pitcairn House in Glenrothes, built *c*.1650 (NGR: NO 2704 0264), and the detached hall of Smailholm Tower in Roxburghshire, remodelled *c*.1645 (NGR: NT 6380 3467) have been subject to modern excavations, and provide some, albeit later, examples which may be compared to Jarlshof.

The ground floor of the two-storey-and-garret Pitcairn was divided into three compartments, the external door led into the central room which had a large fireplace in a substantial cross-wall, the smaller end rooms were accessed from it, and the west gable had a small recessed fireplace (Reid 1981). At Smailholm, three compartments were created from the two of the original hall building next to the tower around 1645. It certainly reached two storeys, perhaps with an attic also,

6 Graemeshall, Orkney, photographed before 1874. *Copyright Orkney Library & Archives*

judging by the position of a roof raggle on the tower. Here, the main access was through a gateway in the outer curtain wall into a narrow courtyard. The hall building was on the north side with a service wing to the south. The excavators suggested that the tower itself no longer fulfilled a primary function at this date and that the central room of the north range had a dual function as hall and kitchen. A large projecting fireplace was built on the south side of this room, from where the end rooms were accessed, and the east room had a small fireplace (Good & Tabraham 1988, 246-8 & 262-4). The large projecting chimneystacks at both Smailholm and Jarlshof could imply that their roofs were originally thatched. Using these later parallels, the ground floor of the north range at Jarlshof could have had two or three rooms as later alterations of its west end may disguise its original arrangement. Also, we cannot discount the use of timber partitions as such evidence is likely to have been overlooked by the antiquarian excavators or may underlie masonry walls. At both Pitcairn and Smailholm, one of the end rooms has a (recessed) fireplace, and if Jarlshof can be seen as a precursor of these later examples, then its east room could have been heated by a fireplace beneath a 'hingin' lum' (canopied flue). At all three houses it is not possible to be certain that the first floor did not contain the main living apartment and that the central ground-floor room functioned as a kitchen only, as the former existence of an external stair cannot be ruled out.[5]

Very few laird's houses, as opposed to tower-houses, survive anywhere in Scotland that are as early in date as the c.1589 Jarlshof and neither is there much in the way of reliable archaeological data. One very relevant example, however, is Bay House in Dysart, Fife (NGR: NT 3033 9202) built in 1585, and, as it is known that William Bruce maintained his Fife links, this probably represents a form with which he would have been familiar. It also typifies the prevailing form of sixteenth-century residences in Fife, described by the RCAHMS (1933, lvi–lvii) as the 'palace' plan, that is long, low, narrow ranges around a courtyard. Bay House was a high status abode, built by Patrick Sinclair, son of Lord Sinclair whose main seats were Ravenscraig Castle near Kirkcaldy and The Hermitage in Dysart (now demolished). Patrick built his house at the Pan Ha', from where coal and salt were shipped across the North Sea to the Low Countries. It consists of two ranges separated by a narrow courtyard and was served by stables and a garden. Geoffrey Hay's reconstruction drawing (7) of the south range shows three compartments on the ground floor, each entered separately from the outside, the east room being the kitchen and the west room a chamber with a recessed fireplace and window. The hall is reached by a forestair and its open roof is adorned with a decorative painted scheme. A covered gallery is thought to have run along part of the north wall and it had a corbelled-out chimneystack on the south side. Two heated rooms, one with a garderobe, are entered off the hall with garret rooms above (Swan & McNeill 1997, 12, 17, 108, 110 & 123). Some remodelling of the north range at Jarlshof created rooms independently accessed from outside, like the ground floor of Bay House, and the extruded fireplace is also a good parallel. The present author has not come across any references to the existence of painted joists or boards in Shetland laird's houses and it seems unlikely that the islands could have sustained such artisans, except perhaps at major buildings such as Muness and Scalloway castles.

JARLSHOF: THE LATER PHASES

The south range at Jarlshof was more substantial than its partner and, as its gables stand close to their original heights, we know that it reached two-storeys-and-garret (RCAHMS 1946, vol. III, 16-17). It had two independently-accessed storerooms on the ground floor, the west one being lit by two small windows. The east one was unlit, had a slightly lower floor level and its door was secured by a drawbar. The absence of fireplaces on the ground floor suggests that the north range served as a kitchen by this date. The principal rooms in the south range were reached by a forestair. The gable fireplaces suggest that there were at least two chambers, though it could have heated one large hall. Alternatively, there is not enough surviving fabric to rule out the possibility of a lateral chimneystack for a third room such as at Bay

A Fifer in the North: William Bruce and the Laird's Houses of Early Modern Shetland

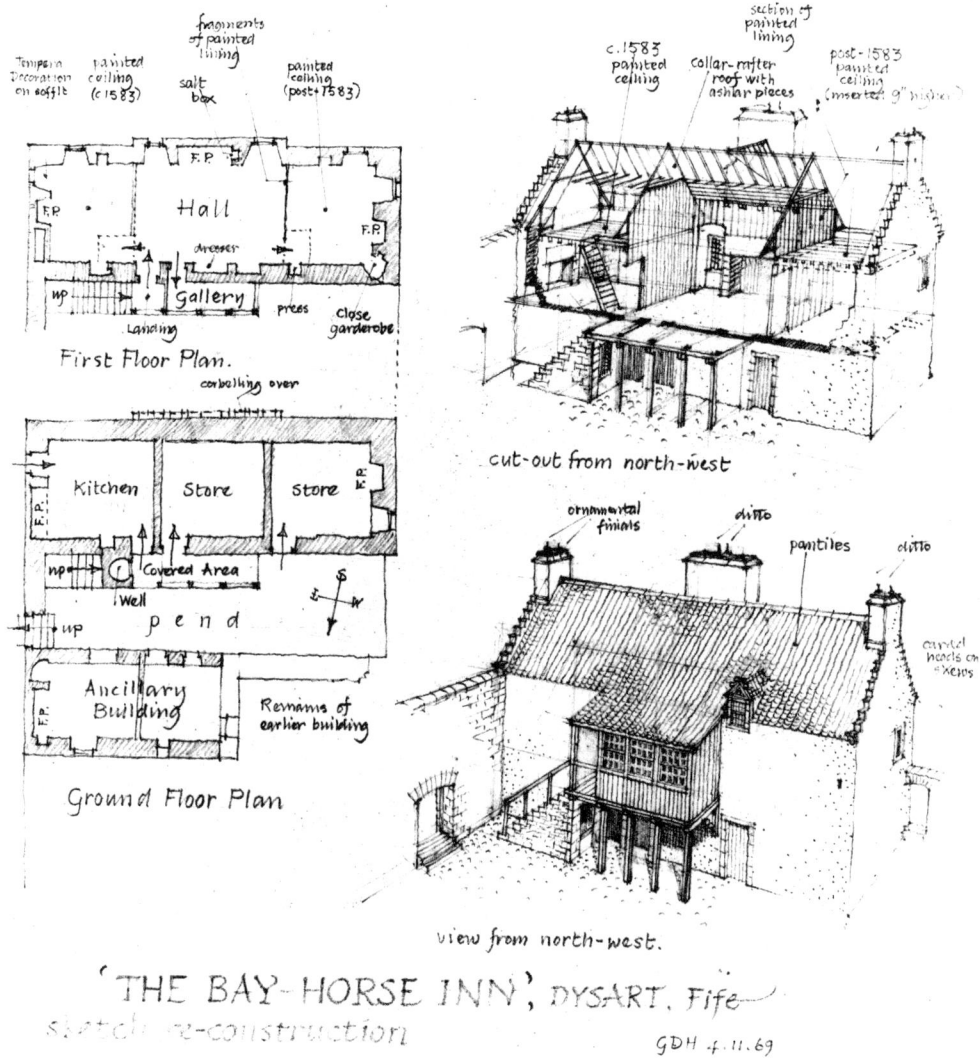

7 Bay House, Dysart, reconstruction drawing by G. Hay, 1969. *Crown Copyright, RCAHMS*

House. At Newhall, the east fireplace was contracted at a later date, and the sill of a south-facing window survives in the west room. Part of a window in the west gable provides evidence of a garret (Hamilton 1953, 35-6; 1956, 197).

The south range has little in the way of dateable architectural features. Its rubble walls are 1.2-1.5m thick, and Hamilton (1956, 197) described the gables as having been 'finished on either side of central chimney 'stalks', with 'a heavy tabling set out on rough corbelling from the wallheads'. The gables are not crowstepped or finished with skews and there is minimal evidence of dressed stonework elsewhere. Thatch or perhaps stone flags may have been its roofing material. The earliest likely date for

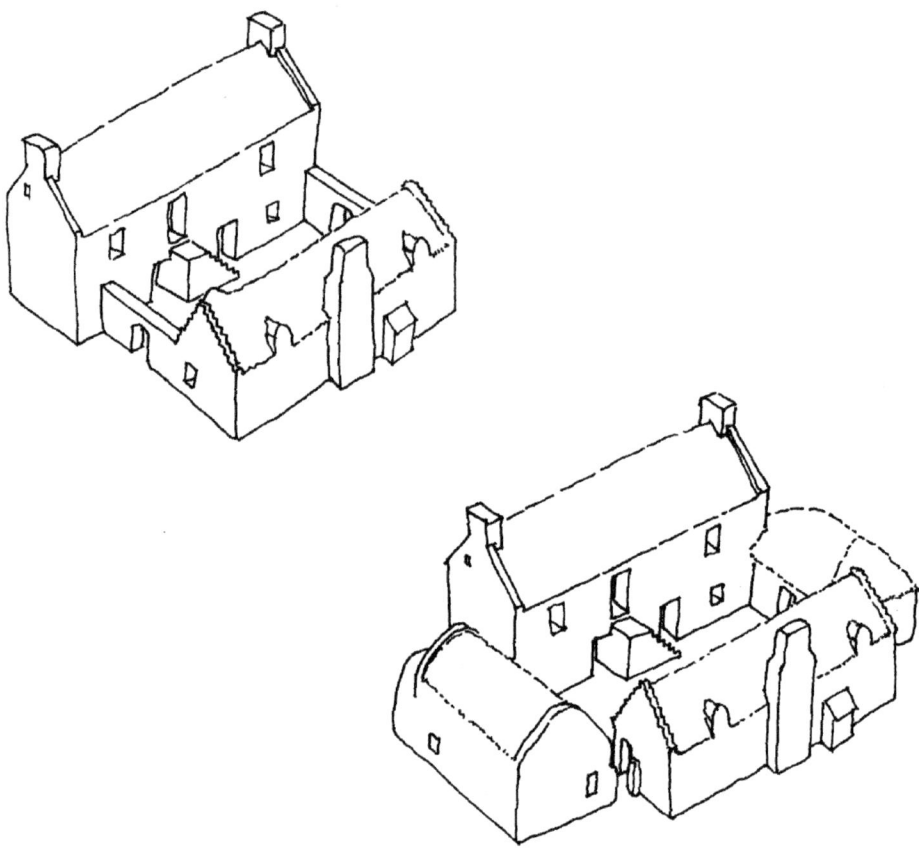

8 Phase II (left) and III (right) reconstruction line-drawings of Jarlshof, to scale. *S. Strachan*

the building of the south range would be after William regained Sumburgh in 1605 or 1609. It is possible that it was the 'new house' referred to in 1617, however. The tight courtyard form prevailed in Shetland throughout the seventeenth century, as for example at the aforementioned Old Haa of Brough, of 1672 (perhaps incorporating earlier work) and Vaila Haa, built in 1696 (NGR: HU 2262 4690). When the south range was built at Jarlshof, it appears that the west side of the courtyard was closed by a screen wall. It is possible that, before the east range was built, there could have been a matching entrance on that side creating a through-route, shown in the Phase II reconstruction drawing (*8*), and similar to Brough (*9*).

The 1609 decreet listed the items that had been stolen from the house and lands of Sumburgh the previous year, and thus gives us a good idea of William Bruce's wealth. Several locked chests are mentioned, variously containing gold and silver (valued at £1,589 Scots), linens including 'Holland claith', and valuable books such

9 The Old Haa of Brough, Yell, in *c.*1896 before the west range (far right in photograph) was demolished. *Copyright Old Haa Museum, Yell*

as the old chronicles and history of Scotland, the Acts of Parliament, the *Denss chronicle* containing the history of Denmark, a world atlas and his rental books. Other items included furniture, such as 10 feather beds (i.e. mattresses), a marshal in the form of four hagbuts and 12 halberds, as well as two meal and two malt girnels and dozens of livestock (Laing 1857, 392-4). This list of stolen goods plus the damage sustained was valued at £8,346 Scots. Even allowing for exaggeration, the contents of the house and lands of Sumburgh far exceed the inventories of his peers, for example, the 1612 testament of Robert Swinton, minister of Walls whose estate, which included five feather beds, was valued at £1,587 Scots. An inventory of William's son Robert survives, drawn up in 1617, to whom William conveyed his estates four years later; incredibly Robert was already worth £32,126 Scots (Donaldson 1958, 81-3).

We can make some inferences about the available accommodation of the house at Sumburgh from the 1609 decreet. The chests that contained the most valuable items are likely to have been kept in William's personal quarters as they would have needed to be kept dry and afforded a greater degree of protection. It is not known whether the doorway at the top of the forestair of the present south range also had a drawbar or how the gate(s) at the screen wall(s) were secured. Four boats and their furniture, each valued at £60 Scots, and 20 double herring nets were also stolen, and so William was deprived of his rightful 'commoditie of the saidis landis of Swonburgh' (fisheries). Two lasts of 'Rochell' and one last of 'Scottis' salt was also listed amongst the items to be accounted for, and, given the vast quantity stolen (36 barrels with a total value of £156 Scots), was probably mostly used to preserve fish for export rather than home consumption. '*Sellars*' (as in a store, not necessarily below ground) and '*skeos*' (a store, usually a distinct building from the house) were often broken into, according to charges in the Shetland Court Book, to steal foodstuffs such as cured fish and meal, '*wadmel*' (a course local cloth) and fishing gear (Donaldson 1958, 50-1 & 96). Assuming that the present south range at Jarlshof had been built by the summer of 1608, it is possible that items such as the salt and nets could have been stored in the unlit east room, rather than, or in addition to, items required to sustain the household. Alternatively, similar provision could have existed in an earlier arrangement of buildings.

William's involvement in commercial fisheries appears to have been wide-ranging. We know that, like other lairds, William rented out land for fishermen's lodgings (otherwise known as booths or '*böds*'), as the exchange Earl Patrick had engineered in 1604 included the transferral of duties owed to William by Fifeshire fishermen lodging in Sumburgh (Shet Docs, no. 391). Tenants were free to fish in Shetland's waters; mainly they caught ling and cod, which they air-dried on beaches or preserved in salt, to exchange with German merchants (of the Hanseatic League) for cash and luxury goods. These merchants also traded from *böds*, for example that belonging to 'Garthe Hemlein' from Bremen who is recorded in 1602 in Dunrossness (Goudie 1904, 208 & 210; Donaldson 1958, 66). Some Scottish and English merchants are also recorded, but in much smaller numbers. In the main, Shetland lairds relied on these merchants to convert rents-in-kind (mainly butter and *wadmel*) into currency. However, a few lairds, such as William Bruce, were trading commodities such as herring and butter directly (Donaldson 1958, 69; Shet Docs, no. 336). William's familiarity with trade should not necessarily be surprising given his strong links with the booming East Neuk fishing ports, and we know that his son, Robert, was particularly active. In 1617 Robert had four boats, each valued at £40, five 'sixareens' (six-man boats), four 'foureens' (four-man boats), a boat 'for passage', and a ship called *The Swanne* valued at £2,000 Scots (Donaldson 1958, 81). The influence of the Hansa was also far-reaching, with Robert able to translate bonds from the 'Dutch' (German) for a decreet relating to the High Court Admiralty in 1627 (Young 1983, 125).

In general, Shetland traders and some lairds only became merchants towards the end of the seventeenth century as a direct result of the withdrawal of the German merchants; their dual-purpose houses were also otherwise known as *böds*, alternatively, they maintained a separate *böd* by the shore. Around the same time, if not before, tenants were bonded, under threat of eviction, into a fishing tenure system whereby they could only fish for their landlord or his nominated merchant (Smith 2000, 68-71). Tenuously, the south range of Jarlshof could be described as a *böd*, but no other merchant *böds* of the early seventeenth century survive to allow for direct comparison. Principal living quarters over store/service rooms is a characteristic shared by the late seventeenth-century merchant *böds* however, and was an arrangement that lasted well into the nineteenth century, as at the Böd of Gremista, Lerwick (NGR: HU 4644 4312) built in 1870 for the fishing station manager, which has a kitchen and salt store on the ground floor. If the ruin at Jarlshof is identifiable with the 'House of Soumbrough' described by Reverend James Kay (1711, 17) as 'a House prettie large formal, and very well situat[ed]', we can conclude that it was still entire and habitable when his account was written in c.1682-8. However, without secure dating for the development of Jarlshof, it is not possible to say conclusively that the present south range was built by William Bruce rather than one of his descendants later in the seventeenth century.

Of the remaining two ranges of Jarlshof, only the east range is now extant. The west range was demolished to allow further excavation of the prehistoric remains, as it was deemed to have 'no architectural or historical merit and could be removed without impairing the value of the site in any way'.[6] Hamilton (1953, 36; 1956, 197) described it has having been of one-storey, extensively rebuilt (probably when two cross walls were inserted) and it had an aumbry in its south gable. One long wall of the east range survives to over 3.7m in height which suggests that it may have reached two storeys. It was lit by three small windows and was entered via the broad 2m-wide doorway facing the courtyard (contracted at a later date); a corn-drying kiln was later inserted into its south-east corner. Kilns of this type were built at the corner of the barn of the farmhouse, occupied in the fourteenth and fifteenth centuries, discovered a few metres to the north-east of Jarlshof (indicated on figure 5). Kilns have also been built in the shells of ruinous buildings, again at the medieval farmhouse at Jarlshof, and in the Kebister teind barn (NGR: HU 4570 4549) in the mid-/late seventeenth century (Ashmore 1993, 23; Owen & Lowe 1999, 301-2). Circular-plan kilns are known throughout Orkney and southern Shetland and continued in use into the twentieth century. As Jarlshof was not excavated to modern standards, the environmental evidence which may have helped to secure a date for the use of the kiln is, unfortunately, lacking. The wide door of the east range and the kiln, which may well represent a rebuilding of an earlier one, makes a barn function most likely and its height suggests there was at least a loft. A 'greit barne' was mentioned in the 1609 decreet (Laing 1857, 392) and the barn and barnyard of 'Soundbruch' are referred to in Margaret Stewart's testament of 1608 (Shet Docs, no. 461). The fourth range most probably functioned as a stable and/or byre for a few milk cows. This arrangement is shown as Phase III in figure 8. The 1609 contract also mentions a bakehouse of William's that was located close to Earl Patrick's house (Shet Docs, no. 480).

CONCLUSION

This study of the ruins at Jarlshof is intended to demonstrate firstly that in the early modern period, there was regular, first-hand interaction between Shetland and the

Scottish mainland; secondly, that the same type of houses were being built in both loci at the same time; and finally, that early modern forms of Scottish secular architecture continued to influence the development of lairds' houses in the Northern Isles. Taller houses with more regular fenestration first appeared in Shetland only in the eighteenth century and form the basis of an article by Mike Finnie (1996). Shetland was dominated by lairds throughout the seventeenth century, and then by both the lairds and a mercantile class in the eighteenth to nineteenth centuries. After the demise of the Stewart earls there were no great magnates resident in Shetland, and the first and last tower-houses to be built there were Muness and Scalloway. Instead the descendants of men such as Laurence Bruce and William Bruce filled the void, shaped the islands and left traces of their lifestyles in documents, ruins and extant houses. At present, a ruin at Voesgrind, Unst (NGR: HP 6220 0203), which possibly dates to the seventeenth century, and the site of a Sinclair house at Brow, Dunrossness (NGR: HU 3863 1407), are being archaeologically recorded and, in the case of Brow, excavated.[7] These should help to reveal much more evidence of the material culture of these important landed men and the context of early modern Shetland society as a whole.

ACKNOWLEDGEMENTS

I am particularly grateful to Allan Rutherford and Richard Fawcett for providing useful comments on earlier drafts of this paper. Thanks to Chris Dyer, Shetland Amenity Trust for information about the recent survey of the laird's house at Brow, Gerry Bigelow for permission to make a copy of the Brow report and Tom Dawson for information about the Voesgrind research. I am also indebted to: Tommy Watt, Shetland Museum & Archives; Mary Ellen Odie, Old Haa Museum, Yell; David Mackie, Orkney Library & Archives; and Bryony Coombs and Michelle Andersson, Historic Scotland for their help with sourcing images. Figures 1, 4 and 5 are reproduced here by kind permission of Historic Scotland, figure 6 Orkney Library & Archives, figure 7 the RCAHMS and figure 9 the Old Haa Museum. Finally, thank you to the Scottish Archaeology Forum organisers for inviting me to participate in the 2005 conference and Lucy Verrill for her editing skills.

NOTES

1   It has been suggested that Busta House (NGR: HU 3451 6680) may date to 1588 as the house of a Hanseatic merchant (Finnie 1990, 64; ('Brae, Busta House Hotel', HU36NW 9.00, CANMORE, www.rcahms.gov.uk/canmore). However, Gifford (1992, 472–3) does not date any of the surviving ranges to before the early eighteenth century. The Giffords

first acquired the lands of Busta at the end of the sixteenth century and c.1650 seems feasible for the origin of the present south wing.
2. The troubled relationship, antagonised by Patrick, between the Bruces of Muness and Symbister and the various septs of the Sinclairs is explored further by Anderson (1999, 47-8) and Smith (1999, 9-10).
3. National Archives of Scotland (NAS), SC21871/2A, 'HM Office of Works, Ancient Monuments Dept, July 1924'; NAS, SC21871/2D 'Jarlshof, Sumburgh, Shetland. Season's Work 1937'; NAS, DD27/949, 'File note to Mr Liddle, Mr Laidler from J.R.C. Hamilton, 26/2/51', Ministry of Works records. And site visit by the present author on 21 September 2006 to read inscriptions in burial enclosure erected at the east corner of the guardianship area in 1951.
4. Bruce (1906, 29-30) suggests that 'it is possible that when the burials took place at Jarlshof the people knew that the ground was consecrated. Close to Jarlshof there were the remains of old walls, recently repaired, enclosing what might possibly have been the remains of an old pre-Reformation chapel, which had been used as a burying-place by the Sumburgh family for many generations. It is possible that this old chapel may have been the Chapel of St Barnaby, known to have been somewhere in the parish'. G. Goudie writing in Mill *Diary*, 1889, xcvi states that it can be inferred from the Rev John Hunter's diary and register of 1734–45 that his Episcopalian chapel, St Barnaby's, was in Dunrossness. However, Goudie acknowledges that the Rev. J.B. Craven, 1883, *History of the Episcopal Church in Orkney*, 1688-1882, 130, placed its ruin in Lerwick. Hunter was patronized by some of the leading families; in 1734 he baptized John, son of Robert Bruce of Sumburgh (Mill *Diary* 1889, 197).
5. At Smailholm, the position of a stair to the upper levels was not positively identified though the excavators hypothesized that the narrow west room may have housed an internal stair (Good & Tabraham 1988, 264). At Pitcairn the excavators were unable to conclusively locate an internal stair position, though two post holes in the central room may indicate supports for a stairway. As only the interior of the building was excavated, a forestair could not be ruled out however (Reid 1981). The burials in the courtyard and the antiquarian clearance of overburden at Jarlshof may have obliterated any evidence for there having been a forestair against the north range.
6. NAS, DD27/949, file note by J.R.C Hamilton, 5/1/51 'The 1950 excavations at Jarlshof and Plans for 1951', Ministry of Works records.
7. T. Dawson *pers. comm.*; Turner, V. 05/08/05 & 06/08/04 'Dellin inta da past...', *Shetland Today* – Shetland Times On-line News, www.shetlandtoday.co.uk/shetlandtimes; Bigelow, Brown & Proctor, 2004.

REFERENCES

Anderson, P.D. 1992, *Black Patie: The Life and Times of Patrick Stewart. Earl of Orkney, Lord of Shetland 1533-1593*, Edinburgh

Anderson, P.D. 1999, 'Earl Patrick and his Enemies', *New Orkney Antiq J* 1, 42-52

Armstrong, W.B. 1882, *Bruces of Cultmalindie, Muness, Sumburgh, and Symbister*, reprinted as a pamphlet from *The Genealogist*, 1st ser, 6 (1882), 162-7 & 205-11

Ashmore, P. 1993, *Jarlshof, a walk through the past*, Edinburgh

Beveridge, E. 1893, *The Churchyard Memorials of Crail: Containing a Full Description of the Epitaphs Anterior to 1800 Together with Some Account of the Other Antiquities of the Burgh*, Edinburgh

Bigelow, G.F., Brown, C.J. & Proctor, R.E. 2004, *Investigation of Archaeological Sites in the Vicinity of the Former Brow Estate, Dunrossness, Shetland*, Gorham, Maine, USA

Bruce, J. 1906, 'Notice of the excavation of a Broch at Jarlshof, Sumburgh, Shetland', *Proc Soc Antiq Scot* 41 (1906), 11-33

Crawford, B.E. 1985, 'William Sinclair, Earl of Orkney, and his family: a study in the politics of survival', in Stringer, K.J. (ed.), *Essays on the Nobility of Medieval Scotland*, 232-53, Edinburgh

Crawford, B.E. 1999, 'The historical setting: Shetland from the pre-Viking age to the modern period', in Crawford, B.E. & Ballin Smith, B., *The Biggings, Papa Stour, Shetland: The History and Archaeology of a Royal Norwegian Farm*, 9-23, Edinburgh (Society of Antiquaries of Scotland Monogr, 15)

Donaldson, G. 1958, *Shetland Life under Earl Patrick*, Edinburgh

Donaldson, G. 1983, 'The Scots settlement in Shetland', in Withrington, D.J. (ed.), *Shetland and the Outside World, 1469-1969*, 8-19, Oxford (Aberdeen University Studies Ser, 157)

Dunbar, J.G. 1960, 'Pitcastle, a Cruck-Framed House in Northern Perthshire', *Scottish Studies* 4 (1960), 113-6

Finnie, M. 1990, *Shetland: An Illustrated Architectural Guide*, Edinburgh (RIAS/Landmark Trust Illustrated Architectural Guides to Scotland Ser)

Finnie, M. 1996, 'An introduction to the haa houses of Shetland', *Vernacular Building* 20, 39-52

Gifford, J. 1992, *Highland and Islands*, London (The Buildings of Scotland Ser)

Good, G.L. & Tabraham, C.J. 1988, 'Excavations at Smailholm Tower, Roxburghshire', *Proc Soc Antiq Scot* 118, 231-66

Goodare, J. 2001, 'The admission of lairds to the Scottish parliament', *Eng Hist Rev* 116, 1103-33

Goudie, G. 1878, 'Notice of two charters in the Norse language found among the papers of the sheriff-court of Shetland', *Proc Soc Antiq Scot* 12, 472-92

Goudie, G. 1904, *The Celtic and Scandinavian Antiquities of Shetland*, Edinburgh

Grant, F.J. 1907, *Zetland Family Histories*, Lerwick

Hamilton, J.R.C. 1953, *Jarlshof, Shetland: Official Guide*, Edinburgh (Ancient Monuments & Historic Buildings Ministry of Works Guides)

Hamilton, J.R.C. 1956, *Excavations at Jarlshof, Shetland*, Edinburgh (Ministry of Works Archaeological Rep 1)

Kay, J. 1711, 'The description of Dunrosenes' in Sibbald, R. (ed.), *The Description of the Isles of Orknay and Zetland. With Mapps of them, done from accurat Observation of the most Learned who live in these Isles*, Edinburgh

Laing, D. 1857, 'A decreit of spulzie, granted by the lords of council to William Bruce of Symbister in Zetland, against Patrick, Earl of Orkney, 4th of February 1609', *Archaeologicia Scotica* 4, 385-98

MacGibbon, D. & Ross, T. 1887, *The Castellated and Domestic Architecture of Scotland. From the Twelfth to the Eighteenth Century* II, Rep 1990, Edinburgh

Mill *Diary*, Goudie, G. (ed.) 1889, *The Diary of the Reverend John Mill, Minister of the Parishes of Dunrossness, Sandwick and Cunningsburgh in Shetland, 1740-1803*, Edinburgh (Scottish Record Society Ser, 5)

Owen, O. & Lowe, C. 1999, *Kebister: The Four-thousand-year-old Story of One Shetland Township*, Edinburgh (Society of Antiquaries of Scotland Monogr, 13)

RCAHMS 1933, *Inventory of Monuments & Constructions in the Counties of Fife, Kinross and Clackmannan*, Edinburgh

RCAHMS 1946, *Inventory of the Ancient Monuments of Orkney & Shetland*, 3 vols, Edinburgh

Reid, J. T. 1869, *Art Rambles in Shetland*, Edinburgh

Reid, M.L. 1981, *Pitcairn House: The earliest known stone-built dwelling in Glenrothes*, Glenrothes

RPC Register of the Privy Council of Scotland, A.D. 1545-1625, Masson, D. (ed.) 1877-98, 1st ser, 14 vols, Edinburgh

Schrank, G. 1995, *An Orkney Estate: Improvements at Graemeshall, 1827-1888*, East Linton

Scott, W. 1871, *The Pirate*, 1st edn 1821, Edinburgh (Waverley Novels Ser., 13)

Sharples, N. 1998, *Scalloway: A Broch, Late Iron Age Settlement and Medieval Cemetery in Shetland*, Oxford (Oxbow Monogr, 82)

Shet Ct Bk, *The Court Book of Shetland, 1615-1629*, Donaldson, G. (ed.) 1991, Lerwick

Shet Docs, *Shetland Documents, 1580-1611*, Ballantyne, J.H. & Smith, B. (eds) 1994, Lerwick

Smith, B. 1978, '"Lairds" and "Improvement" in seventeenth and eighteenth century Shetland', in Devine, T.M. (ed.), *Lairds and Improvement in the Scotland of the Enlightenment*, 11-20, Edinburgh

Smith, B. 1999, 'Earl Robert and Earl Patrick in Shetland: good, bad or indifferent?', *New Orkney Antiq J* 1, 6-16

Smith, B. 2000, *Toons and Tenants: Settlement and Society in Shetland, 1299-1899*, Lerwick

Smith, I.M. 1985, 'Balsarroch House, Wigtownshire', *Transactions of the Dumfriesshire and Galloway Natural History and Antiquarian Society*, 3rd series, 60 (1985), 7-81

Strachan, S. (in preparation), 'Lords or Lairds? A reinterpretation of 'Jarlshof', Shetland, c.1589-1609', *Proc Soc Antiq Scot*

Swan, J. & McNeill, C. 1997, *Dysart: A Royal Burgh*, Dysart

Thomson, W.P.L. 1987, *History of Orkney*, Edinburgh

Young, M.D. 1983, 'Shetland history in Scottish records', in Withrington, D.L. (ed.), *Shetland and the Outside World, 1469-1969*, 119-35, Oxford (Aberdeen University Studies Ser, 157)

10

THE WESTERN ISLANDS: IRELAND'S ATLANTIC ISLANDS AND THE FORGING OF GAELIC IRISH NATIONAL IDENTITIES

Aidan O'Sullivan

INTRODUCTION

It was a summer's day of veiled light and trembling heat. We walked up from the island's small harbour, climbing the path towards the ruined village on the hill-slope above us. Behind us, the ocean was still on the sound between Ireland – from whence we had come – and Blasket Island itself (*1*). The mainland trembled in a false distance of summer mist, the customary sharp outline of its hills lost upon an uncertain sky. I can still remember, more than 25 years later, the sound of the sea, the calls of the sea birds and the glinting of light out on the western ocean. I recall the ruined houses of the village – abandoned then for 30 years – huddled together intimately, looking down onto the fields below, relics of a vanished culture and community (*2*).

I was a young schoolboy then, perhaps 13 or 14 years old, and with my parents on a pilgrimage to the Blasket Islands, County Kerry – one of the most famous places in Ireland and well-known to generations of Irish school children (*3*). Since I had first read Robin Flower's (1944) *The Western Island* (from which I have stolen several phrases above) as part of my Secondary School education, I had become fascinated with the lives, traditions and ways of the people of the Blasket Islands. I had devoured every book about them that I could find, such as Muiris O'Sullivan's (1933) *Fiche Bliain ag Fás* (Twenty Years A-Growing) and Tómas Ó Criomthain's (1929) *An t-Oileánach* (The Islandman). In all that I read in these

The Western Islands: Ireland's Atlantic islands and the forging of Gaelic Irish national identities

1 View of the Blasket Islands from the western end of the Dingle Peninsula, County Kerry. Since the ninteenth century, Irish antiquarians, artists and scholars have looked to the western islands to re-imagine the island of Ireland itself *(Photo: UCD Delargy Centre for Irish Folklore)*

2 The village on the Great Blasket at about 1930. The houses cluster together, sheltered from the Atlantic gales, and overlook their fields and the sea below *(UCD Delargy Centre for Irish Folklore)*

3 The village on the Great Blasket viewing back towards the mainland. An island perspective, as revealed through the island's literature, shows a strikingly different view of island life and identity *(UCD Delargy Centre for Irish Folklore)*

The Western Islands: Ireland's Atlantic islands and the forging of Gaelic Irish national identities

4 Pilgrimage to the Blasket: myself and my father – John O'Sullivan – during a visit to the island in the early 1980s. As it did to generations of other Irish schoolchildren, the Blasket Island literature gave me a sense of the cultural traditions of Gaelic Ireland *(Aidan O'Sullivan)*

and other marvelous books as part of my education, such as Liam O'Flaherty's (1953) *Dúil* ('Desire') and Mairtín Ó Direán's (1961) *Feamainn Bhealtaine* ('May Seaweed', an Irish language short-story collections about island life on the Aran Islands, County Galway) as well as his *Dánta* (a collection of Irish-language poems from the same space; Ó Direán 1980), I felt that these were descriptions of what it was to be truly Irish – to belong to a Gaelic-speaking fishing/farming community on an island off the western seaboard (*4*).

I am no longer so sure of what it is to be Irish, particularly now as our 'island nation' experiences all the tumult and change of economic growth and remarkable inward migrations from Poland, China, the Middle East and west Africa, but at the time I had certainly been convinced by the literature, art and music that my society put in front of me – that Irishness was something that most truly resided on the western islands. My schoolboy belief was no accident – it was the deliberate outcome of a long tradition of Irish scholarship, ideology and, in my case, pedagogy, that stretched back into the early nineteenth century, or perhaps even earlier back into the Middle Ages.

ISLANDS IN THE IRISH NATIONALIST IMAGINATION

Ireland's western islands, situated out on its long Atlantic shore, have long been seen as icons of a true Irishness – the dwelling places of a Gaelic people; pure, clean-living and timeless. From the nineteenth century, islands such as the Blasket

Islands, the Aran Islands, Achill Island, Tory Island and the Iniskeas have been seen as the last surviving bastions of a Gaelic language, culture and identity – resisting the onslaught of a modern, European and, most crucially, English culture. This belief was formed through the nineteenth and twentieth century by two distinct but parallel patriotic movements: that of Romantic cultural nationalism and also the separatist political nationalist tradition that was ultimately to lead to rebellion, the War of Independence, the creation of the Free State and, ultimately, the Republic of Ireland.

Both of these movements actively portrayed the western islands as places of potentially extraordinary cultural, symbolic and ideological power. If nations are indeed 'imagined communities', then it could be suggested that the Irish nation itself was imagined with the help of these geographical places. Through the nineteenth and twentieth centuries, the islands were seen as treasure houses of Gaelic Irish culture and traditions, living sources of inspiration that could be used to reinvent the island of Ireland itself – an island that Irish nationalists believed had sadly fallen from a state of grace into a modern world of materialism, secularism and English culture. The islands were places that had survived intact, because they were remote, through the centuries of English colonialism, plantation and religious oppression on the mainland. They could, therefore, act as wells that could be drawn on to recreate Ireland.

In this paper, to aptly use a maritime metaphor, I am going to tack between archaeology, art history and literature to explore how images of 'islandness' have long been used to forge cultural identities in Ireland. It need hardly be emphasised that other islands in our part of the world have also been similarly used for other nationalist purposes (i.e. of the English-nationalist 'fog in channel, continent cut-off' variety, or the imperialist identity-shaping British tradition of the 'sceptered isle', or 'maritime island nation'). However, it is up to others to investigate those themes.

ISLANDS AS METAPHORS FOR TIMELESSNESS AND CULTURAL RENEWAL

It is well-known that Irish antiquarians, artists, poets and writers used the islands west of Ireland as sources of artistic inspiration and creativity. It is arguable that this originally came about because antiquarian scholars had already suggested that Ireland's western islands, such as the Aran Islands, Blasket Islands and so on, were places where an original, authentic Gaelic Irish culture had survived intact from the distant past (Foster 1977; O'Connell 1994; Kiberd 2000; Zimmerman 2001).

This antiquarian and artistic belief undoubtedly grew up because islands were seen by both in the nineteenth century as physically and culturally remote and conservative places that were safe from the intrusions of the modern world and particularly from English-speaking colonial culture. It is something that can be seen in J.M. Synge's plays and essays on *The Aran Islands*, in W.B. Yeat's poetry, and in Paul Henry's paintings on the Achill Island (Bhreathnach-Lynch 2003). In all of these, the islanders of the west are usually presented as innocents who preserved in their daily work and lives, an epic, stoic tradition that offered an alternative to the norm (i.e. the English-speaking world). By the twentieth century, with the establishment of Irish independence after 1921, and with the foundation of the Free State, it could be argued that the state more actively used the western islands as a resource to rebuild Irish Gaelic culture and identity. Interestingly, as I showed in my introduction, most Irish people's attitudes to islands today can be traced to the uses of the Blasket and Aran island literature in primary and secondary school education in the Irish Republic.

As archaeologists we might wonder what was the role of antiquarianism in this project? I will argue that antiquarians had a significant, if unwitting role. They created, firstly, a sense of the remoteness, cultural distance and uniqueness of these islands. They also created a myth of the antiquity of these islands and the direct link between nineteenth-century populations and the peoples of the remote past. This created a sense of a pure Gaelic Irish ethnicity and identity which could be tapped into by both cultural and political nationalists.

ORIGINS: WESTERN ISLANDS AS PLACES OF SPIRITUAL RENEWAL IN THE MIDDLE AGES

Before tracing antiquarian surveys of the western islands, we should note that the archaeological remains that they inspected were themselves often born of a desire for remoteness and spiritual renewal. Images of islands have long served cultural, symbolic and ideological purposes in the Irish imagination. In Early Medieval Ireland, islands were also seen as timeless, eternal places, potentially located between this world and the otherworld. Most famously, *Tech Donn*, the house of the Celtic God of Death (Donn) was reputedly situated on a tiny islet known as Bull Rock, located in the sea off the modern Dursey Island, County Cork. Indeed, in Early Medieval literature, if it was said that a person had 'gone to the house of Donn' it was understood that he had died. In the late Middle Ages too, the mysterious island of *Hy Brasil* was seen to be a paradise in the Atlantic, even being depicted on Portolan navigation charts up until the fifteenth century (Westropp 1912). In the Early Medieval period, islands were also seen as places of innocence and potential spiritual renewal. Thence, in the fifth and sixth centuries, wandering Irish monks inspired by the writings of St Anthony and the example of the desert fathers themselves, sought a 'desert in the pathless ocean' by setting sail on the Atlantic seaways in order to locate an island for a hermitage or church. The archaeological evidence for this island inhabitation is abundant down the west coast of Ireland (e.g. Marshall and Rourke 2000; Herity 1990; 1995). We gain a sense of the perception of these islands amidst their seascapes when we read Adomnán's seventh-century *Life of Columba*, which is of course set amongst the islands of the west coast of Scotland.

However, it is also worth noting that these islands, or in fact *imagined* islands, were also used for ideological purposes. In the Early Medieval saints' lives (i.e. typically seventh to twelfth century AD hagiographical texts extolling the life and deeds of a hero-saint) and the narrative literature (particularly the *immrama* or voyage tales of the ninth to tenth centuries AD) stories are provided of both saintly and secular heroes who sailed on the western ocean from mythical island to island, surviving attacks by demons and monsters (or resisting sexually predatory women) before returning transformed and spiritually redeemed to the island of Ireland. In these stories the islands out to the west were often places that typified the state to which Ireland would descend if Irish Christianity was not reformed; if women were to have real power in society or if secular authorities were not to heed the dictates of the church (Johnston 2003). In other words, islands were taken to be metaphors for Ireland itself.

THE REDISCOVERY OF THE WESTERN ISLANDS BY ANTIQUARIANS

In a sense, this prefigures in an interesting way something that happened almost 1000 years later. Moving up into the modern era, we can also begin to explore the role of Ireland's islands in the national imagination by tracing their antiquarian rediscovery and the uses to which they were subsequently put. The antiquarian rediscovery of the island has a background in the ideologies of the eighteenth and nineteenth century, when the European Romantic Movement led to a growing interest in, and changing attitudes towards, those peoples and cultures that were different to western European society. It also, as is well-known, led to a growing interest in Europe's own remote past.

In Ireland, inspired by this new interest in the past and a patriotic (but not separatist) desire in particular to establish the antiquity of Ireland past (in opposition to English scholars who derived the origins of Ireland's antiquities from more fantastical explanations), Irish antiquarians were among the first to start visiting the western islands. They were particularly attractive places because of the richness of Early Medieval ecclesiastical remains preserved on places like the Skellig Michael, County Kerry, the Aran Islands, County Galway and Inishmurray, County Sligo. It was also true that many of these medieval sites, with their churches, cross-slabs and saints burials, remained in use in the nineteenth century as places of modern pilgrimage and folk belief. Observing this, and noting the presence of local folklore about saints, antiquarians when they were writing about the antiquities, also tended to refer to the islanders, describing how they were living a primitive form of life (O'Connell 1994).

Antiquarians also saw themselves as heroic agents in this rediscovery of Ireland's timeless past. In 1851, the Irish antiquarian John Windele visited the remote island of Skellig Michael, off the south-west coast (Harbison 1976). In the early Middle Ages Skellig was home to a large community of monks and hermits who left spectacular archaeological remains of stone houses, terraced gardens, cross slabs and oratories. It was also the focus of pilgrimage in the Later Medieval period and is today a designated World Heritage Site. Windele was attracted to the islands because it had some of the best-preserved antiquities on the west coast. His account provides a very detailed description of the ruins on the island. It is interesting that Windele, like many of these antiquarians' writings, also included an account of long and dangerous journeys out to the islands. For example, writing about Skellig Michael, he describes the harsh conditions of the journey: 'For hours we kept beating about and tacking ... but could make no progress westward' (Harbison 1976, 130). Similarly, William Wakeman writing about his visit to Aran Island in 1839 describes how 'At length, after some very lengthened tacks and other nautical measures we were safely landed' (O'Connell 1994, 187). In these accounts antiquarians firstly emphasised the remoteness and then separateness of the islands, and conjured up their own journeys as voyages of discovery to a mysterious civilisation and culture.

THE ARAN ISLANDS, COUNTY GALWAY: ANTIQUARIAN ACTIVITIES IN THE NINETEENTH CENTURY

Antiquarians were interested in these islands almost from the outset of Irish archaeology. For example, the Aran Islands off the west Galway coast were a focus of interest throughout the nineteenth century. George Petrie on his visit to the Aran Islands in 1822 described the well-known cliff-top fort of Dún Aonghusa as 'the most significant barbaric monument now extant in Europe' (Waddell 1994, 84). Romantic images prevailed of the monuments on the Aran Islands, as can be seen in Petrie's famous, romantic painting of the cliff-top fort of Dún Aonghusa placed on a towering cliff overlooking a stormy sea.

Antiquarians would also intersperse their comments on the antiquities with a description of the lives and practices of the islander's themselves – thus establishing a strong sense of continuity with the distant past. Thus, Samuel Ferguson, another well-known antiquarian who visited the Aran Islands, along with his account of archaeological monuments, described the life of the inhabitants, their methods of house-building and thatching, and their work in the fields; all as though they were a barbarian culture themselves (O'Connell 1994, 188).

By the end of the nineteenth century, the Aran Islands were subjected to waves of visits by antiquarians, artists and poets. In particular, Thomas J. Westropp, one of the most famous of Irish antiquarians, wrote several articles on both the island's monuments and people (e.g. Westropp 1895; 1899; 1910). Like most antiquarians, he tended to emphasise a sense of the antiquity and timeless continuity of the islanders' ways of life. Writing about his visit in 1878 to Inis Meáin (one of the three Aran Islands), he stated that

> This island is an extremely primitive place. We saw women grinding meal with querns & weaving the cloth which dyed red or brown forms the staple female dress. The men usually wear blue cloth clothes and scotch caps & 'pampooties' or raw hide shoes of untanned skin laced up at the heel and instep, the wooden home made vessels are of the earliest type and very like the ones in the RIA museum

Westropp 1888

In this way, he was clearly establishing links between the material culture of the islanders (quern stones, wooden dishes) with the prehistoric and medieval objects that he had seen in the Royal Irish Academy Museum and which most antiquaries would have been familiar with (O'Connell 1994, 190). It was a short leap to conclude that these were people living in the past.

INISHMURRAY, COUNTY SLIGO: ISLANDS AS 'LIVING MUSEUMS' FOR ANTIQUARIAN OBSERVERS

Indeed, the antiquarian accounts often seem to view the islands as living museums; places where there was an immense continuity of practice with the past and where the influences of English colonisation and the modern world had less impact. The antiquarian William Wakeman, on a visit to the island of Inishmurray, County Sligo, described it as a 'singularly interesting island, which may in a manner be described as a museum of antiquities relating chiefly to the earlier period of the Irish church' (Wakeman 1885, 185). In writing about the island's remarkable Early Medieval enclosures, churches, crosses and outdoor 'altars', he also created a sense of continuity in linking the islanders' present use of the Early Medieval stone church, known as Teach Molaisse, with its ancient uses, wondering how it had been used by people 'from firbolgian days to our own time' (Wakeman 1885, 221; the Firbolgs were a pseudo-historical people, thought by Late Medieval Irish scholars to be amongst the earliest colonisers of Ireland).

In writing like this, antiquarians helped to create an image of the people of the islands as a society unaffected by mainland political and social upheaval; living an unspoiled, primitive life. Wakeman's account of the people of Inishmurray in 1885 evoked the image of a surviving ancient civilisation in the description of them as a 'fair-haired, comely, well-built race, probably Tuatha De Danann' (again, another mythical, pseudo-historical people) (Wakeman 1885, 178). Wilson Foster (1977) has argued that this led to the belief that there was an ethnic, genealogical link between those who built the ancient archaeological remains and the nineteenth-century populations of the islands. This is despite the fact that there was plenty of historical evidence that many of the island's populations had only been established in the eighteenth and nineteenth centuries by migrants from the mainland. For example, it is suspected that places like Clare Island, County Mayo, Inishmurray, County Sligo and the Blasket Islands, County Kerry may have been largely empty or poorly inhabited in the late Middle Ages (although it should be noted that insufficient archaeological investigations have been carried out to establish whether this is true or not).

It was also probably influential that the nineteenth-century antiquarians were mostly interested in the Early Medieval ecclesiastical monuments on the islands – the various churches, crosses and other religious monuments. This focus also led to the islands as being seen as places to be linked with Ireland's so-called glorious early Christian 'Golden Age'; a period of high artistic achievement before Viking and Anglo-Norman invasions of later centuries. Indeed, this perception was to be profoundly significant in the course of Early Medieval archaeological scholarship through much of the twentieth century. On the other hand, it should be noted that Irish antiquarian scholars (many of whom were of Anglo-Irish origins) generally saw themselves as Irish patriotic scholars dedicated to extolling Ireland's cultural heritage, rather than politically-motivated 'political-nationalists'. It may well be that, while the antiquarians helped to create an image of a timeless, romantic west, this was not a conscious project – and certainly not one with explicitly nationalist intentions.

CELTIC REVIVAL POETS, WRITERS AND ARTISTS CREATE THE HEROIC WEST OF IRELAND

During the Celtic Revival at the end of the nineteenth century, artists and writers sought to create a distinctively Irish literature and both poets and playwrights looked to native sources for inspiration. They found it particularly in the folklore and story-telling traditions of the west of Ireland. Indeed, artists have long seen the west as a metaphor for Ireland itself and this endures in modern literary and artistic endeavours (e.g. Scott 2005).

From at least the mid-nineteenth century, artists, poets and other writers had already been increasingly attracted by the western islands and the stories of the stoic, enduring peasants who lived on them. Increasingly, artists took over the image-making from the antiquarian researchers and began to create new myths about the islands and the islanders. For example, on the advice of W.B. Yeats, the young playwright John Millington Synge (1871-1909) travelled to the Aran Islands and Connemara, and subsequently wrote influential travel writings and plays (e.g. *The Playboy of the Western World*) that communicated a sense of the 'otherness' and primitive, but ruggedly heroic, lifestyle and emotions of the islanders – and indeed the people of the west generally.

Decorative artists also drew from Early Medieval Celtic Irish traditions – sculpted crosses, metalwork and manuscripts – in a reinvention of an ancient artistic style. Decorative artists and painters also became fascinated about various aspects of the western islands – their scenic landscapes, the primitive cultures, the perceived lack of modern materialism and wealth, the harshness and brutality of island life itself and what they saw as the emotional, unpredictable nature of the people. This they could usefully contrast with the sophistication and rigidity of social life back in Dublin, London or other centres of empire. This can all be seen in Frederick William Burton's famous painting of 1841, *The Aran Fisherman's drowned child*. In this scene, the human figures, distributed around a house that has just come upon tragedy, are painted in earthy tones – browns, reds and blacks. The father of the drowned child looks out accusingly to the viewer, while the women grieve in a spectacular, emotionally unrestrained fashion. Both the artist and the viewer could thus encounter the strangeness and 'otherness' of the Gaelic peoples of the west.

THE LONESOME WEST: THE LANDSCAPE PAINTINGS OF JACK B. YEATS AND PAUL HENRY

From the Celtic Revival onwards, and into the early twentieth century, Irish artists began to celebrate the Irish landscape and its lifeways. Most important and hugely influential were the artists Jack B. Yeats (1871-1957) and Paul Henry (1876-1958) who effectively created, from about 1910, a mythic western landscape (Bhreathnach-Lynch 2003; Scott 2005).

Jack B. Yeats created almost on his own the heroic, western peasant, a figure that was far from the poor, disheveled and unruly-looking population depicted by earlier artists (Pyle 2003). In a famous painting from 1905, *The Man from Aranmore*, he depicts a strong, handsome if slightly menacing islandman standing at the end of a pier, at home in his surroundings. In the background can be seen an ancient cross on a small islet. A strongly nationalist artist, he articulated a pride in Irishness and celebrated the life of the ordinary people of the west, and particularly of its islands.

Paul Henry was also of huge significance in the development of a distinctive school of Irish art, but also in the formation of a national Irish identity that drew inspiration from his paintings of western landscapes (Bhreathnach-Lynch 2003). The paintings of Paul Henry evoke a timeless and mystical landscape of the west, particularly those executed on Achill Island, County Mayo, where he spent most of his time (5). He believed that the west of Ireland – its people and their landscapes – represented the 'soul of Ireland'. He depicts men and women digging potatoes, gathering seaweed, cutting turf and fishing, with great empathy and feeling. Henry's papers are not explicitly nationalistic and the artist himself was not politically

5 Paul Henry's *Launching the Curragh*, a typical scene depicting the maritime traditions of the people of Achill Island *(National Gallery of Ireland)*

motivated, but his paintings were certainly used by others, even by the Irish state. Síghle Bhreathnach-Lynch (2003) has suggested that art, like landscape, was used as contested territory in the construction of nationalist ideologies. Indeed, for Irish people today, these images are iconic of both the west and Ireland itself, which is still seen as much the same thing.

Within this growing Irish nationalist hegemony there were also dissenting voices. William Orpen (1878-1831) in particular had no nationalist leanings and was disdainful of the new constructions of Irish identity in the early twentieth century. This seems to be evident in his strange painting *The Holy Well*, from 1916 (the year of Irish Easter Rebellion), which seems almost satirical, but in a veiled way, of Ireland's heroic west. It shows a group of Irish peasants gathering at an ancient holy well beside the sea, while across an ocean sound is a ruined medieval church (on the mainland?). This tradition of going on pilgrimage to ancient church sites on offshore islands remains an aspect of Irish culture today. The stock figures are there: the histrionic priest, the heroic aloof islander standing like Jack B. Yeat's *The Man from Aranmore*, the pure Irish girl; the improbably beautiful men and women divesting themselves of their clothes is some strange ritual. Orpen is known to have been dismissive of the growing emphasis on Gaelic culture in Ireland. Is he here disparaging the Irish peasantry as being superstitious and naïve, and dissenting from the view of Gaelic Ireland? Whatever he is doing, it is striking that even Orpen uses the archaeological imagery of Early Medieval island monasticism in his evocation of Irish Catholic spirituality. Behind the figures in his painting are clochans and decorated cross-slabs that are undoubtedly based on those found on Skellig Michael, County Kerry (Dorothy Kelly *pers. comm.*) (*6*).

By the 1940s, the dream of the Irish revolution was fading in the south. Irish society had closed in; the country became isolated due to its non-participation in the war and the Irish economy had stagnated after a decade of bruising economic war with Britain. Yet still, artists like Gerard Dillon in his 1945 painting *The Little Fields* evoke the west of Ireland and its antiquities, signaling the constant presence of the past in depictions of the west.

THE BLASKET ISLAND LITERATURE, THE IRISH STATE AND THE REINVENTION OF GAELIC IRELAND

The Romantic view of the western islands was in part constructed by artists and by writers like J.M. Synge and W.B. Yeats, who also created an image of heroic islanders, enduring grief, death, suffering and hardship. Yet, interestingly, and almost uniquely on the Blasket Islands, Co. Kerry, it was also created by the islanders themselves. The Blasket Islands are so deeply rooted in most Irish people's perception of the West that they are almost icons of Irishness (*1*). This is largely because in English and Irish classes in Secondary School, generations of school children were all required to read books and short stories about the island, so city children grew up reading about turf fires, fishing and storms (for an accessible introduction to the Blaskets' history and literature, see Mac Conghail 2001).

During the nineteenth century, an astonishing explosion of the population on the Blaskets led to the growth of the island's only village settlement which was situated at the island's eastern end (Mac Carthaigh and O'Reilly 2001). By the 1840s there may have been as many as 4000 people on the island (by the 1950s, after the Famine and subsequent decades of decline, it had dropped to 120). This village was central to the lives of the closely-packed population who were actively engaged in farming for potatoes, oats and barley, while also grazing cattle on the mountain pasture (*2*). The Blasket Islanders also fished for mackerel from currachs, hunted puffins on the cliffs, gathered seaweed and exploited shipwrecks for timber, tea and other products. Indeed, during the Great Famine of the 1840s the Blaskets probably did better than most places on the west coast.

However, the Blasket Islands are particularly famous for the astonishing literary achievements of their inhabitants in the mid-twentieth century; the publication of books and memoirs which seemed to capture an intact Gaelic culture living on the western margins of Europe (see Kiberd 2000 for a critical study of the role and impact of the Blasket biographies).

The Western Islands: Ireland's Atlantic islands and the forging of Gaelic Irish national identities

6 William Orpen's *The Holy Well*, an enigmatic painting depicting aspects of belief and practice amongst the people of the west of Ireland, illustrated with Early Medieval island archaeology, such as the clochans and crosses from the Skellig, County Kerry *(National Gallery of Ireland)*

From about 1910, folklorists, scholars and philologists began to see the Blasket Islands as a place where they could carry out research on a community that seemed to be uniquely connected with Europe's primitive past, and all that might mean in terms of folklore, language, ethnology and economic practices. For some, it was even an opportunity to explore the workings of an alternative, proto-communist society that existed outside of the norms of global capitalism. For the English Marxist scholar of ancient Greece, George Thomson (1977; 1982; 1988), the Blasket Islanders' lifeways and social organisation, with their communally agreed 'kingship' (i.e. one man from the community was democratically 'elected' to lead the village and to represent its needs to outsiders); their sharing of property and resources (a particular reading of the communally agreed land-holding practices known as rundale) and the islanders' heroic endurance of loss and hardship, was a source of idealised inspiration for young men seeking to recreate European civilisation.

Another important scholar was the Englishman, Robin Flower (fondly known to the islanders as *An Bláithín* – 'the flower'), whose book *The Western Island*, published in 1944, describes a culture that he saw as being 'on the verge of extinction – a society, which, though not illiterate, was still in an essentially oral stage and seemed to have retained impressive elements of a proto-historic, European culture'. Flower's book accounts for his visits to the island over about 20 years, from 1910 to about 1930. By the time of his arrival, there were about 150 people on the island, the population having been reduced by emigration, yet he still found it culturally vibrant. He describes the island, its Early Medieval antiquities ('the bright dwellings', as they were known to the islanders, as well as the cross-slabs and ecclesiastical remains scattered around the Dingle Bay area), the village dance, seals and fishing, turf-cutting and the various legends and stories of the islanders. Although all around him there was evidence of the processes of social and economic change (population decline, the introduction of new land-holding practices introduced by the Congested Districts Board), it is striking that even a sympathetic observer such as Flower sought to fit the Blasket Islanders into a timeless past. In one incident he recounts how, when listening to the islanders reciting proverbs, he hears one old woman saying '*Cá'il an sneachta bhí comh geal anuirig*' ('where is the snow that was so bright last year'), whereupon he excitedly explains to them that this was also an old French proverb written down by François Villon some hundreds of years before. One soon to be famous islandman, Tomás Ó Criomhthain, possibly not quite grasping Flower's etymological excitement, remarked 'I've always heard that the French are a clever people, and I wouldn't put it past them to have said that before we did' (Flower 1944, viii).

Interestingly, we also have the voice of the islanders themselves in the 'Blasket Island literature'. Tomás Ó Criomhthain's book *An t-Oileánach* was first published in Irish in 1929, and was translated by Robin Flower as *The Islandman* in 1937. This provides an older man's reflections on the life of the island. Other well-known books were Muiris O'Sullivan's (1933) *Fiche Bliain ag Fás* (translated and published in 1933 as *Twenty Years A-Growing*), a charming account of a youthful life on the island (incidentally, further to the theme of islanders as essentially medieval creatures, it is amusing to note that the online bookstore Amazon.com currently tells us that

Twenty Years A-Growing described a way of life which 'belongs in the Middle Ages' that 'had remained unchanged for centuries'). There is also Peig Sayer's (1936) *Peig*, an autobiographical account of her life transcribed from interviews, describing poverty, memories of the Famine and the inevitability of a mother's suffering. Indeed, generations of Irish school children will remember the book with a sinking heart, as it has many *longeurs* of complaint and misery. It is worth pointing out that some of the biographies were mediated in various ways, either through collaboration with friendly scholars or through editorial censorship prior to publication, so that descriptions of drinking or anything relating to sexuality in the Irish versions were omitted from earliest published editions in English. In any case, these and other books let us see how the islanders themselves perceived the outside world, the seas that surrounded them and their relationships with the mainland. We can sense their culture shock and surprises when they embark on their journeys off the Blasket to the nearby market town of Dingle, where they encountered the land of Ireland itself, with its social hierarchies, wealth and poverty and its money-oriented economy. For the islanders, Ireland was a strange and remote island across the water.

The Irish literary critic, Declan Kiberd (2000), has also noted that, by the establishment of the Irish Republic in 1937, political nationalists began to use the Blasket Islands in an explicit ideological way. In the Irish secondary school curriculum the Blasket Island literature (particularly that of Peig Sayers) and the Aran Island short stories of Liam O'Flaherty and Mairtín Ó Direán were used to project a particular sense of Irishness. Kiberd (2000) has argued that through these island narratives the education authorities attempted to import the real Irishness of the smaller islands back into Ireland. They hoped that the Gaelic culture of the islands could be used to regenerate and renew the bigger island and to restore it to the state of grace from which it had fallen (i.e. after the English had got their hands on the place). I said at the start, it certainly worked on me! I was endlessly fascinated by the Aran Islands, my own identity as a teenager was very much Gaelic Irish (hurling, singing, literature) and it was partly formed by reading stories of Blasket Islanders. Interestingly, for all the fact of their being icons of Irish identity, the Irish government did little to practically and economically support the Blasket Islanders (or indeed other populations of the western islands). The final straw came in winter of 1953, when a young man contracted meningitis, and because of winter's storms, couldn't be got off to hospital. The islanders abandoned the island in November 1953, many of them emigrating to Springfield, Minnesota, USA (Mac Conghail 2001).

CONCLUSIONS

In conclusion, Irish antiquarians certainly had a role in contributing to a growing interest in the western islands, by describing and drawing attention to their archaeological remains and distinct cultural traditions. This inspired, in the nineteenth and early twentieth centuries, a growing fascination amongst artists and writers in the islands, who themselves also helped to create an image of a timeless west. However, this ultimately led to a portrayal of the islands as static, conservative and ageless and Irish nationalists used the islands – both before and after independence – as a resource to try and recreate a Gaelic culture and ethnicity on the larger island of Ireland. Interestingly, it is arguable that all of these images of life on the western islands overlooked the realities of island life through the nineteenth century, essentially a period of utterly transforming social, economic and demographic changes on the islands.

Yet still there is a popular image of the western islands as the places of an unchanging Irish past. In a recent TV programme screened on TG4, the vibrant and innovative Irish-language channel, the programme-makers explored aspects of the life of the modern inhabitants of Inis Mór, the largest of the Aran Islands. Interviews with the Irish-speaking young people of the island revealed the primary concerns of all 'Celtic Tiger' teenagers – music, drink, boyfriends and girlfriends, shopping and world travel. Some of the islanders explained how the island's traditional fishing industry was moribund, with most of the island's fishing fleet operating out of the Connemara port of Rosaveel, while farming had declined to almost the status of a pastime or hobby. Tourism provides most of the islanders' income today; most work in local bed-and-breakfasts, pubs and on the island ferries, or provide bicycles or guided tours of the islands' antiquities in vans that cram onto or near the island's narrow pier upon every ferry's arrival and there compete for the thousands of holiday-makers that visit the island during the summer tourist season (and this is the new reality for many of the other Atlantic islands too; see Royle 2003).

Yet, the TV programme makers also interviewed some of the American, Dutch, French, German, Japanese and other tourists who flock to the island and asked them why they had come. Amusingly, almost all of them said to the camera – while narrowly avoiding being run over by tour vans busily beeping their way around the streets of Kilronan – that they had come to the Aran Islands to see what 'the real Ireland' was like and to see 'life as it was lived long ago'.

REFERENCES

Bhreathnach-Lynch, S. 2003, 'The formation of an Irish school of painting: issues of national identity', in Kennedy, S.B. (ed.), *Paul Henry*, 23-24, Dublin

Flower, R. 1944, *The Western Island*, Oxford

Foster, W. 1977, 'Certain set apart: the Western Island in the Irish Renaissance', *Studies* 66, 261-70

Harbison, P. 1976, 'John Windele's visit to Skellig Michael in 1851', *Kerry Archaeol Hist J* 9, 125-148

Herity, M. 1990, 'The heritage of Ardoilean, County Galway', *J Roy Soc Antiq Ireland* 120, 65-110

Herity, M. 1995, 'Two island heritages in the Atlantic: Rathlin O'Birne, Donegal, and Calder Island, Mayo', *J Roy Soc Antiq Ireland* 125, 85-128

Johnston, E. 2003, 'A sailor on the seas of faith: the individual and the church in The Voyage of Máel Dúin', in Devlin, J. & Clarke, H.B. (eds), *European Encounters: Essays in Memory of Albert Lovett*, 239-52, Dublin

Kiberd, D. 2000, 'The Blasket autobiographies', in Kiberd, D. *Irish Classics*, 520-542, London

Mac Carthaigh, C. & O'Reilly, B. 2001, 'Ó Bhun go Barr an Bhaile: recent settlement on the Great Blasket Island' in Ó Catháin, S. et al (eds), *Northern Lights: Following Folklore in North-Western Europe*, 148-164, Dublin

Mac Conghail, M. 2001, *The Blaskets: People and Literature*, Dublin

Marshall, J.W. & Rourke, G.D. 2000, *High Island: An Irish Monastery in the Atlantic*, Dublin

O'Connell, J.W. 1994, 'The rediscovery of the Aran Islands in the 19th century', in Waddell, J., O'Connell, J.W. & Korff, A. (eds), *The Book of Aran*, 183-194, Kinvara

Ó Criomthain, T. 1929, *An t-Oileánach*, reprinted in English in 1937 as *The Islandman*, (translated by R. Flower), Oxford

Ó Direán, M. 1961, *Feamainn Bhealtaine*, Dublin

Ó Direán, M. 1980, *Dánta 1939-1979*, Dublin

O'Flaherty, L. 1953, *Dúil*, Dublin

O'Sullivan, M. 1933, *Fiche Bliain ag Fás. Baile Átha Cliath*, reprinted in English in 1953 as *Twenty Years A-Growing* (translated by M.L.Davies), Oxford

Pyle, H. 2003, *Jack B. Yeats: Life in the West of Ireland: As it Was*, Dublin

Royle, S.A. 2003, 'Exploitation and celebration of the heritage of Irish islands', *Irish Geog* 36, 23-31

Sayer, P. 1936, *Peig*, Baile Átha Cliath

Scott, Y. 2005, *The West as Metaphor*, Dublin

Thomson, G. 1977, *An Blascaod a Bhí*, Maynooth

Thomson, G. 1982, *The Blasket That Was: The Story of a Deserted Village*, Maynooth

Thomson, G. 1988, *Island Home: The Blasket Heritage*, Wolfboro

Waddell, J. 1994, 'The archaeology of Aran', in Waddell, J., O'Connell, J.W. & Korff, A. (eds), *The Book of Aran*, 75-148, Kinvara

Wakeman, W.J. 1885, 'Inis Muiredaich, now Inismurray, and its antiquities', *J Roy Soc Antiq Ireland* 17, 175-332

Westropp, T.J. 1895, 'Aran Islands', *J Roy Soc Antiq Ireland* 25, 250-274

Westropp, T.J. 1899, 'Dun Aenghus', *Aran J Roy Soc Antiq Ireland* 29, 66-67

Westropp, T.J. 1910, 'A study of the fort of Dun Aenghusa in Inishmore, Aran Isles, Galway Bay: its plan, growth and records', *Proc Roy Irish Acad* 28C, 1-46

Westropp, T.J. 1912, 'Brasil and the legendary islands of the north Atlantic: their history and fable. A contribution to the "Atlantis" problem', *Proc Roy Irish Acad* 30C, 223-260

Westropp, T.J. 1888, 'Notes on Connaught and Clare, especially Aran and Sligo', 1888, *TCD MS*, 973; reprinted as Westropp, T.J. 'Notes on Connaught' (1888), in Ó hEithir, B. & Ó hEither, R. (eds), 1991, *An Aran Reader*, 47-48, Dublin

Zimmerman, G.D. 2001, *The Irish Storyteller*, 357-67, Dublin